Reevaluating Mozambique

Portuguese Literary & Cultural Studies
10 Spring 2003

Reevaluating Mozambique

Center for Portuguese Studies and Culture
University of Massachusetts Dartmouth

This publication was made possible, in part, by a generous grant from the Luso-American Foundation of Lisbon, Portugal.

Portuguese Literary & Cultural Studies
www.plcs.umassd.edu

Portuguese Literary & Cultural Studies is a multilingual interdisciplinary peer-reviewed journal published semi-annually by the Center for Portuguese Studies and Culture at the University of Massachusetts Dartmouth. The journal addresses the literatures and cultures of the diverse communities of the Portuguese-speaking world in terms of critical and theoretical approaches.

Manuscript Policy

Portuguese Literary & Cultural Studies (PLCS) welcomes submission of original and unpublished manuscripts in English, Portuguese, or Spanish appropriate to the goals of the journal. The first page of the submission must include the following: (i), name, mailing address, e-mail address, and appropriate phone and fax numbers; (ii), a brief biography with reference to institutional affiliation, no more than three publications, and current research; (iii), a 100-word abstract of the content of the article; (iv), The article itself may not exceed 20 pages and should be submitted along with the above information in a single digital file. Reviews (no title): 800 words and, (ii), a brief biography. Review-essays (with title): 2000 words and, (ii), a brief biography. All of the information must be in the same language.

PLCS encourages submission of materials in hard copy and 3.5 diskette (in a protected envelope) by mail to:

Portuguese Literary & Cultural Studies
Center for Portuguese Studies and Culture
University of Massachusetts Dartmouth
Dartmouth, MA 02747 USA

Manuscripts should be in accordance with the *MLA Style Manual and Guide to Scholarly Publishing* (latest version) with parenthetical documentation and a list of Works Cited. The author is responsible for the accuracy of all quotations, titles, names, and dates. Notes must be manually typed out at the end of the article (before the list of Works Cited), regardless of whether they were entered as footnotes or endnotes into the word processor.

Subscription Information

The annual subscription (2 issues) for institutions is $80.00 and $40.00 for individuals. Single issues may also be purchased for $25.00. From outside the United States add $12.00 for shipping and handling.

Inquiries should be sent to *Portuguese Literary & Cultural Studies* Subscription, Center for Portuguese Studies and Culture, University of Massachusetts Dartmouth, Dartmouth, MA 02747 USA, or by e-mail to: greis@umassd.edu.

Advertising

Portuguese Literary & Cultural Studies accepts advertising that is of interest to scholars in the field of Portuguese, Brazilian, and Luso-African Studies and Critical Theory. Further information is available by contacting the Center for Portuguese Studies and Culture, University of Massachusetts Dartmouth.

Cover

Design: Spencer Ladd.
ISSN 1521-804X

Printed by RPI Printing, Fall River, MA

Table of Contents

Reviews/Recensões

Introduction: Reevaluating Mozambique

Phillip Rothwell

The 1990s was a decade of momentous change in Mozambique. Years of senseless violence the evolution of which could be traced back to the first colonial moment were finally brought to a close by the timely intervention of the international community. Democracy triumphed over armed conflict with the election of Joaquim Alberto Chissano as head of a newly pluralistic state where human rights would be respected and opportunity encouraged. Yet, behind this complacent, and neocolonially charged, rhetoric of a successful transition to peace and integration into a world community, there lurked a degree of paradigmatic repetition: the nation's self-determined future depended, once again, on interference from abroad. The hoards of international peacekeepers that flooded the southeast African state in the name of peace and development heralded the continuation of a removed and distanced decision-making process that rendered Mozambique once more the compliant periphery to a Western-orientated power base. Indeed, the similarities between the United Nations' peacekeeping operation in Mozambique and the praxis of Portuguese colonialism have been discussed.[1]

The complex issues that led Mozambique into a deplorable state of civil war will continue to be a source of debate and speculation. Without doubt, interference from neighbouring states like Rhodesia and apartheid-era South Africa facilitated the rise of RENAMO, an organization Margaret Thatcher once termed one of the "most brutal terrorist movements that there is."[2] Yet, the FRELIMO government's role in exacerbating, and to a certain extent, laying the groundwork for the conflict, must be acknowledged in any legitimate academic study of the Mozambican civil war. In the early years of the

FRELIMO regime there was a lack of academic work that critiqued the post-independence government. This may be explained by a prevalent sympathy among many Western intellectuals who were blinded by their utopian wish to see Samora Machel's brand of Marxist-Leninism succeed and so remained silent about or simply ignorant of the abuses of the regime. This silence facilitated FRELIMO's powerful propaganda machine, which projected the image of a united and revolutionary Mozambican people who, if given half a chance, would realize a true brand of socialism in Africa. Dissident voices or opposing views were agents of imperialism that the government felt could be legitimately silenced. Those foreign academics and commentators who bought into FRELIMO's rhetoric of socialist revolution failed to see the experiment that Samora Machel foisted on his young nation as yet another imposition from abroad—the replacement of one dated eurocentric system (colonialism) with yet another (Marxism). Furthermore, the hostility that the exponents of scientific socialism harboured against traditional practices in Africa echoed colonialism's contempt for what it deemed to be backwards or uncivilized. The nonsense of imposing a socialist system on a society that had failed to pass through the process of industrialization was always doomed to provoke the opposition of traditional sectors of that society. The roughshod manner in which FRELIMO dealt with that opposition should have been an immediate cause for concern among commentators and the academic community alike. Unfortunately, the hangovers of European colonialism combined with atrocities perpetrated by RENAMO and interference from South Africa to prevent an effective voicing of criticism of FRELIMO or much interrogation of innate government incompetence. Someone or something else could always be easily and attributably blamed for the mess into which the country was plunging, be it the Portuguese legacy or acts of terrorism. FRELIMO policy was never really analysed.

In fact, Mozambique, like the other Lusophone colonies in Africa, occupies the complex postcolonial position of a nation born out of five centuries of occupation by Europe's weakest colonial power. Boaventura de Sousa Santos's work has been instrumental in understanding the true significance of the particularities of Lusophone Africa's process of transition from colonies into neocolonized states. His work is a powerful rebuke to some of the excesses of postcolonial studies, which, as Hardt and Negri have convincingly demonstrated, are often mired in the fashionable politics of fetishized difference and cease to be liberationary once co-opted by the disjunctive flows of a free-market not-so-free-for-all. Talking about Mozambique will always raise to some extent the spectre of a colonial past. But can we effectively talk about Mozambique using the theoretical tools furnished by postcolonial theory? Where precisely is the threatening discursive relevance of Bhabha's menacing mimicry to a colonial system whose rhetoric officially embraced miscegenation and disavowed racial demarcations? How effective is Spivak's voicing of a subaltern to the praxis of Lusophone imperialism in which the colonial masters were often as ignored and silenced by the metropolis as those they purported to dominate?

The peculiarity of Lusophone Africa's colonial experience, as Sousa Santos notes, is Portugal's constant discursive shifting between the role of Prospero and that of Caliban. Portugal may have been the first colonizing power to have reached Africa and the last to depart, but it never really controlled the rules of the colonial game, and spent the better part of the post-partition era playing catch-up to a hegemonic colonialism, the tenets of which were designed to serve British interests. Clearly Portugal's idiosyncratic version of imperialism profoundly affected the shape of post-independence Mozambique.

As Sousa Santos's work on Portugal's semi-peripheral status on the world stage as both an imperial centre and a European margin that failed to undergo the process of industrialization necessary for a truly Marxist revolution implies, Portugal's former colonies were immediately marked by having been the periphery of a semi-periphery. In some ways, that had political advantages: Portugal's economic and political weakness at the time of Mozambican independence prohibited the effective pursuit of a neocolonial agenda by the former metropolis. Also, the manner in which Mozambican independence was finally attained through a popularly supported coup in Lisbon made clear that most Portuguese had grown tired of, or had never wholeheartedly supported, the retention of colonies. In other words, in stark contrast to the experience of what is often taken to be the normative colonialism of the British Empire, Portugal did not have time to make arrangements to neocolonize Mozambique prior to relinquishing its imperial grasp because of the systemic and revolutionary change that simultaneously rocked the former metropolis.

However, the suggestion that Mozambique has thus avoided a neocolonial fate is an oversight. We just need to identify correctly who the pretenders to neocolonization were. The obvious initial answers were a Western-backed South Africa who vied with the Soviet bloc to influence and control the former colony. Yet, with the collapse of communism and the end of apartheid, a more concealed, and thus effective, phase of neocolonization emerged in the guise of the inexorable rise of international capitalism and an influx of NGOs with clear Western-biased agendas.[3]

One of the most effective aspects of the power now wielded by the mechanisms of globalisation over Mozambique is facelessness. We need look no further than Foucault to understand that power is in its prime when disguised and it really is no longer clear who controls the nation's destiny. The co-option of FRELIMO into the free-market system of globalisation even enabled the same faces who had once espoused the state-control of industry and supported the policies of Operation Production, to benefit from a volte-face, profiting from privatisations and the adoption of an extremely brutal version of capitalism.[4] Of course, Mozambique is not alone in its conversion to and active cooperation with the free flow of faceless capital. However, its ruling party has managed to evade much criticism once again through a very effective public relations machine that paints the alternatives as worse, and unswervingly praises FRELIMO's Mozambique as Africa's greatest success story of recent times. The resolution of the armed conflict enabled the international community, embodied in the United Nations, to claim much needed credit for bringing peace after a string of shambolic disasters on the continent.[5] But as Elísio Macamo and Dieter Neubert argue in their article in this volume, the peace that was negotiated in the name of the international community fell far short of what was necessary to assure a positive future for Mozambique. The concept of justice was sacrificed at the altar of expediency in a charade designed to give both parties to the peace process the scent of a legitimacy they ill deserved. FRELIMO needed to be treated as a sovereign government, while the rebel, formerly "terrorist" movement was to play-act the role of a political party with a coherent ideological agenda. In the short term, the game that both sides played bore fruit. There was a cessation of violence, a positive advance by any standards. However, as Macamo and Neubert argue, the long-term consequences of the way in which the peace was constructed are decidedly negative since they have left the FRELIMO cadres with possession of the state, and RENAMO with very little to lose.

The meaningless nature of an increasingly compromised state, whose sovereignty has been abolished by the flows of capitalism, is raised by Branwen Gruffydd Jones. Her interviews of Mozambicans further damage the rosy picture painted of the nominally independent former colony. Her article deconstructs the economic success story proffered by the international community in relation to Mozambique. The real-life experiences of Mozambican workers and peasants gainsay vacuous economic figures espoused in support of the officially sanctioned version of Mozambican development. Gruffydd Jones also brings into stark relief the unsavoury consequences of challenging the official discourse in the newly democratic Mozambique, relating the murder of a journalist who dared to investigate corruption in high places to a trend towards remaining uncritical of the government's betrayal of its people.

There have, of course, always been independent voices critical of corruption and injustice wherever and whenever it has manifested itself in Mozambique. In colonial times, writers and poets used the power of the Portuguese language to construct damning indictments of the effects of the colonial system. A brood of anticolonial poets and writers used the power of the written word to highlight the inequity and racism of a colonial system as it functioned and contradicted its ambivalent, officially colour-blind discourse. Geoffrey Mitchell offers a reading of an important marker in the evolution of Mozambican letters, Orlando Mendes's *Portagem.* Mitchell focuses on Mendes's use of failed relationships as a means of offering a powerful critique of colonial praxis in Mozambique on the eve of the independence struggle. He argues that the image Mendes projects is one of a doomed future, forever beholden to the contradictions of Mozambique's troubled past. The creation of an educational underclass unable to articulate a different reality was one of the most damning legacies of the Portuguese colonial regime, and Mendes is uncompromising in his depiction of a faulty education system. That same faulty system marred Minho almost as much as Maputo, and the real advances both nations made in their education sectors after the Carnation Revolution were remarkable.

FRELIMO's commitment to education was one of the hallmarks of its early administration. There was a definite will on the part of Machel's government to reduce illiteracy and open up the formal education sector to the whole nation. However, the destabilizing effects of the civil war impacted extremely negatively on the education system. Schools and teachers became a favoured target of RENAMO in the darkest moments of the conflict so that in many areas of the country the system ceased functioning. Yet the system FRELIMO adopted—principally because of the need for the rapid training of teachers, but also because of the ideological dictates of its all-encompassing philosophy—was extremely directional and, in essence, flawed. The Ministry of Education wanted to control every single class from the nation's capital, and produced teachers' manuals based on rote-learning and student compliance rather than initiative and the stimulation of intellectual curiosity. Given the limited number of teachers and the consequently huge class sizes, such directionality was seen to be necessary to the rapid placement of poorly trained teachers in classrooms.

The system's greatest flaw, however, was the result of another aspect of the ideology of the early years of the FRELIMO government: the charade of unity. Unity, particularly to Samora Machel, meant that everyone had to speak the same language, Portuguese, the tongue of the nation's former Prospero, who may well have been a Caliban. Unlike Shakespeare's colonial master, the Portuguese had not done very much to bequeath their tongue to those they colonized. One of the great ironies of Mozambican history is the extent to which FRELIMO propagated the Portuguese language; the derisory efforts of the former colonizers palls in comparison. Portuguese was to be the language through which Mozambique imagined itself, and that meant its compulsory use in the classroom. Ideologically speaking, the use of Portuguese was meant to break the power of tribal allegiances and forge the identity of the socialist state. Educationally speaking, the policy was a disaster, and what is worse, it was a disaster that FRELIMO has no excuse for not having foreseen. In the 1950s, UNESCO was already publishing reports that highlighted the dangers of not using a child's mother tongue in the early years of his or her education. In Mozambique, the situation was exacerbated by the fact that the State used legal sanctions to enforce instruction in Portuguese by teachers who often scarcely controlled the language themselves, to pupils entering the system with no knowledge of Portuguese. Unsurprisingly, particularly in rural areas, the system did not work. Dropout rates were high, learning minimal, and teachers frustrated. One reason why the system was retained for so long was because the civil war could be used as a convenient excuse for its failure. Only in the 1990s, when Mozambique's educational policies became increasingly determined by donor agencies, and particularly by UNICEF, was mother-tongue education officially encouraged for the first time since independence. Time will tell if educational achievement improves in the primary sector. What is clear is that the newly pluralistic FRELIMO has stopped persecuting the use of local languages and, as Gregory Kamwendo argues in his article, this opens up a range of possibilities for cross-border cooperation between Mozambique and its African neighbours on terms that are not the by-product of linguistic imperialism.

Mozambique shares a range of languages with its neighbours, providing an opportunity, reasons Kamwendo, for political alliances that do not require the mediating role of former European tongues. He identifies the advantages of pooling linguistic resources at a range of institutional and educational levels, and exemplifies his argument through the case of Chinyanja, a language spoken in Mozambique and Malawi (where it is termed Chichewa).

Language politics in Africa have long been complicated by the arbitrary divisions that resulted from the Berlin Conference of 1884-85. In the era of liberation struggles, Lusophone African liberation movements tended towards Amílcar Cabral's position that "o português [língua] é uma das melhores coisas que os tugas nos deixaram."[6] The stance Ngugi wa Thiong'o adopted in Kenya viewed the continued use of the former colonial tongue as detrimental to a true intellectual liberation. In the case of Lusophone Africa, the cultural association of the "língua portuguesa" with the "pátria" has forever complicated the straightforward assumption of cultural independence through the use of the Portuguese language. Mozambique's great post-independence writers have had to negotiate the difficult terrain of using the Portuguese language and often having a more avid readership in Portugal than in their own nation. The most obvious example of a writer who has been read repeatedly as enriching the "língua" as "pátria" is Mia Couto, the relatively young man who has been catapulted to global prominence, and often problematically read as the voice of his young nation. The secret of his success, according to Patrick Chabal, is his ability to manipulate the medium of the short story. In his article, Chabal argues that Couto understands and appropriates the conventions of the "conto," in part, as a result of his experience as a journalist. Even in his novels, Couto essentially applies the formula he successfully uses in his shorter fiction.

Robert Moser's article focuses on another aspect of Couto's work: his use of the tropes of the epic in a quest to forge a cultural identity. Moser offers a reading of Couto's first novel, *Terra Sonâmbula*, a powerful narrative set in the darkest nadir of the civil war that plays with a number of demarcations: between the written and the oral, between sea and land, between reality and fantasy. Moser's argument that Couto draws on the predominantly Western conventions of the epic is a useful reminder of the complex cultural syncretism that is a necessary and unavoidable aspect of understanding Mozambican contemporary culture.

Another Mozambican author who is receiving considerable international attention is Paulina Chiziane. The fact that she shares the same Lisbon-based publisher as Couto, the prestigious Caminho, in part accounts for and, simultaneously, problematizes her success. While Portugal has never been able economically to neocolonize, in the cultural sphere, Portuguese publishers increasingly determine who are the successful Lusophone African authors. Of course, every writer aspires to the widest possible readership, and Caminho's success in promoting Mozambican writers is a positive aspect of the process of globalisation in that their distribution network enables a greater dissemination of Mozambique's cultural richness. Russell Hamilton discusses Chiziane's intended transnational audience, one that encompasses all seven nations whose official language is Portuguese. Hamilton argues that Chiziane's most recent novel *Niketche: Uma História de Poligamia* communicates a decidedly feminist message and reflects through the author's language, particularly her choice of characters' names, a certain degree of hybridisation characteristic of the processes of globalisation in Mozambique.

Hilary Owen's article focuses on Paulina Chiziane's first novel, *Balada de Amor ao Vento,* and also discusses Chiziane's relationship to the language she uses. For Owen, Chiziane destabilizes a hierarchy that places a nationalist, male discourse in apposition to an essentialized "mother tongue." A result of this destabilization is that Chiziane permits the feminine to transgress into the traditional preserve of what Owen characterizes as male contact zones, and simultaneously transfers part of the blame for a loss of paradise over to men.

Ana Mafalda Leite draws on works by Mia Couto and Paulina Chiziane, as well as Ungulani Ba Ka Khosa, to argue that Mozambique's foremost contemporary authors inherit a poetic paradigm from the voices of a previous generation, most notably, José Craveirinha. The model they adopt foregrounds the restitution of a memory anchored in a localized orality.

The interplay between the oral and the written has long been the polar axis over which debates about what literature from Africa is have been structured. Ana Maria Martinho asserts that the selection of the national canons in Mozambique and Angola is a problematic, but nonetheless often undertaken, exercise precisely because of the important existence of two traditions: the oral and the written. The process of fixing a literary canon has been constantly subject to the vagaries of political fashion, and often tells us more about those wishing to determine what a nation's literature is than about the literary output of a nation.

One Mozambican author of outstanding merit who has been neglected until recently, despite her long literary career, is Lília Momplé. In sharp contrast to the fantastic universes that both Chiziane and Couto create, the work of Lília Momplé, the subject of Claire Williams's article, is grounded on a non-sentimentalising realism intent on portraying and thus critiquing the iniquities of the range of systems, from colonialism through to capitalism, that have been imposed on the Mozambican nation. Williams argues that Momplé's work furnishes an impressive array of social and historical characters, a kind of interlocking jigsaw that, without lecturing or badgering her readers, lays bear the stark injustices under which ordinary Mozambicans have repeatedly laboured.

Despite the critical tone of many of the articles in this collection, today's Mozambique has the potential to become a true success story, not as designated by the outside world, but as determined from within. The fact that critical voices are now raised, as much in the rich cultural output of the nation as in the structures of civil society, raises the possibility of a tangible improvement in the lives of ordinary Mozambicans, since every problem must be recognised before a solution can be reached. Chiziane's interrogation of patriarchal practice, Momplé's portrayal of corruption and abject poverty, Couto's depiction of senseless violence, refashion our image of Mozambique away from the utopian paradise-in-the-making that it never was towards a more profound questioning of the problems that this very young nation faces. What remains to be seen is whether Mozambique will finally be allowed to determine its own destiny or whether that small window between the fall of communism and the obliterating rise of the hegemony of world trade was too brief to permit a meaningful Mozambican identity to come into being.

Notes

[1] See particularly Synge's account for the neocolonial overtones of the UN operation.

[2] Qtd. in Vines, 1.

[3] Margaret Hall and Tom Young have pointed out that even when the perpetrators of NGO discourse employ radical terminology, their underlying beliefs are fundamentally the same as those of the World Bank and Western states. All have "doubts about the capacities of Third World governments" and show "contempt for cultural traditions that do not square with Western notions of 'rights' and 'justice'" (225).

[4] Operation Production was a policy enforced by the Frelimo government, whereby those in urban areas deemed to be engaged in what the state considered to be undesirable activities such as prostitution or vagrancy were forcibly relocated to reeducation camps in the countryside.

[5] The less-than-satisfactory UN operations that immediately preceded the ONUMOZ mandate were the Mission for the Referendum in Western Sahara, the UN operation in Somalia, and the UN verification mission to the Angolan peace process.

[6] Cabral 101.

Works Cited

Bhabha, Homi, "Signs Taken for Wonders: Questions of Ambivalence in Authority under a Tree outside Delhi, May 1817." *Critical Inquiry* 12 (1985): 144-65.

Cabral, Amílcar. *Análise de Alguns Tipos de Resistência.* Lisboa: Seabra, 1975.

Hall, Margaret, and Tom Young. *Confronting Leviathan: Mozambique since Independence.* Athens: Ohio UP, 1997.

Foucault, Michel. *The History of Sexuality: An Introduction.* Trans. Robert Hurley. New York: Vintage Books, 1980.

Hardt, Michael, and Antonio Negri. *Empire.* Cambridge: Harvard UP, 2000.

Ngugi wa Thiong'o. *Decolonising the Mind: The Politics of Language in African Literature.* London: James Currey, 1986.

Sousa Santos, Boaventura de, "Entre Prospero e Caliban: Colonialismo, pós-colonialismo e inter-identidade." *Entre Ser e Estar: Raízes, Percursos e Discursos da Indentidade.* Ed. Maria Irene Ramalho and António Sousa Ribeiro. Porto: Afrontamento, 2001. 23-85.

Spivak, Gayatri Chakravorty. "Can the Subaltern Speak? Speculations on Widow Sacrifice." *Wedge* 7/8 (1985): 120-30.

Synge, Richard. *Mozambique: UN Peacekeeping in Action, 1992-1994.* Washington, DC: United States Institute of Peace Press, 1997.

Vines, Alex. *RENAMO: Terrorism in Mozambique.* London: James Currey, 1991.

Phillip Rothwell is Portuguese Program Coordinator and Assistant Graduate Director in the Department of Spanish and Portuguese at Rutgers, New Brunswick. His book, *A Postmodern Nationalist: Truth, Orality and Gender in the Work of Mia Couto,* is forthcoming from Bucknell University Press. He has published widely in refereed journals on Lusophone African, Portuguese and Brazilian literature and culture.

Articles/Artigos

The Politics of Negative Peace: Mozambique in the Aftermath of the Rome Cease-Fire Agreement

Elísio Macamo
Dieter Neubert

Abstract. This paper discusses the Mozambican post-conflict order that ensued from the Rome peace negotiations. Drawing from an analytical framework that posits a tension between negative and positive peace, it argues that the peace achieved by the Rome negotiations may not be as stable as is generally assumed. The reasons for this are to be found in the negotiation process itself. The paper suggests that peace was bought from the warring parties in exchange for the promise of development aid. While this may have been necessary to bring the conflict to an end, it may have been at the expense of a long-lasting peace that might have included, for example, the settlement of human rights issues.

Introduction

After almost a decade of unremitting violent civil war Mozambique was delivered to peace in 1992 following 18 months of hard negotiating in Rome. The negotiations were facilitated by what C. Pedrick of the *Washington Post*, in its October 10th 1993 issue, called an "unlikely team of amateur peace brokers." This amateur team consisted mainly of the Sant'Egidio Community, an Italian Catholic lay organisation. The peace brokered by the community has been hailed as marking a significant watershed in conflict resolution in Africa.[1] Indeed, not only was it possible to bring the warring parties to the negotiating table but also to encourage them to produce a political agenda on the basis of which the process of negotiation evolved. When eventually a cease-fire agreement was reached, it was secured successfully by the United

Nations all the way up to the holding of elections in 1994, which were generally considered to have been free and fair. It has now been 10 years since the cease-fire agreement and the general opinion is that Mozambique is reaping the fruits of a successful peace-brokerage.

This paper takes issue with this overall optimistic view. To be sure, this optimism is not wholly unwarranted. In contrast to many violent conflicts in Africa, which were the object of international mediation, the Mozambican civil war came to an end.[2] The country has been enjoying a state of peace underwritten by an apparent commitment by the formerly warring parties to preserve the peace and to seek non-violent means of conflict resolution. We argue, however, that Mozambique is living through a peace that is not as shining an example as it is generally held to be. The new political arrangement has left questions of post-war justice unanswered and is upheld by the flow of funds for reconstruction, the so-called peace dividend. The stability of the new order is yet to be tested under political stress such as would be the case if FRELIMO were to be defeated in general elections or if frustrated RENAMO fighters were to stage an uprising. The main thrust of the argument consists in supporting this claim. In so doing we argue that this instability is directly related to the kind of peace that was brokered. In other words, the highly praised negotiation process had a major flaw: in order to commit the warring parties to peace, political, economic and moral trade-offs had to be made, which in the post-conflict order are coming to haunt Mozambican politics. We describe and analyse these trade-offs as "the peacemakers' dilemma." In the following section, we elaborate on this analytical framework. The subsequent section will attempt to reconstruct the conflict, the process of negotiation and the post-conflict order drawing from the analytical insights of the peacemakers' dilemma thesis. This will provide the basis for an assessment of the stability of the kind of peace achieved by the Rome negotiations.

The Peacemakers' dilemma: an analytical framework[3]

If we want to understand processes of peacemaking we need to look at questions of war and peace from a non-normative analytical perspective. In many statements and studies on peacemaking it is assumed that violence does not pay and that peace is a condition for development. The optimism of these programs faces a rough reality. Ongoing conflicts in many places in Africa show that violence pays and offers opportunities for the control of political power and resources. In this context peace-building may be a contradictory enterprise. In addition, the reality of violent conflicts is highly diverse, especially in Africa. Different forms of violent group conflicts bear on the process and the chances of peace-making have to be taken into account in any peace-building enterprise. For the sake of intelligibility we construct ideal types of violent group conflicts and distinguish four main types:[4]

Centralised bi-polar conflicts

1. **Inter-national wars** between nation-states fighting for control over a state and territory.

2. **"Classical" civil wars** between political factions on a national level inside a nation-state fighting for political control of the state and territory.

Decentralised multi-polar conflicts

3. **Local inter-community conflicts** between local warrior and defence communities aiming at the accumulation of wealth, honour, fame, assertion of identity or control over a limited local territory and self-defence.

4. **Warlordism** with political and economic entrepreneurs whose power is based on the violence of armed forces of different sizes (warlords) fighting for wealth accumulation, political influence and sometimes for the control of a limited local or regional territory.

There are further types of violent actors, such as mercenaries, security enterprises or terrorist networks that may play specific roles in the conflicts presented here. And we should bear in mind that actors may change their nature; in real conflicts we may find several types of actors at the same time.

Peace-building itself is a process that includes much more than just an end to fighting. One can usually identify three phases:

1. Crisis management and an end to fighting leading to negative peace (i.e., absence of fighting).
2. Consolidation of peace leading to positive peace (i.e., stable peaceful order).
3. Conflict prevention and de-escalation.

For the analysis of the Mozambican peace-process we shall focus on the conditions necessary for the creation of negative and positive peace. The first step is negative peace, i.e., ending warfare. Generally speaking, the objective of armed conflict is victory, not peace as such. Only victory promises the enforcement of its own objectives while additionally bringing negative peace

(Elwert/Feuchtwang/Neubert 1999b). After victory, positive peace may follow. When victory is no longer a realistic option conflicting parties try at first not to lose the war.

In protracted wars in particular there are groups with a vested interest in their continuation. These are fighting units and their leaders, which we shall call "violence-actors," and other people profiting from the war (war profiteers), such as arms dealers, entrepreneurs controlling important markets of limited goods (e.g., often fuel, food) black market entrepreneurs, or smugglers. They constitute an alliance interested in the continuation of war, which has been termed a "war constituency" (Lederach 1995; Weiß 1997). Fear of defeat and the interests of the war constituency are a driving factor behind a self-enforced dynamic of violence (Elwert/Feuchtwang/Neubert 1999a). Only in cases where both sides see no possibility of winning the war and fear defeat, or when continuous warfare becomes less attractive (e.g., because of dwindling resources) may warring parties consider a negotiated peace as an option. This situation is called by Zartman (1985) a conflict that is "ripe for resolution."

In peace-building, violence-actors play a crucial role. They have a simple, practical veto power. To wit, often a single, well-targeted violent act can stop a peace process by provoking a violent retaliation. Therefore, the decision to end fighting lies in the hands of such actors.

Any peace-building enterprise must consider cost-benefit ratios as well as the motivation of violence-actors for a negotiated settlement (Krumwiede 1998; Calic 1998). We shall call this the "Realpolitik" approach (in its original German sense of radical, non-normative pragmatic politics). To put it differently, all-powerful violence-actors become important partners in peace-negotiations irrespective of their political positions and their role in the war. As we shall note below, this was a crucial ingredient to the Mozambican peace settlement. "Violence-actors" will only agree to peace if peace is more attractive than the continuation of violence. Only under exceptional conditions will all warring parties agree to an end to violence. In such cases, at least two conditions must be met: (1) guarantees that fighters are shielded from enemy attacks and from prosecution; (2) promises of political and economic gains for violence-actors (e.g., participation in the government, access to national resources, support for new enterprises).

Giving up the option of violence carries an extreme risk for the fighters. They relinquish their core resource, one that secured their survival and political and economic success. They subject themselves to a new order. They do this against the background of their former experience, which often tells them that political promises are not usually kept. Therefore, it is no surprise that peace settlements after protracted warfare are rarely about the fundamental political and ideological questions that were originally part of the conflict. What dominates is the interest of military leaders and fighters in securing their position in political, economic and legal terms.

Negative peace is just the first step in a peace process. The main accomplishment is "positive peace" in the sense of building and consolidating a peaceful order. This introduces a new set of necessary actions and objectives (Kühne 1998):

1. Demobilisation of fighters and their reintegration into civilian life.

2. Installation of post-conflict governance including the reconstruction of public order and security, law enforcement and monopoly of violence as well as political reconstruction.

3. Technical reconstruction of infrastructure, clearing of war damages, and economic stabilisation.

4. Legal and psychological reconstruction including the regulation of war crimes, war damages, looted or illegally acquired property and reconciliation.

5. According to Western conceptions of post-conflict, peace-building also includes the accomplishment of the rule of law, social justice, political participation, and a constructive non-violent conflict culture and the control of emotions and instincts (Senghaas 1994, 17-49).

This peace-building sequence may sound self-contradictory. Indeed, for there to be negative peace, incentives and rewards for the war constituency are needed. Yet, positive peace demands the prosecution of war criminals and the regulation of open questions concerning property. As long as violence-actors face the threat of prosecution they will not agree to peace. However, an amnesty encourages a "culture of impunity" that gives legitimacy to crimes committed during warfare. There is a sense in which, therefore, the demands of a negative peace together with the necessary rewards for the fighters would lead to a situation in which violence would pay, after all. This contradiction is what we call the "peacemakers' dilemma."[5] A full, positive peace that includes justice, forgiving and the foundation of a new community will, to some extent, contradict the interests of the violence-actors. However, without their support and agreement a negotiated peace will not be possible.

The situation after a military victory, the peace of the victor as it were (Elwert/Feuchtwang/Neubert 1999b, 21), differs from the situation just described. The victor may, and often does, dictate the peaceful order. Usually, war crimes are prosecuted and open questions concerning property are settled, and even reconciliation may be initiated. However, the defeated party mostly will be pursued legally.[6]

A mere consideration of the violence-actor's cost-benefit ratio (following the "Realpolitik" approach) does not guarantee peace negotiations that will result in actual peace. Successful peace-building is based on core conditions that are not easy to meet. Peace-building requires: (1) Recognisable conflicting parties with military and political leaders that can negotiate and implement peace (control military actions and sufficient command power); (2) leaders who are motivated to negotiate a peace-agreement that considers the specific security, political and economic interests of the opponents; (3) leaders and fighters who will accept post-conflict governance arrangements, including a monopoly of violence not controlled by themselves.

The chances of finding these conditions for peace-building vary according to the type of conflict. In bi-polar centralized conflicts, the core conditions may be established if the leaders are ready for real peace-negotiations. In decentralised multi-polar conflicts, peace-building is much more complicated. However, as long as fighters and leaders see themselves as being responsible for "their people," this concern may impel them to compromises. In cases of warlordism this motivation is lacking. Without linkages to the people, the main issue becomes the interests of leaders and fighters. The risk is that, after a peace agreement, unsatisfied fighters may split away and continue the conflict.

In any case, a peaceful order with a monopoly of violence will rarely be implemented only by agreement; it has to be enforced. The creation of a peaceful order is not (only) a question of negotiated peace but of the existence or creation of a power that is able to keep the monopoly of violence in a defined territory. In a nutshell, a peaceful order goes hand-in-hand with the establishment or the reassertion of a central state power. The kind of peaceful order will depend on the type of state and its political rule.

A classical civil war? The dynamics of armed violence

In this section we start by attempting to classify the Mozambican conflict in terms of our analytical framework. We argue that it is wiser to concentrate on the dynamics of conflict itself rather than on its causes (Elwert/Feuchtwang/Neubert 1999a). We make a distinction between mediation as a formal process and mediation as a substantive process. The former relates to the logistical aspects necessary for mediation to take place, including choice of place, mediators and the order in which issues shall be discussed. The latter refers to the issues that are the subject of negotiation. This distinction is crucial to understanding the kind of peace that the Rome talks granted Mozambique. Indeed, we argue that mediation as a formal process allows us to see the negotiated settlement as a successful example of conflict resolution; mediation as a substantive process refers us, however, to our theoretical premise to the effect that successful mediation often involves the peacemakers' dilemma, with consequences for the post-conflict order. We shall explore the implications of the latter perspective by stressing two aspects of the negotiation process that were central to its success: the active bracketing-off of human rights issues and submission to the financial blackmail of the negotiating parties. We shall conclude the section with a brief checklist of the criteria of positive peace in order to draw attention to the fragility of the Rome peace.

Mozambique's brutal war has been variously described. These descriptions reveal a normative pattern that appears to play a major role in the analysis of the conflict. Accounts of the war tend to distinguish between internal and external factors. Authors who emphasise external factors are more likely to be sympathetic to the Marxist-oriented FRELIMO government that came to power at independence (e.g., Minter 1994; Saul 1993). In the context of the external emphasis, two accounts have been dominant. First, there are those who see the conflict as part of the Cold War. In this sense, Mozambique may have been caught in a proxy war. Secondly, though, the war has also been seen as having been driven by the hegemonic designs of South Africa's apartheid regime. Authors who give primacy to the internal factors have a tendency to play down regional and geo-strategic factors. Instead, they look into politics inside the country itself for an explanation of the war (e.g., Geffray 1990; Hall and Young 1997; Hoile 1994). In terms of these accounts, therefore, the war was a more or less legitimate act of resistance—by political opponents of the regime or by a disaffected rural population—against an illegitimate state power. There is perhaps a third type of description. It gives equal weight to internal and external factors, but rather than seeking to account for the war in normative terms it stresses the devastating effects of the conflict on the country as a whole. William Finnegan's account is a particularly good example of this type of account (Finnegan 1992; see also Gersony 1988).

Our aim in this paper is not to explain the war. Rather, we wish to focus on the dynamics of violence. The typology of conflicts that we presented above may be quite helpful. There is a sense in which the Mozambican conflict could be described as a centralised bi-polar war. In its practical and discursive manifestations it had all the ingredients that could warrant its being labelled as a "classical" civil war between political factions on a national level inside a nation-state fighting for political control of the state and territory. Indeed, the war opposed a government army fighting a conventional war to a rebel army employing guerrilla tactics.

The government army relied on state resources for conscription, training and financing. Its officers and soldiers were trained both in the country and abroad. Training in the country itself was undertaken mostly by Tanzanian, Soviet Russian and North Korean instructors. A considerable number of officers enjoyed training abroad in such diverse countries as Libya, East Germany, Cuba and the Soviet Union. In the later years of the war several contingents of Mozambican army officers were given training by British Special Forces in Zimbabwe. The army acquired its military hardware mostly from the Soviet Union, although the British army also supplied light weaponry in the later stages of the war. In the early years of the war (late 1970s and early 80s), the army's main strategy was defensive. This was a reaction to the guerrilla tactics at the time, which were limited to ambushes and looting raids out of the rebels' main bases in Southern Rhodesia. As the rebels increasingly established themselves in Mozambique, especially in the central provinces, and became more daring in their military campaign, the army switched to an offensive strategy with frequent incursions against rebel strongholds. This strategy was combined with attempts at securing transport routes, economic infrastructure such as bridges, factories and electricity pylons, as well as providing protection to travellers and villagers in the countryside.

The rebels evolved from an initial mercenary stage to a kind of guerrilla army supported by apartheid South Africa and Western right-wing groups with some sort of a political programme. They blended elements of a fairly well organised warlord structure that supported the war effort with looting, forced labour and poaching. A significant source of revenue from the mid-eighties onwards was protection money. They were able to extract this from the British multinational Lonrho as well as from Malawi. They were created by the Southern Rhodesian secret service towards the end of the seventies to counter the activities of Zanu-PF in Mozambique and to undermine the support given to the former by the latter. With majority rule in Zimbabwe in 1980, they moved their bases to Mozambique. They established their headquarters in a mountainous area in Central Mozambique. Training and military supply were taken over by the South African Army Intelligence Services, which would remain loyal to the rebels throughout the conflict, even after the signing of a non-aggression pact between Mozambique and South Africa (Stiff 1999). In the early years of the conflict the rebels avoided engaging the army directly. They aimed their activities at economic infrastructure and carried out raids and terrorist acts against the civilian population. During these raids and attacks on the civilian population, the rebels conscripted fighters into their ranks and procured food and consumer goods. The latter, together with ivory from felled elephants and different types of hides, would be exchanged for other consumer goods as well as for weaponry through an intricate trading system involving middlemen in Malawi and South Africa (Vines 1996).

By the mid-eighties, the rebels' military campaign had been largely successful. They had been able to spread their activities to the whole of the country, severely undermining economic activity in the countryside and curtailing the movement of people between cities. Contrary, however, to overly romanticised accounts of an efficient guerrilla force of highly motivated and well-trained fighters enjoying the support of the rural population against a demoralised, under-equipped and inefficient government army (e.g., Cabrita 2000; Hoile 1994), the main success of the rebels seems to have been its staying power. In other words, the rebels were successful in that the government army was unable to defeat them militarily. They relied on a well-articulated military structure (for details see Geffray 1990; Gersony 1988; Hoile 1994; Vines 1991). They had a communications systems superior to that of the government which allowed them not only to co-ordinate their campaigns well but also to intercept and interfere with the government army's communications systems (Cabrita 2000). In spite of their military strength, the rebels never controlled territory. Some authors suggest that this simply did not fit into their military philosophy, which relied heavily on mobile and flexible fighting units (Geffray 1990; Vines 1991). Other authors point to the lack of a coherent political project, which would have been necessary to rally the population behind the rebels. The territory under the control of the rebels consisted of their strongholds and their respective perimeters. Most accounts of the internal organisation of these areas suggest that civilians living there were neither followers nor supporters of RENAMO but rather captives or villagers who were expected to grow food for the fighters (Geffray

1990; Gersony 1988; Minter 1994). Civilians were an efficient human shield against government army air raids.

In the months following the signing of the Nkomati Accord, the non-aggression pact between South Africa and Mozambique in 1984, the government, aided by a much better equipped and trained Zimbabwean expeditionary force—with British SAS commandos—launched an all-out offensive against the main rebel strongholds in Central Mozambique. Most of them were overrun, forcing the rebels to disperse and break into very small units. These campaigns dealt severe blows to the rebels without, however, seriously curtailing their military activities, which became even more brutal.[7] While the rebels were never able to recover military initiative as in the period immediately before the intervention of the Zimbabwean army, they managed to keep their disruptive potential throughout the country. From 1987 to 1989/90 the war was technically a stalemate. The joint Mozambican/Zimbabwean forces could hold the rebels in check, but were unable to seriously limit their activities in the country at large. The rebels, for their part, had had to give up their strongholds, but were able to reorganise and set forth their campaigns.

The politics of peace-building

Towards the end of the eighties, it had become clear to many that neither party could win the war. A number of factors accounted for this. On the government's side, the war effort was sapping resources that were dearly needed elsewhere. There are estimates according to which it was costing Mozambique and Zimbabwe nearly a million dollars a day to keep the joint force. Donors were pressing for a negotiated solution to the conflict as a precondition for further structural adjustment funds and emergency relief. In the eighties, the country found itself in the throes of a severe drought that claimed hundreds of thousands of lives and displaced around 4 million people. Internally, there were growing calls for a negotiated settlement. The churches played a prominent role in such calls, but there were also similar calls from within the ruling FRELIMO party.[8] On the rebels' side, the Nkomati Accord had, in spite of continued covert support from South Africa, placed severe constraints on RENAMO. Concerted military offensives by the joint Mozambican/Zimbabwean force had taken the initiative away from the rebels. The drought was taking its toll on the traditional logistics of the guerrilla fighting units, which could no longer rely on looting and forced labour for food procurement (Hume 1994; Della Rocca 1997; Vines 1996). There were also calls on the rebels to prepare for a negotiated settlement. These came from South Africa, the rebels' main backers, and sympathetic African governments such as the Malawian and Kenyan.

Previous attempts at ending the conflict peacefully had ended unsuccessfully, apparently because they had failed to take the rebels seriously. The earliest attempt was made in the run-up to the Nkomati Accord, when the South African government arranged for the rebels to acknowledge the legitimacy of the Mozambican political order, including its head of state, Samora Machel, in exchange for amnesty and reintegration into Mozambican society. Indirect talks are said to have taken place, mediated by the then South African foreign minister, Roelof "Pik" Botha (Cabrita 2000). These plans never came into fruition owing to differences within the rebel movement, which at the time was locked into bloody internal conflict.[9] After the Nkomati Accord, the government combined its military strategy with an amnesty policy. While many rank-and-file rebel fighters heeded the amnesty call, it had no significant impact on the leadership. The most prominent figure to surrender was Constantino Reis, a highly controversial person, who had defected from FRELIMO in the early eighties to join the rebels only to be later accused of having been a member of the government's security services (e.g., Cabrita 2000).

Mozambique's growing dependence on Western foreign aid, which was essential both for structural adjustment as well as for emergency relief operations, gave an impetus to a process of economic and political liberalisation. Political liberalisation reached its climax in 1990, when a new liberal democratic constitution was passed following a broad consultation process. Although not calculated to appease the rebels, whom the government continued to label "armed bandits," thereby denying them political legitimacy as negotiating partners, this political move was an important preliminary to the peace process. In their various attempts at formulating a political agenda, the rebels had often insisted on a liberal democratic political order as the aim of their struggle. Confronted with this *fait accompli*, they had trouble justifying the war to the international community and this must have played a major role in predisposing them to a negotiated settlement.

The Mozambican war was ripe for resolution (Zartman 1985). The military options had become limited, risky and costly. Economic resources to fuel the war had become scarce, popular support had declined dramatically[10] and a sort of political platform that could serve as the basis for negotiation had come into existence.

The Rome negotiations

We shall look first at the formal structure of the mediation of the Mozambican conflict. Cameron Hume, a deputy chief of the U.S. mission to the Vatican at the time when peace negotiations took place in Rome and an official observer for the American State Department, has written a straightforward and well-balanced account of the talks (Hume 1994). His account describes the process and seeks to uncover the reasons for the success of the mediation. Between July 1990 and October 1992, twelve rounds of talks were held at the Community of Sant'Egidio in Rome involving representatives of the FRELIMO government and the RENAMO rebels. They were mediated by this lay Catholic community, building on initiatives to bring peace to the country undertaken by the churches in Mozambique dating back to the mid-eighties.

Hume breaks the negotiating process into five conceptual parts. In the first part, which covered the first three rounds of talks between July and December 1990, the negotiating process consisted of getting dialogue started. The single most important issue that was discussed throughout the first three rounds was the status of the negotiating partners. As Hume points out, traditional diplomacy is mainly concerned with conflicts between states. The Mozambican conflict, however, opposed a state to an insurgent movement. By agreeing to talk, the government of Mozambique had largely acknowledged the rebels' status as a negotiating partner. Nonetheless, it was at pains to keep the façade of negotiating as a sovereign entity by consistently rejecting the involvement of the United Nations as a peace-broker. The rebels, for their part, were inexperienced diplomatically and politically, had few resources to match those the government could muster for its negotiating team, and were highly suspicious. They were concerned with their personal security and wary about talking to the government directly. They insisted throughout on the presence of mediators who would ensure not only the good faith of the government but also fair negotiations. Eventually a formula was reached with Zimbabwe and Kenya serving as mediators on behalf of the government and the rebels with the Community of Sant'Egido as facilitator.

The second part spanned rounds four, five, six and seven between January and October 1991. It dealt with the nitty-gritty of the negotiating process. Hume groups these rounds under the heading "ordering the peace process." He thereby drew attention to the fact that it was during this period that the parties focussed on the steps required to achieve peace. A major issue at the time was the timing of discussion of political and military issues. After very difficult negotiations, during which both parties threatened to withdraw, the so-called Protocol I document was signed on 18 October 1991. Not only did it lay down the framework within which talks would proceed, but it also defined an agenda that would henceforth structure the process.

The third part consisted of rounds eight and nine. Although little direct contact took place between the negotiating parties, agreement was reached on 12 March 1992 concerning the electoral law for the elections that would follow a cease-fire agreement. In the fourth part, round ten, the framework, to use Hume's words (p. 95), was expanded to include institutions and governments that had the leverage to enforce whatever agreement was reached. For the first time since the start of talks in Rome, the government and the rebels negotiated directly with one another: the Mozambican head of state and the rebel leader met in private all night long to settle outstanding issues before signing, in August 1992, a declaration committing themselves to peace and thanking the mediators for their role in bringing them together. The final part of the peace talks consisted of rounds eleven and twelve. It worked out compromises on military issues, including the technical details concerning demobilisation, the formation of a new unified army and overall security for former rebels. It ended with the signing of the General Peace Agreement on 4 October 1992 in Rome.

This brief tour through the formal structure of the negotiating process as it took shape in Rome brings into bold relief what is actually involved in such procedures. Mediation, as Hume clearly shows, was crucial to bringing violent conflict to manageable proportions through de-escalation. All through the process mediators sought to bring the negotiating partners to set the conditions for negative peace, i.e., the absence of fighting. Negative peace is not an end in itself, but rather a step towards a higher goal, namely positive peace. In the Mozambican conflict the important preconditions for negotiating a negative peace had been met. There were recognisable political parties and identifiable military and political leaders ready and willing to negotiate for peace. As we have seen above, the Mozambican conflict developed into a classical civil war opposing a state and a rebel guerrilla movement. Furthermore, both parties displayed a coherent and well-structured hierarchy with leaders strong enough to impose themselves on their followers. On either side of the conflict there seemed to be enough motivation to pursue negotiations as the better alternative. To be sure, at times both parties seemed to misunderstand the whole process. This apparent misunderstanding reflected, in fact, contrasting negotiating strategies, which were to prove unrealistic. FRELIMO sought to use the peace process as a way of accommodating the rebels without relinquishing power. As for the rebels, who did not seem to have any long-term objectives, the peace process was a highly effective way to secure political recognition internationally. The Italian ambassador to Mozambique at the time reports, for example, on a long and bitter conversation he had with the Mozambican President in which the latter castigated the mediators for seeming to take sides with the rebels. The President's wrath had apparently been caused by the mediators' inability or unwillingness to force the rebels to accept peace on the government's terms (Della Rocca 1997).

The politics of negative peace are nonetheless much more complex than Hume's neat account might suggest. As mentioned above many peace settlements are less about political and ideological issues at the root of the conflict than they are about securing the position of military leaders and fighters in political, economic and legal terms. This holds true for Mozambique. Much of what Hume describes as starting the dialogue involved precisely helping the parties to define themselves in ways that would help them secure claims in a post-conflict order. In the initial rounds of negotiations, the government was concerned to project the impression of being the representative of a magnanimous sovereign state stretching its hand to nationals gone astray. Behind this "impression management," there were hard political calculations, which included securing further international recognition for the purpose of maintaining its role as the manager of overseas development assistance. Acknowledging Mozambique's sovereignty under FRELIMO rule was the price the mediators had to pay to secure the government's commitment to peace. In the short and medium term, this was a moderate price to pay in comparison to what it would take to secure the rebels' acquiescence. Indeed, the mediators were faced with a formidable task. There were three important sets of issues at play, namely the political, the diplomatic and the financial.

First, throughout the civil war the rebels had failed to develop a political profile and programme. Authors who account for the war in internal terms often assume that the alleged rural dissatisfaction with post-independence modernisation strategies constituted the rebels' political programme. The argument is misleading. It seems to suggest that the rebellion grew out of this dissatisfaction, when in fact the rebels came much later to articulate it as part of the things for which they were fighting. When steps towards a negotiated settlement of the Mozambican conflict gained momentum, the rebels' main concern was to develop a political profile. They commissioned a South-Africa-based German constitutional lawyer, Prof. Andre Thomashausen, to draft statutes for the movement as well as to write up a constitution for a post-conflict Mozambique. On several occasions, the rebels approached some Western governments for support in political matters. Cameron Hume has remarked that RENAMO's negotiators in Rome seemed more comfortable discussing military matters than political ones. In 1991, the Italian government funded the first RENAMO congress ever (Vines 1996), a move calculated by the rebels to give its negotiating position more political weight. As the peace process unfolded, the rebels became increasingly confident on political issues, even if oftentimes they were caught out of step by the government, which in its own reforms had gone much further than the rebels' anti-communist rhetoric would have expected. The mediators recognised that the success of the talks hinged largely on the rebels' ability to articulate political positions. The money and effort that they invested in this was well spent.

Second, the rebels were internationally isolated. With the exceptions of South Africa, Kenya and Malawi, virtually no other country overtly supported them. South Africa did it by virtue of its own pariah status at the time as well as due to the fact that it had taken control of the rebels after the demise of the white minority regime in Rhodesia. Kenya did it out of hostility towards the FRELIMO government and because of the internal Mozambican lobby.[11] Malawian authorities were also extremely hostile to the Mozambican government[12] and had struck deals with the rebels for the safety of the Nacala corridor, Malawi's lifeline to the world. For successive American administrations, the Mozambican rebels were little more than terrorists, even at the height of anti-communist sentiment during the Reagan administration. An official State Department report labelled RENAMO "Africa's Khmer Rouge" (Gersony 1988). There was a ban on RENAMO leaders' visits to the US. Britain was also hostile to the rebels. It went further than the US in granting the Mozambican government military assistance against RENAMO. The rebels saw the peace process as a welcome opportunity to break out of their international isolation. In the early rounds of the talks, they repeatedly raised the issue. At times, they would justify their reservations against certain Western countries on the grounds that they were biased towards the government. One particularly cunning strategy the rebels deployed to this end was the insistence that mediators and foreign dignitaries wishing to consult with the rebel leader do so in his stronghold in Mozambique.

Finally, the rebels were in dire need of money. As de-escalation set in, the rebels were faced with worsening logistical problems coupled with the rather exacting financial price attached to participation at the talks in Rome. Their negotiators had to travel and be lodged. Often they lacked such bare necessities as pencils and notebooks,[13] not to mention technical equipment that would allow swift and reliable communication with the leadership in the Mozambican bush.

Getting the rebels to the negotiating table also meant meeting their financial needs. The rebels' top negotiator in Rome is quoted as having said that there is "no democracy without money" (Vines 145). The rebels' demands for money rose from USD$3 million in December 1991 to USD$10-12 million by June 1992. The Italian government had been footing most of the bill for the peace process, including the rebels' Rome telephone bills between January and July 1992 at USD$60,000 and the flight costs of the rebels' London lobbyist, a film crew, and exiled rebel supporters to visit rebel-controlled areas in Mozambique (Vines 144). Alex Vines writes of Italian spending on the peace talks as "…an astute reading of probably the single greatest interest RENAMO had, namely to extract maximum material, rather than political benefits from the peace process" (Vines 145). It is well known that the rebels made the signing of the cease-fire agreement conditional upon payment. The Italian ambassador to Mozambique at the time of the negotiations sent a fax to his superiors in Rome on 21 April 1992 in which he informed them that the rebel leader had threatened that the talks might not evolve in a positive way if his movement's demands for financial assistance were not met (Della Rocca 231). Funds subsequently pledged by the Italian government never materialised as an angry rebel leader would reveal in 1993 at a press conference in Maputo (Vines 152). According to him, Italy had promised his movement USD$15 million for signing the cease-fire. Furthermore, relations between the rebel leader and Tiny Rowland, Lonrho's chief executive, chilled over precisely financial matters. Apparently, the rebel leader demanded a payment of USD$6-7 million as a precondition for signing a peace accord (Vines 146). Lonrho, which during the war had struck protection deals with the rebels, went out of its way to meet the rebels' financial needs. The rebel leader frequently travelled on Lonrho's executive jet to Malawi and Kenya for consultations. After the signing of the peace accord, a considerable number of leading rebels were accommodated free of charge at Maputo's Cardoso Hotel owned by Lonrho.

In a sense, negotiating peace for Mozambique was more than just an exercise in textbook mediation. It was an exercise in pretence. The mediators pretended that they were dealing with an intact sovereign state on the one hand and a legitimate political opposition on the other hand. The fact that the peace negotiations themselves were proof that the Mozambican state was not as sovereign and as intact as it pretended to be was a necessary fiction for the success of mediation. The same argument applies equally well to the rebels, whose inability to formulate a coherent political programme and obvious attempts at blackmailing their way into a post-conflict political order flew in the face of the aura of respectability attached to the Rome peace talks.

The substantive agenda of the peace talks centred on the peacemakers' dilemma. It revolved around the tension between negative peace and positive peace. The purely technical aspects of positive peace did take place as planned. Demobilisation, for example, took place on schedule, even if initially RENAMO only demobilised fighters from marginal areas such as Niassa and Inhambane. Later it transpired that the government and RENAMO had both attempted to keep "hidden armies." The moves were aborted by the soldiers themselves, who were war-fatigued and feared being excluded from the process of demobilisation. Disarmament also got off to a bad start, as RENAMO only surrendered poorly maintained and old weaponry (Vines 1996). Both the government and RENAMO continued to maintain undeclared weapons stores, a small fraction of which were located and destroyed by the UN (Vines 155). In the run-up to the first elections in 1994, there were numerous violent incidents, 374 overall, involving former fighters. In one such incident a government minister along with 200 other people was kidnapped and held hostage by former combatants. Under the provisions of the General Peace Agreement, demobilised soldiers were to be given a monthly cash subsidy for 18 months funded by the international community, a demobilisation card, civilian clothing, food for the journey back home and three months' salary in advance. In addition, the government pledged a six-month subsidy to be disbursed by the authorities of the demobilised soldiers' home areas or of an area of their choice. The formation of the national army took much longer than envisaged. In fact, contrary to what had been planned, no unified army was on the ground by the time elections were held in 1994.

Technical reconstruction of destroyed infrastructure started even before the elections. It was part of the national reconstruction programme that donors had committed themselves to financing once peace had been achieved.

There have been very critical voices against the politics of aid to Mozambique. These have stressed its inappropriateness and insufficiency (Hanlon 1991; 1996) and its problematic neo-liberal assumptions (Abrahamsson and Nilsson 1995). Whatever the relative merits of the practice of development aid in Mozambique, it is obvious that structural adjustment has provided a framework for the management of reconstruction activities in the post-war period.

However, with the exception of the return of church property confiscated by the FRELIMO government during its revolutionary phase as well as the return of—or compensation for—nationalised property, not much else has happened on this score. Neither the government army nor the rebels have been held accountable for looted or illegally acquired property. In spite of the fact that FRELIMO and RENAMO regularly hurl accusations against each other on war atrocities, these have not, as yet, been regulated in the form of prosecution of war criminals or a nation-wide reconciliation initiative on the South African model.

While it is fair to assume that the Mozambican conflict was ripe for resolution, available evidence suggests that the achievement of negative peace held important aspects of positive peace hostage to the negotiated settlement. Two aspects are worthy of note, both affecting the government as much as the rebels.

There seems to have been an assumption that successful mediation, measured according to whether negative peace had been achieved, would have to bracket off human rights issues. Neither the government, nor the rebels, stood in a good light as far as these were concerned. The history of FRELIMO is one characterised by serious human rights abuses, which have never been properly discussed in Mozambique. FRELIMO shares with other liberation movements a general contempt for the rights of individuals held to be opposed to its ideological goals. During the liberation war, executions of adversaries as well as violent purges seem to have taken place as a matter of routine (Cabrita 2000; Chilcote 1972). In the period immediately before and after independence, political opponents were jailed, "re-educated" and even executed on grounds that hold little legal water. When the political system was opened up in the early 1990s, there were a few attempts, especially by the relatives of the victims, to reopen the files. These bore little fruit. Throughout the post-independence socialist experiment, FRELIMO had a tendency to treat human rights in a cavalier manner by subordinating basic human rights issues to the ideological goal of constructing a socialist society. People were sent to so-called "re-education camps,"[14] or rounded up and forced to leave their homes and relatives and start a new existence elsewhere in the country. Corporal and capital punishment were reintroduced after having been abolished at independence. In the late seventies and early eighties, there were public executions of "enemies of the state," a category that lumped together captured insurgents and racketeers. While these human rights abuses never took place on as massive and genocidal a scale as in Cambodia under the Khmer Rouge, a regime FRELIMO identified as a "natural ally," they followed, at times, a similar fanatical ideological logic.

The RENAMO rebels were even worse. They rank amongst the most brutal guerrilla movements Africa has ever seen. Their terrorist repertoire included the routine maiming of victims chillingly documented by Lina Magaia, a Mozambican journalist (Magaia 1988). RENAMO directed its violence principally against civilians, ambushing vehicles and trains, looting and burning to the ground entire villages and small towns and sowing landmines on a massive scale in the rural countryside. Living on communal villages or being a member of a FRELIMO organisation was reason enough to be the target for RENAMO's brutal reprisals. The substantive agenda of the peace talks circumvented these issues in the interest of negative peace. During the negotiations, the mediators were too weary to address such issues. No provisions were made for these problems after the peace process was completed.

The second aspect related to the substantive agenda concerns the political economy of peace itself. Peace was in the interest of both parties to the conflict. Nevertheless, it had to be sold to them. As far as the government was concerned, peace was intimately linked to the prospect of a steady flow of development aid. Donors had made it clear to the government of Mozambique as early as 1984 that aid would only be forthcoming if the country could move towards peace. The Nkomati Accord was a preliminary that was soon to be followed by economic liberalisation and later political opening. Peace held out the promise of a state in control of the flow of development resources. FRELIMO's adamant refusal to form a government of national unity after narrowly winning the first multiparty elections in 1994 effectively allowed it to reap the benefits of peace in the form of control over development aid. The only concession that FRELIMO made to RENAMO was the offer to the latter's leader of the special status of "Leader of the Opposition," a position that entailed a state salary, benefits and protocol treatment.

As for the rebels, it is clear that peace meant much more than just an end to fighting. Not only did they seize the opportunity offered by the negotiations to make up for their financial shortcomings, but they also sought to secure their livelihood in post-conflict Mozambique. Within the framework of the cease-fire, a UN Trust Fund was set up in 1993 to aid political parties in the initial stages of democracy. Western goverments raised as much as US$17 million for RENAMO to transform itself into a political party. Its middle-ranking officers benefited from US$250,000 earmarked for them as handouts every month (Vines:152). Illiterate military leaders were integrated into the new national army as high-ranking officers. Leading RENAMO members found themselves sitting on commissions and institutions that placed them in a position to fend for themselves and their followers. The major prize, however, went to the leadership in the form of control over the resources flowing to the organisation as part of the peace deal.

Conclusion: The rebels who did not lose the war, but lost the peace...

The Rome peace negotiations brought a bitter and brutal war to an end. While it is perfectly legitimate to see them as an example of a very successful peace negotiation, caution should be exercised. They were able to bring peace about because they recognised the reality of violent armed conflicts. While basic political issues are important, more down to earth considerations have to be taken into account if peace negotiations are to be successful. Politics were central to the Mozambican conflict. The idea that the conflict was about democracy or the return of the country to its own cultural traditions was a usable one, both for the warring parties as well as for interested observers. It served the purpose of giving coherence to efforts to making it solvable.

However, the main thrust of the negotiation process did not consist in laying the ground for democracy to work. Rather, it consisted in winning the warring parties over to the cause of peace. The main bait used by the international mediators to lure the warring parties into negotiations was the promise of development aid to be channelled through a democratic and peaceful Mozambican state. In this, however, there lay a dilemma that casts its shadow over the post-conflict order. Peace negotiations aimed at bringing about negative peace and in order to do so they had to gloss over basic human rights issues such as the atrocities that were committed during the war, the destruction of property and the general arrested development of the country. Violence, both for the ruling FRELIMO party as well as for the insurgent RENAMO rebels, paid.

The basic assumption underlying the outcome of the Rome negotiations is that there were neither winners nor losers. Yet the facts contradict this assumption. The warring parties were bribed into a settlement, but the ruling FRELIMO party won the day. Since the biggest prize was the development state, by winning the first general elections in 1994 and surviving through the transitional stage to the second general elections in 1999, FRELIMO was able to keep the state firmly under its control and dictate the terms of the post-conflict order. Although the Rome peace treaty provided for a strong RENAMO voice in the post-conflict political order through its representation in major national institutions such as the National Electoral Commission and the Armed Forces, FRELIMO has been able to set the pace by virtue of its control of the state.

To add to RENAMO's difficulties it has been unable to make the transition from a rebel movement into a political party. Here again the Rome negotiations can be regarded as having played a significant role. Indeed, as part of the peace deal, the RENAMO leadership was placed in a neo-patrimonial position with regards to its own constituency. The United Nations Trust Fund as well as the cash handouts paid to the leaders gave the latter considerable financial power, which they have used to entrench their position. Most internal conflicts within RENAMO have been over the distribution of financial resources. The RENAMO leader has often been accused of using the party's treasury as private property. Meanwhile, RENAMO's chief negotiator in Rome, Raul Domingos, has left the party for reasons related to accusations of financial mismanagement rather than for political differences.

Coupled with this, RENAMO failed to develop a clear political profile. This might not be unrelated, once again, to the terms of the Rome peace agreement. Given that the major prize promised by the peace settlement was the state, RENAMO concentrated its energies on capturing it. In the process, the rebels neglected basic political work such as establishing structures at the local level. In 1998, Mozambique held council elections,[15] which were boycotted by RENAMO. In this way, it might have missed a golden opportunity to establish itself as a political force with political responsibilities within the context of local-level politics. There are signs that this has dawned on RENAMO, as it prepares to contest the next council elections. Whether this indicates a significant departure from the obsession with state power remains to be seen. The highly centralised nature of Mozambican politics has played a role in promoting state fixation. In a context where all taxes are levied and distributed by the central authorities, real political power can only be wielded by those who control the state.

It is in this sense that it can be said that RENAMO did not lose the war, but lost the peace. Its effective military campaign was a useful resource to win political accommodation in a post-conflict Mozambique, but the benefits of peace in the form of the development state went to the former enemy. All that RENAMO has been left with is the empty shell of a neo-patrimonial political organisation without enough funds to keep up the pretence. The Rome peace agreement seems to have come to its limits. It secured stability through the injection of development aid to the FRELIMO-controlled state and money to RENAMO, both of which mixed with the post-war reconstruction boom to foster a sense of optimism. This money is running short and will not be enough to buy RENAMO's acquiescence. The next elections may be a very strong test of the Rome agreement. Should FRELIMO win, there will be even less for RENAMO. Should RENAMO win, FRELIMO might fall into a crisis as a state party without a state. It seems that the post-war arrangement faces its major test.

It is not surprising that RENAMO's political discourse has become more aggressive in tone. Already at the last elections RENAMO cried foul, accusing the ruling FRELIMO party of fraud. Even now, in the run-up to council and parliamentary elections, the tone has been highly charged, with RENAMO warning that the only way it can fail to win the elections is if the ruling FRELIMO party commits fraud. This warning is not only indicative of the deep mistrust that underlies Mozambican politics at the moment, but also reflects the terms of the Rome peace deal in a significant manner. An important party to the peace deal is getting desperate, and this might not augur well for the future of peace in Mozambique.

Notes

[1] The celebratory literature includes Alden 2001; Cabrita 2000; Chan and Venâncio 1998; Della Rocca 1997; Synge 1997.

[2] Most recent civil wars did not achieve peace even when peace agreements were signed (e.g., Liberia, Sierra Leone, Angola, D.R. Congo). The few cases where civil wars were actually terminated were mainly due to the victory of one side (e.g., Uganda, Biafra).

[3] See Neubert 2003 for an elaborate discussion.

[4] Violent group conflicts shall be differentiated with regard to: the actors involved and their (political) objectives, the specific type of warfare, financial resources for war, and the internal structures of warring parties, including command-structure, professionalization, and with regards to links between fighters and a given population.

[5] A compromise is a regulation that offers amnesty to those who acknowledge their guilt.

In South Africa this was the case for violent acts committed out of political motives. As a result, the political leaders de facto had good chances for an amnesty and only the lower officer ranks and the rank and file risked criminal proceedings.

[6] From the perspective of the defeated, the new peace order is forced and seen as one-sided (e.g., the war crime tribunals in Rwanda or ex-Yugoslavia are criticised by the defendants).

[7] A particularly chilling sign consisted in massacres, such as in Homoíne and Manjacaze where 400 and 90, respectively, were slaughtered by roving Renamo gangs.

[8] There was, for instance, an anonymous letter written by Liberation War veterans calling for talks with our "brothers" in the bush (Anonyme 1988).

[9] I remember a chilling conversation in 1997 with a former vice-president of Renamo—an academic based in the U.S. It took place at a Lisbon Hotel and was a never-ending list of executions, assassinations and threats that took place in South Africa, Malawi and Portugal over the political leadership of Renamo and control of its funds [EM] (see also Vines 1991).

[10] Alex Vines reports that the Minister of Defence complained at a Frelimo Party Congress that an increasing number of young people were refusing conscription (Vines 1996).

[11] Kenya gave refuge to a considerably large Mozambican dissident community from the liberation struggle years.

[12] This hostility seemed to stem from Banda's, Malawi's first president, territorial ambitions; Banda had coveted parts of Mozambique and seems to have struck deals with disaffected former Portuguese settlers to achieve this.

[13] Della Rocca writes: "A l'exception des armes, la Renamo est dénuée de tout matériel et de toute facilité technique essentielle: elle manque de médicaments, d'essence, de chaussures, d'énergie électrique, de papier, de bics, de moyens de transport et de passeports. Après une séance de négociation, alors qu'il se prépare à retourner dans la forêt, [Raul] Domingos [the rebels' chief negotiator in Rome] doit mettre à exécutio des listes d'achat d'objets les plus variés, allant des crayons aux piles, qui le retiennent longtemps dans les supermarchés de Rome" (p.232).

[14] André Matsangaíssa, Renamo's first leader, as well as Afonso Dhlakama escaped from such a camp to Southern Rhodesia.

[15] Albeit in 33 cities and towns.

Works Cited

Abrahamsson, Hans, and Anders Nilsson. 1995. *Mozambique, the Troubled Transition: From Socialist Construction to Free Market Capitalism.* London, Atlantic Highlands, N.J.: Zed Books.

Alden, Chris. 2001. *Mozambique and the Construction of the New African State: From Negotiations to Nation Building.* Basingstoke: Palgrave.

Anonyme. 1988. "Lettre des Anciens Combattants." *Politique Africaine* 29.

Austin, Kathi, and William Minter. 1994. *Invisible Crimes: U.S. Private Intervention in the War in Mozambique.* Washington, DC: Africa Policy Information Center.

Cabrita, João M. 2000. *Mozambique: the Tortuous Road to Democracy.* New York: Palgrave.

Chan, Stephen, and Moisés Venâncio. 1998. *War and Peace in Mozambique.* Houndmills, Basingstoke, Hampshire; New York: Macmillan Press; St. Martin's Press.

Chilcote, Ronald H. 1972. *Emerging Nationalism in Portuguese Africa: Documents.* Stanford: Hoover Institution Press, Stanford University.

Della Rocca, Roberto. 1997. *Mozambique: de la Guerre à la Paix – Histoire d'une Médiation Insolite.* Paris: L'Harmattan.

Elwert, Georg, Stephan Feuchtwang, and Dieter Neubert, eds. 1999a. *The Dynamics of Violence – Processes of Escalation and De-escalation in Violent Group Conflicts.* Berlin: Duncker & Humblot.

———. 1999b. "The Dynamics of Collective Violence – An introduction." *The Dynamics of Violence – Processes of Escalation and De-escalation in Violent Group Conflicts.* Ed. Georg Elwert, Stephan Feuchtwang, and Dieter Neubert. Berlin: Duncker & Humblot. 9-31.

Finnegan, William. 1992. *A Complicated War: the Harrowing of Mozambique.* Berkeley: U of California P.

Geffray, Christian. 1990. *La Cause des Armes au Mozambique: Anthropologie d'une Guerre Civile.* Paris: Karthala; Credu.

Gersony, R. 1988. *Mozambique Refugee Accounts of Principally Conflict-Related Experiences in Mozambique.* Washington: State Department.

Hall, Margaret and Tom Young. 1997. *Confronting Leviathan: Mozambique since Independence.* Athens: Ohio UP.

Hanlon, Joseph. 1991. *Mozambique – Who Calls the Shots?* London: James Currey.

———. 1996. *Peace without Profit: How the IMF Blocks Rebuilding in Mozambique.* Oxford; Portsmouth, N.H.: Irish Mozambique Solidarity & the International African Institute in association with J. Currey; Heinemann.

Hoile, David and Mozambique Institute. 1994. *Mozambique, Resistance and Freedom: a Case for Reassessment.* London: Mozambique Institute.

Hume, Cameron. 1994. *Ending Mozambique's War – the Role of Mediation and Good Offices.* Washington: US Institute of Peace Press.

Magaia, Lina. 1988. *Dumba Nengue, Run for your Life: Peasant Tales of Tragedy in Mozambique.* Trenton, N.J.: Africa World Press.

Minter, William. 1994. *Apartheid's Contras: an Inquiry into the Roots of War in Angola and Mozambique.* Johannesburg; London; Atlantic Highlands, N.J.: Witwatersrand UP; Zed Books.

Neubert, Dieter. 2003. "The 'Peacemakers' Dilemma'. The role of NGOs in processes of peace-building in decentralised conflicts." *In Search of Peace: Contemporary Processes of Ideological, Social and Legal Reconstruction after War and Disruption. Hart Onati Series on International Law and Society.* Ed. M.-C. Foblets and T. v. Trotha. Oxford: Hart.

Saul, John S. 1993. *Recolonization and Resistance: Southern Africa in the 1990s.* Trenton, NJ: Africa World Press.

Sift, Peter. 1999. *The Silent War – South African Recce Operations 1969-1994.* Alberton: Galago.

Synge, Richard. 1997. *Mozambique – UN Peacekeeping in Action 1992-94.* Washington: US Institute of Peace Press.

United Nations. 1995. *The United Nations and Mozambique, 1992-1995.* New York: United Nations Dept. of Public Information.

Vines, Alex. 1991. *RENAMO: terrorism in Mozambique.* London; Bloomington: Centre for Southern African Studies, University of York, in association with James Currey; Indiana UP.

———. 1996. *RENAMO: from Terrorism to Democracy in Mozambique.* York, [England]: Centre for Southern African Studies, University of York.

Zartman, William. 1985. *Ripe for Resolution. Conflict and Intervention in Africa.* New York, Oxford: Oxford UP.

Dieter Neubert is Professor of Development Sociology at the University of Bayreuth. He has written extensively on African political sociology, knowledge and development work. His most recent publications include:

Neubert, Dieter, ed. 2002. *Postkoloniale Transformation in Afrika. Zur Neubestimmung der Soziologie der Dekolonisation.* Berlin: Lit Verlag (with Anna-Maria Brandstetter).

Elwert, Georg, Stephan Feuchtwang, & Dieter Neubert, eds. 1999. *The Dynamics of Violence – Processes of Escalation and De-escalation in Violent Group Conflicts.* Supplement of the journal *Sociologus.* Berlin: Duncker & Humblot. 290 pp.

Neubert, Dieter. "A Development Utopia Re-visited. Non-Governmental Organisations in Africa." *Sociologus* 47: 51-77.

Elísio Macamo is Assistant Professor in Development Sociology at the University of Bayreuth. He has written on religion, work and disasters in Africa. His most recent publications are:

Macamo, Elísio, ed. 2002. *Unraveling Ties – From Social Cohesion to New Practices of Connectedness.* Frankfurt am Main: Campus (with Shalini Randeria, Yehuda Elkana and Ivan Krastev).

Macamo, Elísio, ed. 2003. *Entsetzliche soziale Prozesse – theoretische und empirische Annäherungen.* Hamburg: Lit Verlag (with Lars Clausen and Elke Geenen).

Macamo, Elísio, and Dieter Neubert. (2003). "When the post-revolutionary state decentralizes – the reorganization of political structures and administration in Mozambique." *Revista do Centro de Estudos Africanos* 4 [Lisboa] (in press).

Appearances and Realities of Post-War Reconstruction in Mozambique[1]

Branwen Gruffydd Jones

Abstract. Mozambique is widely promoted on the world stage as a success story. The international community celebrates Mozambique's success in achieving lasting peace after decades of war; in implementing economic and political reforms; attaining impressive and steady economic growth; and promoting peace, democracy and reform in the region of southern Africa. But what is the reality underlying this shining image of success and post-war reconstruction? This article seeks to expose the stark contrast between the discursive portrayal and celebration of Mozambique's post-war path towards democracy, growth and development, and the concrete reality of ever increasing inequality and the rise of systematic corruption and organized crime. The article first presents the dominant portrayal of Mozambique, giving examples from various discursive sites (official reports of international organizations, governmental documents, the media, etc.). The article then turns to explore the reality of Mozambique in the current period, focusing on two definitive aspects of Mozambique's post-war condition. First, it describes the growing inequality that characterises Mozambican society today, the ever-growing wealth alongside widespread poverty and social exclusion in both urban and rural areas. It then considers the entrenched culture of corruption and violence that has arisen in the context of neo-liberal reform, exemplified most tragically in the assassination of journalist Carlos Cardoso in 2000. The analysis draws on various sources, including interviews conducted by the author in 1999, official reports and documents, and the media.

The thought typical of any age has the primary function of hiding the realities of that age and perpetuating its evils.[2]

Mozambique: Africa's success story

There is a particular image of Mozambique that is currently promoted on the international stage, by and for the international community. This is an image of peace, stability, democracy, reform, and growth, with a government that displays political will and commitment to poverty reduction. It is an image of an "African success story," which goes as follows. A country wracked by a brutal "civil war" for more than a decade, which left it "one of the poorest countries of the world," over the past decade Mozambique has set out on a path towards reconstruction and development. The "mistaken" economic policies of the "socialist" period after independence were abandoned long ago and Mozambique has joined the rest of the world in opening up its markets, privatising businesses, and welcoming foreign investment. The former one-party system has been reformed into a multi-party democracy, and a healthy civil society has emerged. While the sustained effort and commitment of Mozambique's government and peoples are applauded for bringing about this success, Mozambique is also held up as an example of successful international intervention and cooperation in Africa. This was clear first during the peace process of the early 1990s, and more recently in the co-operative manner in which government policies are formed in consultation with the donor community and private sector as well as local civil society. Thus in 1998 the UK Department for International Development affirmed that

> good progress is being made. Macro-economic management is sound and the economy is growing at about 8%. The Government of Mozambique is committed to reducing poverty. [...] Democracy is functioning [...]. The Government promotes a constructive and open relationship with the donors. The prospects for an effective development partnership with Mozambique are good. Britain should expect to be involved long-term. (DFID 1)

When the UN Security Council met in New York in January 2000 to discuss its engagement with Africa, the Deputy Secretary-General to the Security Council, Louise Fréchette, proudly claimed:

> Mr. President, if there is one country in the world where the efforts of the United Nations—in peacemaking, peacekeeping and peace-building—have made an incontrovertible difference, I suggest that Mozambique would be that country. Let no "Afro-pessimist" say, therefore, that you in the United States, or we in the

Secretariat, or any of the members of this Council, are wasting our time in trying to help Africans solve their problems.[3]

The European Parliament's Commission on Development and Cooperation has recently observed:

> Since the end of the civil war and the first democratic elections in 1994, Mozambique has become one of the most successful nations of mainland Africa in terms of economic development and reconstruction, with an annual growth rate of 9% between 1995 and 1999. With 60% of its GDP financed by development cooperation, Mozambique has operated an efficient management and execution of the funds concerned, and has thus been able to benefit twice (in 1999, and again a few days after the end of the mission) from the IMF/World Bank initiative for heavily indebted poor countries (HIPCs) for reduction of their external debt. (European Parliament 2)

Paul Fauvet sums up the prevailing view: "Since peace came in 1992, the image of Mozambique has been transformed from that of an economic basket case to an African 'success story.'" (12).

At the forefront of the government's reform and development programme is its commitment to poverty reduction. This is seen in the recent establishment of the *National Plan for the Reduction of Absolute Poverty*, which was drawn up in consultation with Mozambican civil society and consists of a policy framework through which to achieve a significant reduction in the level of absolute poverty over the next decade.[4] A central component of the poverty reduction policy is sustained economic growth: "For a poor country such as Mozambique, rapid economic growth is an essential and powerful tool for poverty reduction in the medium and long-term" (GOM *National Plan* 2).

It is widely admitted that Mozambique's economic growth is beginning from a "low base," but nevertheless Mozambique has witnessed remarkable recovery and economic growth since the end of the war in 1992. During the late 1990s and into the twenty-first century the portrayal of Mozambique's apparent success is epitomised in the celebration of its "double digit economic growth" and "single digit inflation" by the Mozambican government,[5] Western governments and donor agencies,[6] international organisations,[7] and commercial banks.[8] Mozambique has been heralded by the international press as an "emerging market," one of the world's fastest growing economies.

The Economist Intelligence Unit forecast that Africa would be the fastest-growing region in 2001, with Mozambique leading the way.

This is the appearance of Mozambique's path of success in post-conflict reconstruction and growth, as promoted by the international community. In this globalising era when everything is for sale, national economies themselves are now being "marketed," put on display as attractively as possible to catch the attention of global investors. Here is Mozambique's brand image provided by one such image-broker, Summit Communications, an organisation that specialises "in promoting the image of countries internationally":

> **Healthy Economy Set To Take Off**
> With a government firmly committed to liberalization, Mozambique's economic potential is looking up. In agriculture, transport and industry, new reforms and an active private sector are driving major expansion, while the newly-created tourism ministry has the enviable task of promoting one of Africa's most idyllic and little known destinations.
>
> Today's Mozambique is characterized by a political stability that combined with swiftly advancing liberal economic reforms is bringing hopes of a prosperous future. Implemented by a government keen to cooperate with the private sector and woo foreign investment, those reforms have brought double-digit growth alongside single-digit inflation.[9]

The notion of "growth" is one of the many organic metaphors that infuse the ideological discourse about "development," which consists of a particular way of thinking about and describing processes of social change in different parts of the world, primarily the so-called Third World. This discourse emerged in the post-war years of the twentieth century and has been re-invigorated in recent years. But the type of "growth" produced by neo-liberal development policy today is more analogous to the growth of cancerous cells than that of any healthy plant or animal. The "double-digit economic growth" experienced by Mozambique in recent years is not a sign of a healthy society or of a healthy economy, if we are to retain any notion of economic development as having something to do with increasing the capacity of a society to meet the needs of its members: "in use-value terms the drive for unlimited growth would appear not as a sign of a healthy economy, but as a cancer on the body politic" (Collier, *Value* 9). Mozambican journalist Paul

Fauvet has underlined that Mozambique's is a "growth with poverty" (12). It is also a growth with enormous wealth—but not the kind of wealth that produces a rich society, only rich individuals.

The lived experience of "double digit economic growth"

The contrast between the enthusiasm with which Mozambique's post-war reconstruction is portrayed in the various discursive sites of the international community, and the concrete experience of that same process for ordinary Mozambicans, is stark. The gulf between the discursive and the concrete is matched only by the ever-growing gulf between rich and poor in Mozambique. The former vision of an independent Mozambique no longer characterised by "the exploitation of man by man" has given way to a current reality of daily insecurity and lack for the majority, alongside ever new heights of luxury and consumption for the few. The extremes of inequality are visible and prominent; Mozambique has become a place of different worlds alongside each other. This is evident along two dimensions: first in the difference between the worlds of the city and the countryside; second in the growing contrast of wealth and poverty within the towns and cities.

The majority of Mozambicans live in the countryside. While there is significant differentiation within and between different regions, most experience broadly similar conditions of life, arising from their basic situation of being dependent for the most part on what they can produce: they are "direct producers" in a liberalised market economy. They produce with their own "sweat and blood," using family labour and hand tools. They sell what they can—ground-nuts, maize, cassava, cotton, beans, perhaps some cashew nuts. They sell their produce in local markets or to passing traders, to get money to buy "*bens da primeira necessidade*"—*kapulanas*, shoes, second-hand clothing,[10] cooking oil, pots and pans, machetes, salt, soap and washing powder, and so on.

In their own words the people living in the countryside are *camponeses* or *Moçambicanos*. In the words of the prevailing development discourse they are "small-holders" or "micro-entrepreneurs." According to this discourse they are also, most of them, "poor," "absolutely poor" and even, "ultra poor":

> Given that more than two out of every three Mozambicans live below the reference poverty line, there is a case for distinguishing a notion of ultra-poverty, which can help us to focus on the poorest among the poor. (MPF 57-8)

The aim of government policy, supported by the international community, is to reduce this rural poverty through the promotion of economic growth and the creation of dynamic rural markets. The liberalisation of markets is assumed to liberate the rural producers, enabling them to respond to price incentives and increase their income:

> Price incentives, and therefore market liberalisation are important to rural poverty reduction. [...] Given the extent and depth of rural poverty, measures to improve rural livelihoods are the first foundation of the national strategy for poverty reduction. An appropriate incentive environment for agriculture through the full liberalisation of agricultural markets [...] will raise smallholder incomes and create rural employment both on and off farm. (GOM *Poverty Reduction* ii, 14)

For most Mozambicans living in the countryside, however, the concrete reality of the competitive market in rural Mozambique, the actual experience of so-called "price-incentives," is not an experience of liberation but of chronic insecurity and lack:

> These days production is not forced. Each one decides how many *machambas* to plant each year. It is not controlled by anyone. And we manage to produce. The problem is this, when we take our produce to the shops, we arrive there, we get—I don't know, maybe a million *meticais*, two million, but that money serves for almost nothing, for the *camponês*. We produce a lot, but the problem is this. We go to sell our produce and receive money, but what we can buy—we can buy virtually nothing, it is only enough perhaps to buy a *kapulana* for our wife, and the husband has to remain as he is, with nothing, only at least giving some respect to his wife. [...] The problem for us *camponeses*, is that the traders do not respect the work of the *camponês*. For example, they come with a price—who knows how the price is established, whether it is established centrally, who knows, but the *camponês* has nothing to do with it, has no say, he is only told—"look, we have come to buy your produce for such-and-such." He can say nothing. So he is obliged to go along with that price. He cannot set the price, let us say, in relation to his own blood, the work of his own blood. He cannot say—"the price of this is so much." Because he is the one that knows, he is the one who produced, and knows how he produced. And so it is him that can establish the price. But these days—this does not happen. The prices are established elsewhere, and so the traders arrive here, and buy, and the *camponês* has nothing to do, is not able to complain. On

the contrary, we would remain with our produce in our house until it rots there. So in fact we are obliged to sell at whatever price. Whether we like it or not, we have to sell at whatever price.[11]

Here, these days [...] the produce we sell is undervalued. In terms of the prices of the traders, it is very low, in relation to the things we need to buy from the shops. So for someone to buy a bar of soap, for example, which costs 10,000M, you have to take a lot of produce, because when you take one kilo it is not enough to buy a bar of soap. Because the price of a kilo of ground-nut is very low, so you have to take many kilos of ground-nut in order to be able to buy just one bar of soap. And then what about clothes for your wife, clothes for the children, you have to take so much produce. This is our difficulty, here in the countryside. .[...] The money has very little value, whereas in the past the money was small but it had a lot of value—with 100 *escudos* you could buy something. Now with 5,000M you can't buy anything. There is no balance between the money and the goods. [...] The prices vary, they differ, according to how much produce you have, and when. Someone can sell their ground-nut for 4,000M a kilo. Then there will come a time—after the ground-nut is over—the same traders come wanting to buy for 5,000M, 6,000M. But after it is over! [...] they have their tactics. The government doesn't manage to establish a fixed price for the whole season. [...] If a person has nothing, they need money that instant [...] say, you want to buy some soap, some rice, some sugar, because you don't have any [...] your child is ill, you want to take her to hospital [...] the guy offers 4,000M—"do you want to sell, or not?" You say—"but, I'd sell if it was 5,000M." So he doesn't buy, he goes away. And when this happens—you say "wait, wait, come back, I'll sell!"[12]

In many respects life in urban areas is very different from that in the countryside, but for many Mozambicans these different worlds share a basic condition of economic insecurity and insufficient satisfaction of needs. In towns and cities many Mozambicans live in the *bairros* surrounding the centre. For those lucky enough to have a regular job in the manufacturing or service sector the wages are generally pitifully low.[13] Many companies have closed, temporarily or permanently, while workers are still owed months of pay.[14] Some work in domestic employment, as *empregados domésticos* for richer Mozambicans or the expatriate community. Others try to gain some money by buying goods from traders and selling them on the street—any type of good they can acquire: batteries, shower curtains, brightly coloured pens, plastic rucksacks, plastic drinking bottles, children's toys, belts, cotton thread, boiled sweets, chewing gum, packets of biscuits, skin-lightening cream, watches. These are the "*vendadores da rua*," often young children, roaming the streets with goods in their hands, trying to sell to passers-by. The problem for the ordinary Mozambican during this post-war period, in urban areas as in the countryside, is how to live, how to get by:

> The life of the people [...]—let me say this, during the war, things were very difficult. There were no clothes, there was nothing; when this war—when Mozambicans were fighting each other—stopped, in this period now, now there are clothes, in the shops. But even so, life has become difficult. Well—some people have things—as also in other countries, it isn't everyone who has, is it? Some have, some don't have. [...] The problem we face these days is not a lack of clothing. It is a lack of employment. So—it becomes very difficult: how a person can get by, work things out (*resolver a vida*). There are many there, sitting, who have nothing to do. [...] So life becomes very difficult. How to get by, throughout the year, is very difficult. [...] Really, here in Mozambique, we are in a really bad situation. Especially here in Nampula. Here in Nampula things are really bad.[15]

> These days life is very complicated, things are very expensive to buy, and the money these days is worth nothing. Even if I have a lot of money—but that money—it isn't enough even to be able to buy something that will last—it will only buy something that will last for one day. For example with 100 *contos*[16] you go to buy some food, the food won't last you a week. So our money today doesn't have value. Even if you have a lot, see? But that money won't have much impact. These days, the main difficulty is that each person struggles in order to have things. This is what is most difficult—how to have. Yes. And so a person finds a contradiction, between his needs, and his capacities, you find a contradiction when you need and you don't have the capacity. These days this is the problem, this is the issue. [...] the struggle between wanting and being able. The difficulty of life these days is this. Yes. Each person is struggling to have things. But it is not easy to have things these days.[17]

The town of Angoche on the coast of Nampula Province used to be a vibrant and busy commercial centre, a place of importance and activity, with two cashew factories, a rice-processing factory and a fish-processing factory. Now none of these factories are functioning, as a result first of the war and then as a result of the post-war liberalization.[18] The town has a forlorn and desolate atmosphere and the livelihoods of thousands in the area have been sacrificed in the name of market efficiency:

> *Former cashew factory employee:*
> First I worked at the factory in Nacala [...], then I was transferred here when it was *Caju de Moçambique.* Then it became *Angocaju.* I worked all the years, from Nacala to here, for twenty-five years. I even became a mechanic.
>
> *Second former cashew factory employee:*
> I began to work in 1988. Here, in Angoche, when it was *Caju de Moçambique.* [...] I worked in the raw-material store, we had to weigh the *castanha*, the raw material as it entered the warehouse. Later I became a security guard. And then I was made redundant—let us say—with nothing. Now, as the factory has stopped working, some are really suffering, they have no means of livelihood. Others go to fish, but you don't earn anything, fish doesn't bring any money, [...] yes, he is one of these, see? (*pointing to the first man, who had fish scales all over his hands and was holding a small fish*) he is selling fish, you see? A mechanic!! Many people don't have any work, and so there are no people to buy. People don't have money because no one has any work. And so because of this there is no good life.
>
> *First:* Because of this things are bad. I live with nine people at home. I have five children.
> *Second:* There are many people who have their families to look after. I have six children. And so people go to fish, they can fish, but there is no one to buy the fish, because no one has money.
> *First:* It didn't used to be like this. There were at least three factories functioning, or two [...] now—life is not good. It is not normal. There were around 1,500 people working at the factory—in the beginning, around 1974, it was 4,000, but lately only 1,500. Now all these people are left with nothing. They go around with empty hands. [...] Each worker has more family—three, four, five, six [...] life is difficult, visibly, as you can see—[*showing all around*].
> *Second:* Things are miserable, because we have to rely on fishing. Artisanal fishing, small scale—not industrialised, mechanised, like *Angopeixe* [The former fish-processing plant]. And so this fishing—truly people cannot manage. As you can see—[*pointing to the mechanic*].
> *First:* I have been there since the early morning—from five in the morning until now [*around midday*] I haven't even made 10,000M. And my children are wait-

> ing for me. And they still haven't eaten, the first meal—they still haven't had breakfast. It is like this for most people. This is how things are.[19]

As we walked back through the *bairro*, we passed through the market, past rows of stalls where each person was selling small piles of small fish, small onions, garlic, tomatoes, nails, flour, rice, sugar—all in small, small quantities. The *Secretário* of the *bairro* said to me: "you see, all these people are selling and no one is buying, in our market."

These are just some glimpses into the everyday reality of Mozambique's current neo-liberal order as it is experienced by ordinary Mozambicans in towns and the countryside—by peasants, unemployed former factory workers, domestic employees, *vendadores da rua.* The concrete lived experience of other groups of "socially excluded" in Mozambican society has been explored recently in important research conducted by Carlos Serra and a group of researchers at the *Centro de Estudos Africanos* at Eduardo Mondlane University.[20] Their research documents the conditions, experiences and views of various social groups and social worlds in Mozambique—drivers and passengers on Maputo's *chapas*[21] (Matsinhe); *lixeiros,* people who hunt through the city's rubbish tip for food, clothing and anything that can be recycled or sold (Colaço 2001); patients at Nampula's Psychiatric Hospital (Monteiro); *esmoleiros*, beggars in the city of Nampula (Aquimo); the world of the *barracas* in Maputo (Colaço 2000). In doing so this work brings into the focus of academic inquiry the reality that is experienced by the majority of Mozambicans today, those for whom notions of "double-digit economic growth," "participation," "poverty reduction," and "price incentives" remain abstract and empty phrases with little bearing on their lives.

So where is the evidence of the much-lauded double-digit economic growth? It is not in the factories, which lie silent with locked gates, leaving workers unemployed and empty-handed. Is it perhaps in the shining new shops, cafés and restaurants blossoming in the cities? In the shining new Mercedes automobiles, the 4x4 Pajeros and Isuzos parading the pot-holed streets of the city centres? In the space of a few months in 1999, two huge new shops opened in Nampula, with enormous glass shop-fronts and marble facing, selling a daunting array of household goods and equipment, tools, and mechanical parts. At the same time a new ice-cream parlour opened, which would have looked at home in any smart European or North American high-street. These small islands of luxury, plenty, and consumption stand out starkly against the surrounding dusty pot-holed roads and cracked pavements. The *vendadores da rua* watch from the darkness as 4x4s drive up and well-dressed passengers descend to enjoy an evening ice-cream.[22] Who is it that enjoys such treats, who is it that buys the wide-screen televisions, DVD players and microwave ovens on display in Nampula's marble-faced, air-conditioned sale-rooms? Who is it that fills up their brand new Nissan Patrols in the smart BP fore-court? And where does the money come from?

In Maputo the same processes take place but on a larger and faster scale—more hotels, more supermarkets, bigger shopping centres, appearing almost overnight. Their marble and glass façades shine in the sun while, across the pot-holed road, piles of rotting, stinking litter overflow from the old metal bins all over the cracked, broken pavements. Clearly there are some very wealthy people in Mozambique. But what is the source of their wealth? It does not seem to come from production in Mozambique. Mozambican society includes within it some exceedingly wealthy people; but it is not a wealthy society. The recent observations of writer and journalist Mia Couto articulate the profound contradictions of Mozambique's post-war economic growth:

> The biggest disgrace of a poor nation is that, instead of producing wealth, it produces the rich. But rich without wealth. In truth, it would be better to call them not rich but well-off. The rich are those who possess means of production.
>
> A rich person is one who generates money and provides employment. A well-off person is simply one who owns money. Or who thinks he does. Because, in truth, it is money who owns the person. The truth is this: our "rich" are too poor. What they have, they do not keep. Even worse: what they exhibit as theirs, is the property of others. It is the produce of robbing and shady deals. They cannot, however, these well-off people of ours, relax and enjoy the benefits of all that they have robbed. They live obsessed by the fear that they could be robbed.
>
> The biggest dream of our new-rich is, in the end, very small: a luxury car, some ephemeral *cintilâncias*. But the luxury vehicles are not able to dream very much, jolted by the pot-holes in the streets. The Mercedes or the BMW cannot fully realize their brilliance, occupied as they are with navigating between bulging *chapas* and pitted roads. The existence of good roads is dependent on a different sort of wealth. A wealth that serves the city. And the wealth of our new-rich was born from the opposite process: the impoverishment of the city and of society. (Couto 7)

The neo-liberal reforms of the past decade have enabled processes of cancerous "economic growth" in Mozambique, which produce not a wealthy society but only wealthy individuals, with wealth born from the impoverishment of society.

The political economy of double-digit growth: the growth of wealth and corruption

In pursuit of economic growth, since the mid to late 1980s the government of Mozambique has embarked on a programme of structural adjustment and liberalisation. This has included currency devaluation; one of the most extensive and rapid programmes of privatisation in Africa;[23] liberalisation of the market internally and externally through the removal of fixed prices and state-controlled marketing institutions and the removal of import and export tariffs; reform of the tax system and property laws to create an environment attractive for private business and, above all, foreign investment. All of this has been directed closely by the international financial institutions of the World Bank and International Monetary Fund and the donor community, which has met with varying degrees of criticism, resistance, and acceptance on the part of the Mozambican government and so-called "civil society." This process and context of neo-liberal reform, which has been embraced by some of the Mozambican political and economic elite and accepted reluctantly by others, has caused or provided the conditions of possibility for specific forms of economic activity and accumulation through which private individuals and groups gain at the expense of society. These include large-scale financial fraud, drug trafficking, money laundering, smuggling, and other forms of organised illegal activity. It is these forms of accumulation that help to account for some of the visible manifestations of extreme wealth alongside growing poverty and insecurity outlined above, which over the past decade have come to be a definitive condition of Mozambican society.

Over the past five years or so, increasing evidence has emerged that practices of fraud, organised crime and corruption have become embedded within Mozambican society at a high level. As public criticism and attention mounted so too did a culture of violence and a routine disregard for justice and public integrity, on the part of many economic and political actors. These tensions, structural symptoms of the neo-liberal transformation of Mozambique's political economy, culminated in the assassination of the investigative journalist and political activist Carlos Cardoso on November

21, 2000. This tragic murder was only one part of an ongoing struggle between social forces in Mozambican society that has grown up in the context of neo-liberal reform. This is a struggle between those seeking to further the collective interests of Mozambican society and those seeking to pursue personal gain with no regard for collective social costs. Few societies are free from such tensions, but over the past couple of decades the reorganisation or "adjustment" of society, in Mozambique and throughout the world, has created conditions that structurally favour the latter and hinder the former. And all this has been brought about under the guise of precisely the seductive, technocratic discourse of economic growth and prosperity examined above.

The rapid and widespread programme of privatisation, initiated in the mid-1990s, enabled foreign investors and members of the Mozambican elite to acquire assets easily and cheaply, with easy access to credit lent to the government by international economic institutions but disbursed by commercial banks. Many of the privatised enterprises have subsequently shut down while many of the original loans have not been paid back, so-called "non-performing loans." In the mid-1990s the state-owned banks were privatised, under the direct insistence of the World Bank and the IMF.[24] Joseph Hanlon has examined in detail the way in which the very hasty privatisation of the two main banks paved the way for future mismanagement. Over the next few years, the Banco Comercial de Moçambique (BCM) and Banco Popular de Desenvolvimento (BPD, which became Banco Austral) generated enormous losses.[25] When it came to raising new capital to rescue the banks, the government, which owned a percentage of the shares, was forced to sell treasury bonds equivalent to about 80 million USD$, at high levels of interest (over 22%). The cost of servicing this internal debt is now greater than servicing Mozambique's international debt.[26]

The most significant instance of bank fraud came to light in 1996, when it emerged that 144 billion *meticais* (about 14 million USD$) had been "siphoned" from a Maputo branch of BCM by means of a sophisticated scheme that exploited the bank's weak internal accounting procedures. Formal investigation into the 1996 bank fraud was slow and ineffective. It transpired that the process had been deliberately delayed and disorganised by members of the Public Prosecution Office, apparently acting to protect the suspects by preventing the case from proceeding and destroying key evidence from the case file. Ever since this fraud came to light there has been ongoing collusion between networks of criminals associated with the suspects and high-level officials in the Attorney General's office, the police and the prison service, from disrupting the fraud investigation to smuggling mobile phones into the cells of suspects detained in the high security prison. The embedded corruption has been accompanied by the systematic and ongoing use of violence and threats to attempt to silence or get rid of "inconvenient" lawyers, journalists, judges, and members of the Attorney General's office.[27]

Hanlon has explored numerous other practices of fraud based similarly on exploiting the weak internal banking procedures that have enabled fraudulent payments and the transfer of funds to foreign bank accounts. He estimates that the cost to the Mozambican economy from the combination of bad loans, incompetent management and fraud following the bank privatisations amounts to more than 400 million USD$.[28] Bank fraud is not the only area in which some high-level individuals in the government and the legal system facilitate illegal economic activity. Networks of criminals are involved in significant levels of drug trafficking, money laundering, trade in stolen cars, and other forms of illegal trade, which are made possible by protection or cooperation from police and customs officials, who are bought through bribes.[29] Gastrow and Mosse observe:

> Money laundering activities in Mozambique are linked primarily to drug trafficking. The profits of the Mozambicans involved in the trafficking amount to millions of US dollars each year. Some of this money is spent on items such as houses and luxury cars, but the traffickers also convert large portions of their proceeds into properties and businesses in the legitimate economy to generate profits or to sell at a later stage without arousing suspicion. It is suspected that this money has contributed to the upsurge in the construction of new buildings in Maputo, Nampula and Pemba. The investment in hotels and tourism is strategic because it is relatively easy to declare more clients than have actually been serviced and thereby disguise profits earned from illicit drug trafficking (9).

While the productive elements of Mozambique's economy continue to deteriorate, leaving thousands unemployed, parasitic forms of private accumulation thrive. Most Mozambicans do not have ready access to clean drinking water and must walk for over an hour to reach the nearest health unit.[30] Meanwhile the rate of construction of new hotels in Maputo since the mid-1990s is such that the Association of Mozambican Hotel Companies complain their profits are falling because there are now far more rooms than clients.[31] This is the reality of Mozambique's success story of rapid economic growth, and it is not the result of development policy gone wrong. On the contrary, it is the normal outcome of neo-liberal reform that is entirely abstracted from the concrete concerns and needs of human societies and concerned only about the growth of international capital. The up-beat promotion of Mozambique's success and prosperity on the international stage will be of little comfort to the peasants, the *vendadores da rua*, the unemployed factory workers, who struggle daily to make ends meet. But this discursive portrayal of Mozambique's condition is not intended for them; it is intended for foreign investors. What matters in the current global development era is not the satisfaction of human needs but the satisfaction of international credit ratings.

Notes

[1]This article draws on research that was funded by the UK Economic and Social Research Council (grant numbers R00429734736 and T026271069) and additional support from the University of Sussex, which is gratefully acknowledged. I thank the following for their various support and discussions which helped in writing this article: Gabrielle Anthmer, Dulce Bastos, Soila Hirvonen, Peki, Phillip Rothwell, Julian Saurin, Carlos Serra, and all those who facilitated my research in Mozambique.

[2] Collier, *Being and Worth* ix.

[3] Press Release DSG/SM/82 AFR/205 SC/6797, 31 January 2000.

[4] See Government of Mozambique 2001.

[5] In February 2002, President Joaquim Chissano told an audience of American investors that "in spite of the severe floods that affected the country for two consecutive years in early 2000, in the last five years Mozambique has shown steady high GDP growth rates in a sustainable manner. As a matter of fact, GDP growth between 1996 and 1999 averaged around 10%, inflation declined from a high two digits level in 1995 to a mere single lower digit at the end of 1999. Last year GDP grew by 14.9%. We are very proud of our accomplishments in Mozambique. The job creation, the ability to successfully attract new foreign investment, and the ability to sustain real double-digit economic growth has consistently earned Mozambique a place among the top economic performers." Address to the Corporate Council on Africa, February 25 2002, http://www.uspolicy.be/Issues/Africa/chiss.022602.htm. In December 2002 the Finance Minister Luisa Diogo reported that Mozambique's double-digit growth rate recorded in 2002 is expected to continue in 2003 ("Mozambique set to continue high economic growth: minister," Dec 24 2002, Agence France Press, http://quickstart.clari.net/qs_se/webnews/wed/ag/Qmozambique-economy.RX11_CDO.html).

[6] The US Government Trade Department's "Country Commercial Guide" for Mozambique at the end of 2001 stated that "Mozambique's macroeconomic policy reforms have led to double-digit GDP growth over recent years ... GDP growth for 1999 was approximately 10 percent, and has averaged in double digits during the past three years. The government expects the economy to continue to expand at a rate between 7-10 percent over the next several years, combined with low inflation rates" (*Mozambique Country Commercial Guide FY2001*, Ch. 1, http://www.usatrade.gov/Website/CCG.nsf/).

[7] "The World Bank's International Development Association (IDA) and the International Monetary Fund (IMF) agreed today that Mozambique has taken the steps necessary to reach its completion point under the enhanced framework of the Heavily Indebted Poor Countries (HIPC) Initiative. Mozambique becomes the third country to reach this point (after Bolivia and Uganda). [...] a return to near double-digit growth is expected during 2001." Press release, *The World Bank Group*, September 25, 2001. http://wbln0018.worldbank.org/news/pressrelease.nsf/. The UN Secretary-General's report on the *Implementation of the Programme of Action for the Least Developed Countries for the 1990s* (1999) reported: "Twenty of the least developed countries achieved GDP growth rate of 5 per cent or more in 1997, with three countries (Equatorial Guinea, Mozambique and Rwanda) recording double-digit growth" (UN 3).

[8] See "Quarterly Update for Mozambique," December 2002, Economics Division, Standard Bank of South Africa http://196.8.88.70/research/UMOZ0212.PDF.

[9] "About Us," http://www.summitreports.com/. Summit Communications produce "high-quality, informative sections that are distributed with *The New York Times* and are aimed at influencing public opinion, generating awareness and stimulating response. The result is an effective connection between nations, consumers, vendors, and investors."

[10] Known popularly as "calamidades," because second-hand clothing was first distributed during the war by the *Instituto Nacional de Gestão das Calamidades* (National Institute for Disaster Management).

[11] Group interview, Minicane, Muecate, Nampula, 30 July 1999.

[12] Group interview, Minheuene, Muecate, Nampula, 2 July 1999.

[13] In 2000 the minimum monthly wage was around $30 (450,000 *meticais*) which was too low to support a family. A worker on the minimum wage spent 35% of his monthly salary on travelling to and from work (*Mozambiquefile* June 2000, p. 9). The minimum wage was enough to buy only 38.8 per cent of a very basic "basket of goods for the average five member family," consisting of 9 kilos of maize flour, 1.5 kilos of rice, 1.5 kilos of vegetable oil, 1.5 kilos of beans, 1.5 kilos of brown sugar, 2 kilos of second grade fish, and 4.5 kilos of vegetables per person per month. As emphasised in *Mozambiquefile*, this "basket of goods" is a very bare minimum with no expenditure on clothing, transport, education or health (*Mozambiquefile* July 2000, p. 21).

[14] Workers of many companies have been unpaid for months. In 2000, according to Joaquim Fanheiro, general secretary of the largest trade union federation, more than 13,000 workers lost their jobs (*Mozambiquefile* June 2001, p. 18).

[15] Interview with *empregados*, Nampula city, 18 June 1999.

[16] 100,000 *meticais*.

[17] Interview with a domestic guard, Nampula city, 11 June 1999.

[18] The story of the destruction of Mozambique's cashew processing industry by World Bank-imposed liberalisation of trade in raw cashew nuts is notorious and has drawn considerable international attention; unfortunately there is no space to tell it here. The process was closely followed and documented over years by Carlos Cardoso's newspaper *Metical*, and also by *Mozambiquefile*. See also Hanlon, "Power without responsibility." By 2000 nearly all of the former cashew processing factories in Mozambique had shut down leaving over 90% of the 11,000 former cashew factory workers unemployed (*Mozambiquefile* June 2001, p. 18).

[19] Interview with two unemployed cashew-factory workers, Angoche, Nampula, 22 June 1999.

[20] For details of the research project, *Sociedade Civil Precarizada em Moçambique*, see http://www.cea.uem.mz/pesqinfo/.

[21] *Chapas* are privately owned minibus taxis in Maputo.

[22] See Colaço, "Tradição e modernidade" 159 for discussion of the views of people in the *barracas* in Maputo regarding the city's smart restaurants and bars.

[23] Around 1,000 formerly state-run enterprises were privatised (*Mozambiquefile* July 2000, p. 3). For analysis of the privatisation process see Cramer, and Pitcher.

[24] See Hanlon, "Bank corruption becomes site of struggle in Mozambique."

[25] *Mozambiquefile* various editions. See Hanlon, "Bank corruption" for a detailed analysis of the processes that led to the losses.

[26] *Mozambiquefile* January 2002.

[27] In December 1997, José Lima Félix, the Portuguese manager of the International Bank of Mozambique (BIM), was killed. At the time it was said to be motivated by car theft but it is now suspected that he was murdered because of his investigations into money laundering. On November 29, 1999, there was a failed attempt to assassinate Albano Silva, the chairman of the Legal Council of the Bar Association who was acting as lawyer for BCM investigating the 1996 fraud. In July 2000, the Attorney General, Antonio Namburete, was sacked by President Joaquim Chissano, following allegations that he had assisted in undermining the investigation of the bank fraud. The following year under the direction of the new Attorney General Joaquim Madeira a number of corrupt members of the Public Prosecution Office in the capital and the provinces were removed from office. On 22 November 2000, Carlos Cardoso was murdered as he drove home from work. The key actors in his murder are suspected to have orchestrated the 1996 theft of 144 billion *meticais* from the BCM. This was one of the many instances of fraud and corruption that Cardoso and his newspaper *Metical* investigated and campaigned about over months. On February 14, 2001, there was an attempt to assassinate Assistant Attorney Albino Macamo, who had been working with Madeira investigating and dealing with corruption in the Office of the Attorney General. Madeira was convinced that the attempt on Macamo's life was by organised crime. On 18 April 2001, the Secretary General of the Attorney General's office, Orlando Generoso, was held up and threatened with death by three armed men, when he stopped his car on Avenida Eduardo Mondlane in the centre of Maputo. On 19 April 2001, a journalist from Radio Moçambique, José João, received an anonymous death threat by phone after writing a news item on drug trafficking and illegal imports. On 28 April 2001, a journalist for *Mediafax* (an independent daily paper) was savagely beaten in a Maputo suburb. As no attempt was made to rob him the motive was suspected to be an attempt to silence his journalist activity. On 11 August 2001, Antonio Siba-Siba Macuacua was murdered. His body was found at the bottom of the stairwell of the multi-storey building of Austral Bank's headquarters in downtown Maputo. Siba-Siba was a highly respected economist who was appointed by the Central Bank as chair of the provisional board of directors of Austral Bank in 2001, when the shareholders pulled out after admitting the true scale of accumulated losses to be over 150 million USD$. Siba-Siba was directing the investigation into the bank's financial state and chasing up "bad debts." In September 2002, Antonio Frangoulis, former head of the Criminal Investigation Police in Maputo, received death threats from the escaped murder suspect Anibal Antonio dos Santos ("Anibalzinho"). Most recently, during the Carlos Cardoso murder trial in December 2002, a series of threats were made to several witnesses and officials in the Public Prosecution Office, including threats made to the presiding Judge, Augustino Paulino, in an attempt to disrupt the process of the trial and protect the suspects (*Mozambiquefile* various editions).

[28] Hanlon "Bank corruption."

[29] The activities of organised criminal networks are documented in Gastrow and Mosse.

[30] According to the recent Survey of Basic Indicators of Well-being published by the National Statistics Institute in October 2001; see *Mozambiquefile* November 2001.

[31] *Mozambiquefile* August 2001.

Works Cited

Aquimo, L. 2001. "*Esmoleiros* da cidade de Nampula." *Estudos Moçambicanos* 18: 181-200.

Colaço, J. C. 2001. "*Lixeiros* da cidade de Maputo." *Estudos Moçambicanos* 18: 25- 74.

———. 2000. "Tradição e modernidade nas barracas do Museu em Maputo." *Conflito e Mestiçagem.* Ed. C. Serra. Maputo: Livraria Universitária.

Collier, A. 1999. *Being and Worth.* London: Routledge.

———. 1994. "Value, rationality and the environment." *Radical Philosophy* 66: 3-9.

Couto, M. 2002. "Pobres dos nossos ricos." *Savana* 13 December 2002.

Cramer, C. 2001. "Privatisation and Adjustment in Mozambique: a 'Hospital Pass'?" *Journal of Southern African Studies* 27 (1): 79-103.

Department of International Development (DFID). 1998. *Mozambique Country Strategy Paper.* DFID Information Department, London.

European Parliament Committee on Development and Cooperation. 2001. *Report on the Mission of a Delegation of the Committee on Development and Cooperation to Mozambique.* 14-18 September 2001, Brussels.

Fauvet, P. 2000. "Mozambique: growth with poverty." *Africa Recovery* (United Nations) 14 (3).

Gastrow, P., and M. Mosse. 2002. "Mozambique: Threats posed by the penetration of criminal networks." Paper presented at the Institute of Security Studies Regional Seminar, Organised Crime, Corruption and Governance in the SADC Region, Pretoria, April 2002. Government of Mozambique, 2001, *The National Plan for the Reduction of Absolute Poverty, 2000-2004 (PARPA).* Maputo.

Government of Mozambique. 1995. *The Poverty Reduction Strategy for Mozambique.* Maputo.

Hanlon, J. 2002. "Bank corruption becomes site of struggle in Mozambique." *Review of African Political Economy* 91: 53-72.

———. 2000. "Power Without Responsibility: the World Bank and Mozambican Cashew Nuts." *Review of African Political Economy* 83: 29-45.

Matsinhe, V. 2000. "Quando tradição e modernidade se mesticizam nos chapas da rota Hulene Xipamanine." *Conflito e Mestiçagem.* Ed. C. Serra. Maputo: Livraria Universitária. Ministry of Planning and Finance (MPF), Government of Mozambique, Eduardo Mondlane University, and International Food Policy Research Institute, 1998, *Understanding Poverty and Well-Being in Mozambique: The First National Assessment 1996-7.* Maputo.

Monteiro, H. 2001. "Com os doentes do Hospital Psiquiátrico de Nampula." *Estudos Moçambicanos* 18: 75-160.

Mozambiquefile, various editions.

Pitcher, M. A. 2002. *Transforming Mozambique: The Politics of Privatization, 1975–2000.* Cambridge UP.

United Nations. 1999. Implementation of the Programme of Action for the Least Developed Countries for the 1990s. Report of the Secretary-General, A/54/269 and Corr.1.

Branwen Gruffydd Jones is Lecturer in International Relations and Politics at the University of Aberdeen, Scotland, UK. She was previously ESRC Post-Doctoral Research Fellow at the University of Sussex, UK, where she completed her doctoral thesis about rural poverty in Mozambique. Her recent publications include "The civilised horrors of over-work: Marxism, imperialism and development of Africa" (*Review of African Political Economy* 95 [2003]) and "Globalisation and the freedom to be poor: from colonial political coercion to the economic compulsion of need" (*Portuguese Studies Review* 10 (1) [2002]).

(Lost) Love, Eros and Metaphor: Colonialism, Social Fragmentation and the "Burden" of Race in *Portagem* by Orlando Mendes

Geoffrey S. Mitchell

Abstract. Orlando Mendes's 1965 novel *Portagem* traces the tragic life of the bi-racial protagonist, João Xilim. Using the metaphor of frustrated and empty human relationships, Mendes illustrates the socio-political fragmentation of colonial, Mozambican society on the eve of the war for independence. Racial, economical and educational divisions introduced by Portuguese colonialism are the factors that contributed most significantly to Mozambique's pre-independence state of affairs. The poor education of rural Mozambicans not only prevented their ability to articulate their grievances but also undermined the anti-colonialists' attempts to unite the colonized against Portuguese hegemony.

> [João] não tem mulher, nem filhos, nem amigos. [...] Foi sempre ele, o mulato, um homem clandestino [...]. Por toda a parte ele encontrou gente que anda à toa, rejeitada pelos brancos e pelos negros. Deserdada pelas duas raças puras. (*Portagem* 169-170)

In the mid-nineteenth century, the French philosopher and racial theorist Count Arthur de Gobineau stated in *The Inequality of the Races* that "[It is impossible] that the civilizations belonging to racially distinct groups should ever be fused together. The irreconcilable antagonism between different races and cultures is clearly established by history [...]" (179). Known for his often-paradoxical racist theories, Gobineau proposed that miscegenation is useful only in order to achieve civilization but once attained, continued miscegenation will cause civilizations to degenerate (Gobineau 179). Although Gobineau's apprehensions regarding sustained miscegenation did not deter him from marrying a Creole, his polemical theories illustrate the racial and social problematic that Mozambican author, Orlando Mendes, wished to deconstruct and criticize in his 1965 novel, *Portagem.* Born to Portuguese émigrés, Orlando Mendes was one of Mozambique's most notable literary figures, primarily as a poet and as a writer of fiction. Having rejected an opportunity to pursue a brilliant scientific career in Europe, Mendes opted to return to Mozambique in order to pursue scientific research in the countryside on behalf of the government (Araújo Medina 166-167). *Portagem* reflects the period in which Mendes's work in rural Mozambique exposed him to scenes of racial oppression, poor education and abject poverty.

Originally written in the 1950s, *Portagem* gained considerable repute as a realist critique of socio-racial injustices attributed to colonialism. The biracial protagonist, João Xilim, is the illegitimate offspring of a Portuguese coalmine owner, Campos, and his African mistress, Kati. Written in the tradition of the *bildungsroman, Portagem* traces the socio-economic and race-related hardships that João must endure from childhood to young adulthood. Throughout the text, Mendes portrays a cross-section of Mozambican society by deploying a heteroglottic variety of authentic-sounding voices. Nevertheless, it is frequently obvious that these voices, and indeed the characters, are contrived in order to advance Mendes's socio-political agenda. His strident criticism of the marginalization of some sectors of Mozambican society due to racial and class constructs surfaces throughout the novel and the ambiguous *dénouement* intentionally leaves the reader with a sense of a tragic and uncertain future not only for the characters but for Mozambique as well. The themes of tragedy and solitude resonate throughout *Portagem* and arise primarily out of the failure of all intra- and inter-racial relationships. It is my contention that these frustrated relationships function as a metaphor that signals the fragile and fragmented state of Mozambican society on the eve of the struggle for independence.

Since Mendes developed an early interest in Marxism and anti-fascism, an intellectual affinity shared by many of his anti-colonialist compatriots, it stands to reason that the majority of the relational conflicts in *Portagem* originate in the racial and class structures established by colonialism. Mendes deploys the metaphor of troubled human relationships in *Portagem,* particularly those that ultimately fail or are thwarted due to discrimination and social mores, in order to illustrate the unstable and fragmentary state of colonial Mozambican society. Creating a metaphor out of human relationships is not a new idea. Some scholars, such as Latin Americanist Doris Sommer, typically understand the successful union of otherwise incompatible literary characters as a metaphorical amalgamation of regional, economic and political differences. In her book *Foundational Fictions* (1991), Sommer focuses on a canonical corpus of nineteenth-century Latin American "national romances," a term that she defines as "[...] a cross between our contemporary use of the word as a love story and a nineteenth century use that distinguished the genre as more boldly allegorical than the novel" (5). Sommer further posits that both the authors and the readers of these national romances assume an allegorical relationship between the personal and political narratives (41). Moreover, the ever-present erotic element serves simultaneously as a literary mechanism to unite the characters as well as a hook to maintain the readers' interest. Although Mendes also includes in *Portagem* the same elements that are representative of Latin American foundational romances, he approaches concepts such as nation and unity as an unattainable goal given the social and political conditions resulting from colonialism. On the literary level, the reader senses this pessimism through failed human relationships. If, as Frederic Jameson has stated, all third-world texts are necessarily allegorical and should be read as national allegories, then *Portagem* certainly portrays a bleak image of colonial Mozambique (Jameson 69). Mendes does not hesitate to reveal his preoccupation with Mozambique's lack of direction as a national community.

The novel opens with signs of fragmentation within the family unit with a combative exchange between Alima, an elderly black woman who refuses to leave the land of her birth, the Ridjalembe, and Kati her daughter. Alima represents a traditional Africa that resists European colonialism. Kati, who symbolizes the betrayal of African culture, visits the poor and ailing Alima in order to bring her food, keep her company and ultimately to convince her to abandon Ridjalembe in order to live in the newer settlement of Marandal. In this relationship, Alima berates Kati for embracing the language and culture of the colonizers: "Tu só gosta de falar língua de branco, não é?... E aprendeste a mim a falar também, não é? [...] Vocês gosta de branco mas branco só quer a preto só pra gastar o corpo de ele" (8). The reference to the language of the colonizer while defending the language of the colonized suggests the binary opposition "europhone elite / noneurophone populace" proposed by

Kwame Appiah (143). On the one hand, Kati's acceptance of the colonizer's language and her move to the Marandal signal the necessity of adapting to the status quo in order to survive, yet it also indicates a betrayal of her people and her great-great grandfather, a former slave. This binary opposition of the resistant mother Alima and the acculturated daughter Kati is an oblique reference to the *Regime do Indigenato*, a policy instituted by Salazar, which, according to Allen and Barbara Isaacman, legalized the racial, economic and cultural subordination of most Africans (39). Furthermore, the Isaacmans add that:

> The tiny minority who could read and write Portuguese, had rejected "tribal" customs, and were gainfully employed in the capitalist economy were classified as *assimilados* [assimilated]. In principle, they enjoyed all the rights and responsibilities of Portuguese citizens. Africans and mulattoes who could not satisfy these requirements had to carry identity cards, fulfill stringent labor requirements, and live outside European areas. These persons, known as *indigenas* [indigenes], were not considered citizens, and they remained subject to customary law. (39)

In addition, by referring to the Portuguese material interest in the African "body," Alima is not only alluding to the forced labor practices of colonialism (*chibalo*), she is also hinting at the sexual alliances between white men and African women, and the bi-racial offspring that these unions will generate.

Alima's negative opinion of interracial relationships reflects the opinion of literary characters in other Mozambican narratives such as Ungulani Ba Ka Khosa's *Ualalapi* (1987). In this anti-historical parody of official Portuguese discourse, the protagonist King Ngungunhane prophetically reveals the contempt that will be directed at the offspring of interracial relationships: "E por todo o lado, como uma doença que a todos ataca, começarão a nascer crianças com a pele da cor do mijo que expelis com agrado nas manhãs. Serão crianças da infâmia" (119). Although Ngungunhane is speaking to Africans, he also implies that even whites will reject these "crianças da infâmia." Similarly, in José Craverinha's poem "Ao meu belo pai ex-emigrante" (1974), the bi-racial subject acknowledges his Portuguese and African roots but notes that he will never be white enough for the European:

> E na minha rude e grata
> sinceridade não esqueço
> meu antigo português puro

que me geraste no ventre de uma tombasana
eu mais um novo moçambicano
semiclaro para não ser igual a um branco qualquer
e seminegro para jamais renegar
um glóbulo que seja dos Zambezes do meu sangue.
(Ferreira 329)

Given the period of political and social turmoil in which Craverinha wrote the poem, it comes as no surprise that the author only emphasizes the marginalization of the bi-racial by the Portuguese and not that by Africans. However, when applied in tandem, both *Ualalapi* and "Ao meu belo pai ex-emigrante" effectively demonstrate the unenviable, middle position in which the bi-racial resided in Mozambican society.

In *Portagem*, João Xilim is the bi-racial product of the type of interracial relationship to which Alima alludes. While waiting for the arrival of his legitimate, Portuguese wife, Laura, Campos arranged for Kati to satisfy his sexual needs as well for "simples entretenimento" (Mendes 34). The result of the sexual relationship between Campos and Kati is, of course, João. For Kati, there is no possibility of a legitimate, long-term relationship with Campos since her skin color and social class present an insurmountable obstacle. Frantz Fanon, quoting from Mayotte Capécia's *Je suis Martiniquaise*, affirms this problematic encountered by women of color: "[...] a woman of color is never altogether respectable in a white man's eyes. Even when he loves her" (42). Despite knowing *a priori* that marriage with Campos is out of the question, Kati believes their sexual relationship to be advantageous for her despite the obvious imbalance of power in terms of race, class and gender. In her essay on race and film, Dina Sherzer addresses the issues of imbalance of power and the exploitation of the native woman:

> Sexual policies were really about maintenance of power and domination, the inheritance of White property, and the threat to the homogeneity of the social group. But, though mixed marriages were discouraged, the sexual exploitation of the native woman was a common practice in colonial society, as native women were frequently used as concubines, servants, and playthings for Europeans. (230)

Kati undoubtedly has few choices but to acquiesce to Campos's advances. Her service to him is perversely reminiscent of the *chibalo*, which was a colonial system of quasi-slavery or forced labor. The relationship is further complicated by Kati's untimely pregnancy and subsequent arranged marriage to Uhulamo, whose silence Campos purchases with the foremanship of the mine. Despite the appearance of legitimacy, this marriage is simply a front to conceal João's illegitimacy. Furthermore, since Laura is homely and lacks "quaisquer encantos para seduzir o marido" it is understood from the text that Kati will continue to serve as Campos's mistress (Mendes 34).

Two important aspects of Portuguese colonialism are at play in these and subsequent scenes in *Portagem* where the racial and relational dynamics between Africans and white men are concerned. First is Gilberto Freyre's concept of lusotropicalism, which proposed that the Portuguese colonizer was particularly suited to adapt to his environs and to effect the colonizing process through miscegenation with women of color (*miscibilidade*). Lusotropicalism also implies that these colonized women of color passively and willingly entered into sexual relationships with the Portuguese colonizer. In *Casa-grande e senzala* Freyre indicates that "Quanto à miscibilidade, nenhum povo colonizador, dos modernos, excedeu ou sequer igualou nesse ponto aos portugueses" (83). Freyre later adds that all Brazilians bear the influence:

> Da mulata que nos tirou o primeiro bicho-de-pé de uma coceira tão boa. Da que nos iniciou no amor físico e nos transmitiu, ao ranger da cama-de-vento, a primeira sensação completa de homem. [...] Já houve quem insinuasse a possibilidade de se desenvolver das relações íntimas da criança branca com a ama-de-leite negra muito do pendor sexual que se nota pelas mulheres de cor no filho-família dos países escravocratas. [...] Conhecem-se casos no Brasil não só de predileção mas de exclusivismo: *homens brancos que só gozam com negra.* (343, emphasis mine)

The same inability to become sexually aroused by white women not only occurs with Campos but also with the aging and unappealing, white bar owner, Esteves, who not only steals away João's legitimate, mulatto wife, Luísa, but also later marries his first love, Campos's daughter Maria Helena. Although doubly legitimate in that Maria Helena's marriage to Esteves is legal and socially acceptable, the relationship is unfulfilling and unhappy. Esteves's penchant for women of color apparently causes frequent bouts of impotence that prevent a healthy, intimate bond with Maria Helena. The desire for women of color while seeking legitimacy in marriage with a white woman suggests Freyre's reference to an old Brazilian saying: "Branca para casar, mulata para f…, negra para trabalhar" (85). Esteves's lust for women of color, particularly bi-racials such as Luísa, actually leads him down a slippery path to a kind of emotional and sexual enslavement similar to that which director Carlos Diegues portrays in his cinematic rendition of the legendary slave-woman Xica da Silva of colonial Brazil. Although Luísa initially resists Esteves's amorous advances because she wishes to remain loyal to João, she ultimately acquiesces primarily due to the influence of her mother, Esteves's persistence, and his willingness to support her financially in return for sexual favors. This is now the second instance where a white man and a woman of color have betrayed João. This cycle of betrayal is curiously Freudian in that it mirrors the disappointment, and perhaps the jealousy, that João experienced when he discovered his mother's intimacy with Campos. Esteves, a paternal figure, competes with João for the attentions of Luísa who, in many ways, is a mother to João. In fact, Luísa supports João financially since discriminatory hiring practices prevent João from securing steady and compensatory employment. This longing for the mother while simultaneously desiring to kill the father looms large in the relationships that João experiences with Kati and Luísa and metaphorically suggests the desire to abolish colonial patrimony in order to restore Mamana Africa to her original purity.

The second important aspect of Portuguese colonialism is the powerlessness of both the woman and the man of color, although the (desired) body of the former can prove to be an important manipulative tool. As Robert Young states in *Colonial Desire*, "Colonialism was a machine: a machine of war, of bureaucracy and administration, and above all, of power […]. Colonialism […] was also a desiring machine" (98). In the first case, the women of color are the objects of desire for both the white, Portuguese men as well as for African men. This is evident in all of the love triangles present throughout the novel. Furthermore, in all of these love triangles, not only is the woman of color the object of desire but the man of color, particularly the bi-racial, is the object of rejection and betrayal. As Fanon asserted in the case of French colonialism in the Caribbean, the objective of the woman of color was to become "whiter" through sexual relationships with the white man and to avoid returning to her blackness through a union with a man of color (47). This cycle of rejection and solitude begins in the first chapter of *Portagem* when Alima reveals Kati's betrayal of her African roots in order to undergo the process of acculturation.

Although the first love triangle involving a white man (Campos) and an African woman (Kati) produces the most profound and long-lasting effect on the bi-racial protagonist, the other relationships that João either observes or directly experiences also leave indelible scars on his psyche. Before proceeding further with the interracial, heterosexual relationships, it is important to point out that even the majority of the homosocial relationships that João and other characters experience ultimately end in failure. The term "homosocial," explains Eve Sedgwick, "is a word occasionally used in history and the social sciences, where it describes social bonds between persons of the same sex" (1). In *Portagem*, all of João's relationships with white men center on mutual contempt and on competition for the affections of African and bi-racial women. Homosocial relationships between other African men are equally disastrous, often ending in death or estrangement of some variety. João never experiences a father-son relationship with Campos nor does Mendes elaborate on any details relating to the relationship between João and Uhulamo. While serving on a cargo vessel after initially abandoning the Marandal, João befriends Jaime, a black sailor who does not know the identity of his father and whose mother is a prostitute. This homosocial relationship is short-lived as Jaime simply disappears and never returns to the ship. Furthermore, while in prison for attacking Luísa for an affair with a Portuguese soldier, João meets Izidro, a violent black prisoner who hates and mistrusts João because of his racial impurity. The homosocial bond transforms from animosity to friendship only when João proves his loyalty and Izidro is mortally wounded during a prison riot. Perhaps the most intimate and promising homosocial relationship that João experiences is with the bi-racial fisherman Juza, who later commits suicide upon learning that his mulatto girlfriend, Beatriz, has betrayed him with his white rival, Borges. As we shall see later, the amorous relationship between Juza and Beatriz closely parallels that of João and Luísa.

The theme of failed and/or complicated, unhappy heterosexual relationships continues after the first chapter in which Kati's strained relationship with her mother, Alima, reveals the former's acquiescence to the exigencies of Portuguese colonialism and miscibility. Campos calls João, whom the former knows to be his illegitimate son, to the big house in order to be a playmate for his legitimate daughter, Maria Helena. Childlike innocence initially ignores racial differences until Maria Helena's mother, Laura, delineates them clearly: "Este moleque parece-me esperto demais. Além disso, é mulato. E não gosto nada desta raça. São mais falsos que os pretos. –Os moleques pretos são tão estúpidos, mãe!..." (13). It is initially evident that Maria Helena has learned to mimic her mother's racial prejudices but her childhood innocence continues to see João in a somewhat egalitarian fashion. Maria Helena and João soon begin to share a mutual attraction despite the racial and socio-economical barriers that separate them. Nevertheless, since the narrator only seems to know João's thoughts at this point in the novel, the reader gets the impression that Maria Helena is less infatuated than João. The reality of João's subordinate status in the big house returns as Campos sends him to work in the mine with the other black workers. Circumstances will continue to impede reconciliation between João and Maria Helena whose innocent romance is temporarily thwarted by fate for several years.

When Campos's death and the fate of the mine finally reunite João and Maria Helena in an ephemeral, erotic encounter, Maria Helena is unable to escape her mother's racial indoctrination. Circumstances once again force João to abandon the Marandal for the city. Maria Helena's rejection of João suggests not only her conformity to social mores relating to class and to race but more particularly to the unwritten but well-established rules governing interracial, erotic unions, especially to those between a man of color and a white woman. Undeniably, unions between a white woman and a man of color contrast markedly with the inverse scenario. In a footnote relating to *Je suis Martiniquaise*, Fanon indicates that the former scenario has a romantic aspect and is based upon an act of giving whereas the latter is often understood as violence against the woman of color (46).

Although Mendes decries the marginalization of all Africans, the fact that he does not develop this brief, sexual encounter with the degree of depth that he employs with the novel's intraracial relationships betrays a subconscious fear of African male sexuality. The fear of the sexually potent Other who is capable of seducing the white woman was often a fear in the European metropolis during the colonial period (Scherzer 230). Furthermore, Sander Gilman asserts that the nineteenth-century, European mindset perceived black sexuality as "[…] a corrupted and corrupting sexuality. […] Blackness evokes sexuality, and sexuality (*pace* the late Freud) evokes death" (124). Although *Portagem* is a twentieth-century novel, the social constructs relating to race and class reveal a mindset that had remained unchanged for nearly a century. For Maria Helena this brief sexual encounter is much more negative and personally and socially shameful than it is for João. Though Maria Helena faults herself for her weakness, she places the majority of the blame on João who, in her view, has doubly disgraced her. She is now unworthy of a legitimate marriage, which is to say with a white man of her class. Consequently, after the mine goes bankrupt she has few options but to marry Esteves. Though not specifically stipulated in the text, the general theme of the novel, the metropolitan fear of the sexuality of the Other, and the previous discrimination of Africans and bi-racials strongly suggest that Maria Helena attributes her unworthiness not simply to the loss of her virginity, but more particularly to the loss of her virginity to a man of color.

In the failure of João's relationship with Maria Helena, Mendes is not simply exposing the hypocrisy of lusotropicalism but is also referring to the economic interests of the Portuguese colonists. In the seventeenth century, the Portuguese crown instituted the system known as the *prazo*, which was a tract of land given to settler families in Mozambique that they would govern in a feudalistic fashion. The legal heir to the *prazo* was the eldest daughter who would then have to marry a Portuguese subject born in Portugal. The purpose of the *prazo* system was to ensure the permanence of the settler community in Mozambique and to hinder the accumulation of capital by the Mozambican indigene (Mittleman 24). Although the *prazo* was a feature of early Portuguese colonialism in Mozambique, the feudalist mentality that it created endured for centuries and greatly influenced Mozambican social formation. In *Portagem* it is clear that social factors such as race, class and feudalistic tradition play a key role in preventing the realization of a successful relationship between Maria Helena and João.

The final series of failed relationships in *Portagem* occur in the second half of the novel. The primary factor that causes these relational failures is the white fisherman, Borges, who goes by the appropriate moniker "Coxo." As with the aging and unattractive Esteves, whom, because he is white, society considers superior to João, this word-picture suggests the implementation of the blueprint of the physical imperfection of the white rival who succeeds in stealing the woman of color from the African male. After his release from prison, João manages to rediscover his love for Luísa despite her previous unfaithfulness. Once reunited, Luísa becomes pregnant—a symbolic event that testifies to the sincerity of her contriteness. However, circumstances, unemployment and forced relocation by white developers trigger the premature birth and subsequent death of their infant daughter. This "bocadinho de esperança perdido" foreshadows subsequent tragedy with respect to João and Luísa's relationship and further serves as a metaphor of unrealized national unity (Mendes 124). João then takes up commercial fishing as an apprentice to the mulatto, Juza, whose mulatto lover, Beatriz, reminds the reader of Luísa before forsaking her lascivious and wanton lifestyle. It turns out that Juza becomes the only real friend that João has ever known while Luísa and Beatriz share a relationship that could be considered homosocial. During this time, João and Luísa have a second child, this time a son whom they name Zidrito, after the black prisoner, Izidro. Names are often symbolic in *Portagem* as we have already seen with Coxo. This is also the case with Izidro and Zidrito. According to Terry Jones's website *Patron Saint Index*, in the Catholic tradition there are many Isidores (Izidro in Portuguese) who have been canonized as saints by the church. It is quite interesting to note that most were martyrs and one of these was an African convert from the Congo whom white colonists beat to death. This African Isidore corresponds appropriately to Mendes's Izidro in that after the latter is fatally shot during a prison uprising, he takes the blame for the murder of a white prison guard committed by João. Even João treats Izidro, his former enemy, as a saintly figure. When Izidro dies, João leans down and piously closes Izidro's eyes: "E o velho sentenciado [Izidro] olha para o mulato [João Xilim] com uma tão angustiada súplica, que este de novo se debruça sobre o seu corpo, agora acabado, para lhe fechar os olhos piedosamente" (Mendes 77). Although João's gesture in naming his son Zidrito is an effort to pay homage to the deceased prisoner, the subliminal suggestion here is that hope for a better future will most likely be unrealized given that Izidro's life was tragic and ended in prison.

Tragedy is ubiquitous in *Portagem* and it looms on the horizon when Borges initiates his conquest of Juza's bi-racial companion, Beatriz. She already has questionable motives for staying with Juza and she thus is a likely candidate for relational betrayal. Only Luísa knows the truth and, ironically, it is she who advocates informing Juza of the betrayal while João cautions her to remain silent. João's silence is particularly disturbing since one would think that he, of all people, would wish to inform his friend of Beatriz's infidelity. It is apparent that João's desire to maintain the economic status quo gets the better of him at the expense of Juza's dignity and well-being. When Juza discovers the truth about Beatriz's infidelity through another bi-racial who also happens to be a friend of João, he plans to avenge himself. After purchasing a new fishing boat, appropriately named "Esperança da gamboa," Juza takes Beatriz out for the maiden voyage, scuttles the boat and drowns them both. As with other symbolic events interspersed throughout the plot, the act of scuttling the boat foreshadows the inescapable trajectory toward personal and universal tragedy in unrealizable relationships.

The death of Juza and Beatriz marks the end of João's brief period of economic stability and relative happiness. Without the new skiff and Juza and Beatriz, João and Luísa are unable to turn a profit in their fishing venture. Furthermore, Luísa once again becomes pregnant, which soon limits her participation in the fishing business. Since the economic outlook is dire, João and Luísa consider the most drastic of measures: an abortion and possible financial assistance from Luísa's former, white employers. This latter suggestion infuriates João who retorts: "À gente branca tu não pede nada! [...] Que é que teu pai fez por ti? O meu nunca me fez nada!" (157). Once again, Orlando Mendes addresses the economic effects of Portuguese colonialism in Mozambique. Forced relocation by white developers, commercial competition with white entrepreneurs and exploitation of all varieties leaves people of color completely at the mercy of the colonizers.

Their economic difficulties force João to go to the city to find employment. Luísa's solitude puts her in a vulnerable position, one that the sexual predator, Coxo, cannot resist. In their first encounter, Luísa begs Coxo to help them, which he agrees to do. Shortly thereafter, Coxo visits Luísa in her seaside shack and seduces her despite her advanced state of pregnancy. The text is particularly interesting at this juncture in that it superimposes João's fatalism on Luísa who seems physically, but not mentally, paralyzed to resist Coxo's sexual advances. On a subsequent occasion, Coxo once again attempts to seduce Luísa but this time her guilt forces her to resist and cry out for João. Like a scene from a soap opera, it is at this precise moment when João returns home from the city and discovers what is happening. After giving Coxo a thrashing, João insults Luísa, accuses her of betraying him again and he abandons her for the last time. In his absence, Luísa gives birth but both she and her baby soon die from starvation. When João's anger finally subsides and he returns to the shack, he finds Zidrito alive on his bed, Luísa dead on the floor and his infant daughter buried. This tragic ending bears some resemblance to the nineteenth-century Brazilian novelist José de Alencar's *Iracema*, despite the absence of the hopeful expectation of a new race and national destiny embodied in João and Luísa's son, Zidrito. In *Iracema,* Moacyr, the product of miscegenation between the Tabajara princess Iracema and the Portuguese *conquistador* Martim Soares, retains his Otherness but must undergo a process of acculturation in Portugal in order to be acceptable. In *Portagem,*

Zidrito and João will continue in a "destino comum," one marked not by the hopeful expectation of a new nation but rather one hobbled by discrimination against the African.

Because the metaphor of failed relationships points the reader to a fragmented, Mozambican society marked by the marginalization of the African, it now becomes necessary to explore the reasons behind Mendes's emphasis on the negative in his allegorical work. Though its presence is somewhat subtle throughout *Portagem*, the role of education is an integral aspect of Mendes's concern with the fragmented and illiterate working class. According to Allen and Barbara Isaacman, after the implementation of Salazar's *Estado Novo*, the colonial regime in Mozambique presided over the second highest illiteracy rate in Lusophone Africa (52). For Mendes, then, education is the main ingredient necessary to achieve political consciousness and, hence, to successfully implement a united front against colonial hegemony. For, as Benedict Anderson appropriately states, a sense of nationness and national community cannot be separated from political consciousness (135). Without a sense of social and political union, any attempt to articulate a sense of nationness will be thwarted. Anderson's assertion echoes the sentiments of nineteenth-century Cuban independence leader José Martí who, in his essay "Mi raza" ("My Race") forcefully and articulately confronted the white *and* black racism that prevented the unification of the Cuban people against Spanish colonialism. Cuba, like Mozambique, was a settler colony in which the colonizers not only occupied all of the positions of importance within the socio-political framework but also exploited the African population. Spanish colonization in the Americas, like its Portuguese counterpart, produced a variety of social and racial divisions that prevented, in Martí's words "[...] la ventura pública, y la individual" (Martí 100) ("[...] public and individual happiness"). Similar to Martí's project of social unification, in *Portagem* Mendes intends to suggest that poor education and the marginalization of the African underclass will prevent social and political integration and thus will diminish the likelihood of the successful eradication of Portuguese colonialism in Mozambique.

In *Portagem*, the uneducated, Mozambican underclass constitutes what Marx described as "[...] an incoherent mass scattered over the whole country, and broken up by their mutual competition" (17). However, Mendes correctly understood that since the vast majority of Mozambicans were, at best, poorly educated, they would be unable to coherently and uniformly articulate their grievances against Portuguese colonialism. Therefore, it was necessary for the anti-colonial intelligentsia to act as a spokesperson for the marginalized underclass. In addition, the substandard level of education among the predominantly African underclass also proved to be an obstacle for the anti-colonialist intelligentsia. Because of this, Orlando Mendes did not direct his literary work at the uneducated masses but rather at the Portuguese colonists. In an interview with Patrick Chabal, Mendes affirmed:

> Para quem é que nós escrevíamos? Temos uma população moçambicana com 95 por cento de analfabetos. Portanto, ao povo moçambicano nós não podíamos dirigir directamente. Escrevíamos evidentemente para os colonialistas. Porquê? Porque era uma maneira de nós marcarmos uma posição em nome do povo moçambicano, que não era capaz de se exprimir, nem era receptivo às nossas propostas e às nossas mensagens. [...] Éramos uma espécie de transmissor do pensamento que nós julgávamos que o povo moçambicano tinha, primeiro pela sua resistência e depois pela luta [armada], pela situação a seguir. (76)

It is further likely that Mendes directed his work at the literate minority of Africans who not only had the ability to speak to and for the uneducated populace but who also possessed the intellectual skills necessary to advocate reform in political, economic and social policy in Mozambique. Mendes's work, therefore, served to give a voice to the marginalized, uneducated masses that were incapable of redressing their grievances to the colonial regime.

The practical applications of the poor education of the rural African and bi-racial population do not escape Mendes's attention in *Portagem.* The novel presents the reader with convincing evidence of this inferior level of education in the grammatically incorrect discourses of João and his grandmother Alima. In fact, Mendes novelizes the people's resistance to the anti-colonialists' message due largely to discriminatory educational practices advocated by Lisbon. Of course, the result of the resistance and suspicion is social and political fragmentation among the non-elites, both acculturated and non-acculturated.

Despite the disproportionate number of uneducated Africans and biracials in *Portagem*, one of the novel's most interesting characters is Abel Matias, who makes only a brief appearance during the latter half of the novel. When Matias realizes that his new friend, João, is unemployed, his discourse turns political, highlighting the injustices of the white, colonial regime:

> "Os brancos fazem o que querem com a gente. E a gente é que estamos na nossa terra. [...] Eu moro na cidade. Só converso com gente dali. Mas, aqui, fora da cidade, as pessoas ainda têm vida pior. E há de haver gente que está farta e anda a pensar que é preciso os negros e os mulatos mandarem na sua terra." (128-129)

Matias's standard Portuguese serves as an identifiable sign that he is one of the few educated, acculturated Africans. Furthermore, the fact that Matias lives in the city underscores the binary opposition city / countryside nurtured by Portuguese colonialism. One of the many unfortunate features of this system was to force Mozambican rural dwellers into a subordinate position (Saul 43). Matias's reason for befriending João becomes apparent when he asks João to gather some of the other unemployed locals for a political meeting. Although he agrees to do so, João's lack of education and his unconscious resignation to his subaltern caste cause him to completely misread Matias's noble motives. Furthermore, João's equally uneducated acquaintances remain cynical and suspicious, and rather than listen to Matias's socio-political ideas and become active in the anti-colonial momentum, they simply rob him. Additionally, since João set up the meeting in the first place, these men are also suspicious of him and they consequently tell him to leave and never come back. This seemingly disconnected meta-plot is particularly significant in that it presents colonial realities as well as Mendes's preoccupation with the rural masses whose lack of education hinders the anti-colonialists' attempts to unite them against the colonial regime.

What then can the reader conclude from *Portagem*? As a national "romance," *Portagem* does not offer the hope of a unified Mozambique as the voiceless and uneducated masses advance slowly toward revolution. Rather, as a neo-realist novel subtly accentuated with Marxist overtones, *Portagem* purports to expose and condemn social injustices inflicted by the Portuguese colonizers upon rural, colonized Africans. In Orlando Mendes's opinion, colonialism in Mozambique has little to show except social fragmentation along educational and racial lines. In order to illustrate his well-delineated ideology and pessimism regarding Mozambique's future, Orlando Mendes's employs the metaphor of failed intra- and inter-racial relationships, both amorous and homosocial. Rather than implementing a literary strategy of a hopeful future marked by social and political unity through what Doris Sommer calls "cross-over" relationships, Mendes's intent is to focus on unrealized love and friendships as well as on other negative aspects of Mozambican social reality. This approach stresses upon the reader, who was more than likely one of the colonizers or an educated *assimilado*, that discriminatory practices that marginalized an enormous sector of Mozambicans must be eradicated. To unite the voiceless underclass that consisted primarily of the poor and uneducated Africans against the minority bourgeoisie required a minimum level of education that would lead to the political and social consciousness necessary to confront the colonial hegemony. Despite the institution of a socialist state following independence in 1975, the relics of colonialism nevertheless continued to haunt Mozambique's future as the nascent nation plunged into civil war. Similar to the myth of Sisyphus, Mozambique was doomed to repeat the cycle of social and political fragmentation inherited from Portuguese patrimony.

Works Cited

Anderson, Benedict. *Imagined Communites: Reflections on the Origin and Spread of Nationalism.* New York: Verso, 1996.

Appiah, Kwame. "Out of Africa: Topologies of Nativism." *The Bounds of Race: Perspectives of Hegemony and Resistance.* Ed. Dominick LaCapra. Ithaca, NY: Cornell UP, 1991.134-163.

Araújo Medina, Cremilda. *Sonha Mamana África.* São Paulo: Epopeia, 1987.

Ba Ka Khosa, Ungulani. *Ualalapi.* 2ª ed. Lisboa: Caminho, 1990.

Chabal, Patrick. *Vozes Moçambicanas: Literatura e Nacionalidade.* Lisboa: Vega, 1994.

Craverinha, José. "Ao meu belo pai ex-emigrante." *50 Poetas Africanos.* 2ª ed. Ed. Manuel Ferreira. Lisboa: Plátano Editora, 1986. 329-332.

Fanon, Frantz. *Black Skin, White Masks.* Trans. Charles Lam Markmann. New York: Grove Press, 1967.

Freyre, Gilberto. *Casa-grande e senzala.* São Paulo: Récord, 2001.

Gobineau, Arthur de. *The Inequality of the Races.* New York: Howard Fertig, 1999.

Isaacman, Allen and Barbara. *Mozambique: From Colonialism to Revolution, 1900-1982.* Boulder, CO: Westview Press, 1983.

Jameson, Frederic. "Third-World Literature in the Era of Multinational Capitalism." *Social Text* 15 (Fall 1986): 65-88.

Jones, Terry H. *Patron Saints Index.* Catholic Community Forum. 27 Feb. 2003 <http://www.catholic-forum.com/saints/sainti12.htm>.

Kosofsky Sedgwick, Eve. *Between Men: English Literature and Male Homosocial Desire.* New York: Columbia UP, 1985.

Martí, José. "Mi raza." *Letras Fieras.* La Habana, Cuba: Letras Cubanas, 1981. 100-102.

Marx, Karl and Frederick Engels. *The Communist Manifesto.* Ed. Frederick Engels. New York: International Publishers, 1989.

Mendes, Orlando. *Portagem.* São Paulo: Ática, 1981.

Mittelman, James H. *Underdevelopment and the Transition to Socialism: Mozambique and Tanzania.* New York: Academic Press, 1981.

Saul, John S. "The Context: Colonialism and Revolution." *A Difficult Road: The Transition to Socialism in Mozambique.* Ed. John S. Saul. New York: Monthly Review Press, 1985.36-74.

Scherzer, Dina. "Race Matters and Matters of Race." *Cinema, Colonialism, Post-Colonialism:Perspectives From the French and Francophone World.* Ed. Dina Scherzer. Austin: U of Texas P, 1996. 229-248.

Sommer, Doris. *Foundational Fictions: The National Romances of Latin America.* Berkeley: U of California P, 1991.

Young, Robert. *Colonial Desire: Hybridity in Theory, Culture and Race.* New York: Routledge,1995.

Geoffrey Mitchell is a Ph.D. candidate in Spanish at Tulane University in New Orleans, Louisiana. He is currently an instructor of Spanish and Portuguese at The University of Southern Mississippi.

On Cross-Border Languages and Cross-Border Collaboration between Malawi and Mozambique

Gregory Kamwendo

Abstract. One glaring consequence of colonial history is the placement of people speaking one language into different countries. Mozambique is no exception in this regard. With reference to one of its neighbours, Malawi, the two countries have languages such as Chichewa (also known as Chinyanja), Chilomwe, Chisena and Chiyao cutting across their borders. The two countries, however, differ in terms of the statuses and degrees of corpus-planning treatment given to the cross-border languages. For example, the two countries use different orthographies for their cross-border languages. Another profound difference is that the language known as Chichewa in Malawi is called Chinyanja in Mozambique and other Southern African countries. This paper observes that it is not uncommon for neighbouring countries to set up cooperation agreements to handle the effective management of cross-border resources such as water and wild life. As an analogy, this paper argues that cross-border languages are resources that also deserve cross-border cooperation or collaboration in their management and development. It is in this spirit that the 1997 Harare Intergovernmental Conference on Language Policies in Africa (UNESCO 2002) urged African countries to cooperate in the management and development of cross-border languages. The current paper observes that this cooperation is largely lacking between Malawi and Mozambique. There is, therefore, the need to increase the level of cooperation between the two countries. Attempts are made in this paper to account for the current state of affairs. In addition, the paper outlines some of the benefits that can be gained from cross-border cooperation. The current state of the cooperation on cross-border languages is then subjected to a SWOT (Strengths, Weaknesses, Opportunities and Threats) analysis. The paper ends with the way forward. It has to be acknowledged at the very beginning that this paper is written from a Malawian sociolinguist's point of view.

1.0 Introduction

After the partition of Africa by European powers in 1884, political boundaries were drawn on the African map. One result of this process was that people of the same ethnolinguistic background found themselves separated and then placed in different colonial spheres of influence (Asiwaju 1985; Chumbow and Tamanji 1998; Elugbe 1998). This colonial occurrence has led to the existence today of a number of languages that cut across national boundaries. Such languages are commonly known as cross-border languages, a term favoured by Legere (1998), UNESCO (2002) and others. Other scholars prefer to use the term transborder languages (for example, Chumbow and Tamanji 1998, Chumbow 1999). Today, cross-border languages are a common phenomenon in Africa. In this paper, my focus is on cross-border languages that are shared between Malawi and Mozambique as neighbours. It is worth mentioning that Malawi shares its borders with three countries, namely Mozambique, Tanzania and Zambia. It is with Mozambique that Malawi has the longest border.

The paper is organised as follows. First, I present an overview of the political and language situation of each country in sections 2.0, 2.1 and 2.2. To appreciate the different language policies adopted by the two countries, we have to understand the socio-political backgrounds against which language planning is done in each country. My second task is to assess the level of the two countries' cooperation with regard to the development and management of the cross-border languages. The degree to which this cooperation can be successful is determined by the political climate surrounding the two countries. This is the main argument that I advance in section 3.0. A third and related task is to discuss the benefits that can be achieved through cooperation between Malawi and Mozambique. My fourth task will be to conduct a SWOT analysis, and the final task will be to map out the way forward, taking into consideration important recommendations such as those adopted by Namibia, South Africa, Angola, Botswana and Zambia (Legere 1998); the Intergovernmental Conference on Language Policies in Africa (UNESCO 2002); and Malawi's second national symposium on language policy for education (Pfaffe 2000).

2.0 The Language Situation in Malawi and Mozambique

Due to the lack of systematic and comprehensive nationwide language surveys in most African countries, accurate and reliable language data are hard to find. Often, the language data are a matter of estimates, some of which are far from satisfactory. The absence of language surveys has meant that many countries do not have up-to-date information on the number of languages, the dialects of the languages and their degrees of mutual intelligibility; the geographical spread of the languages; the numerical strength of the speakers of each language; and degrees of language loyalty, shift, death and maintenance. Without the existence of an accurate picture of the language situation of a country, national development planners cannot make judicious decisions. Given the importance of language surveys in overall national-development planning, some countries are either proposing to conduct language surveys, or they are in the process of conducting them. An example of the latter case is Tanzania (see Legere 2002) where a language survey is currently underway.

2.1 The Language Situation in Malawi

Malawi, because of its British colonial history (1891 to 1964), has retained English as the main official language. As such, Malawi belongs to the Anglophone linguistic group of African nations. As the main official language, English is the key language of government business, including education, the media, the judiciary and the legislature. Proceedings of the legislature are conducted in English only; thus, aspiring members of parliament have to demonstrate competence in English before they are allowed to run in elections. In the school system, the medium of instruction in the first four grades is Chichewa, the national language. From grade five onwards, English takes over as the medium of instruction. As a subject, English is offered from grade one. The dominance of English is also felt in the mass media. The locally printed papers are predominantly in English. The same dominance of English is also in existence on the country's sole television channel, Television Malawi. The national radio, the Malawi Broadcasting Corporation (hereafter MBC) has reduced the dominance of English by featuring Chichewa significantly. Since 1994, five local languages have been introduced on MBC for use in newscasts. These languages are Chitumbuka, Chiyao, Chisena, Chilomwe and Chitonga. Chitumbuka used to be broadcast on MBC until 1968 when the broadcasts were discontinued in line with Malawi Congress Party convention resolutions. It has to be mentioned that during the first thirty years of independence (1964-1994), which is also called the Banda era, government policy granted official status to only one local language (Chichewa). The rest of the local languages received no official recognition. In having Chichewa as the national language, the Banda regime hoped to unite Malawians of various ethnolinguistic origins. With the demise of the Banda regime, the new government has ushered in a culture of linguistic liberalisation through which local languages other than Chichewa have the chance to enter the official domains. The second act of linguistic liberalisation in post-Banda Malawi has been the dissolution of the Chichewa Board and its replacement by the Centre for Language Studies. Thirdly, the government of Malawi in 1996 proposed the introduction of mother-tongue instruction in grades one to four. This proposal has not yet been implemented but preparations for the implementation are underway (see Pfaffe 2002).

2.2 The Language Situation in Mozambique

Like Malawi, Mozambique has not had any language survey since its attainment of independence from Portugal in 1975. As such, accounts of the language situation in Mozambique are to be found scattered in various books and journals. Whilst gathering information for this article, the author was lucky to come across a number of informative sources in English. The most comprehensive picture of the language situation in Mozambique is given by Lopes (1998). Other helpful sources available are Lopes (1997), Langa and Chambale-Mshotola (1998), Gadelii (2001), Katupha (1994), Matusse (1997), and Stroud (2002). Given that a comprehensive language atlas of Mozambique is lacking, it is an uphill task to give the exact number of languages found in Mozambique (Lopes 1998).

The official language of Mozambique is Portuguese, a consequence of colonial history. When FRELIMO formed the first post-independence government in 1975, it was noted that there was no dominant local language that could work as a national language. This contrasts sharply with the situation in Malawi where at the time of independence in 1964, a nationwide lingua franca, Chichewa, was in existence. In the absence of a dominant local language, Portuguese became the common linguistic denominator for the peoples of Mozambique. The FRELIMO government hoped to forge national unity through Portuguese, which is an ethnically neutral language. Today, Portuguese is the language of the government machinery. Portuguese is also the dominant language of the mass media and education (Lopes 1998).

3.0 Cooperation between Malawi and Mozambique

Before discussing cooperation between Malawi and Mozambique with regard to the management and development of cross-border languages, it is important to mention that politics is a crucial factor regulating the type and degree of cooperation any two countries can forge. For example, one cannot expect countries that are at war to collaborate in matters involving cross-border issues. Nor can one reasonably expect countries that have stormy relations to work in collaboration on cross-border matters such as language. To understand how after many years collaboration may now be possible, I will start by giving a brief account of the politics of the relations between Malawi and Mozambique. When Malawi gained its independence from Britain in 1964, it soon found itself isolated by other African countries who accused it of collaborating with the colonial and white minority regimes in Mozambique, Rhodesia (now Zimbabwe) and South Africa. Malawi's then-president, Dr. Hastings Kamuzu Banda, was accused of betraying the liberation cause through his association and collaboration with the oppressive colonial regimes of Southern Africa. Banda's response was that his country's economic survival was dependent on these countries. He argued that the best approach for Malawi was not to isolate the white minority regimes or to be engaged in supporting armed-liberation movements but to engage in contact and dialogue. Banda adamantly asserted that for the economic survival of Malawi, it was necessary to make "alliances with the devil" (Short 1974; McMaster 1974). To this end, Malawi established diplomatic relations with the apartheid regime of South Africa in 1967 and collaborated economically and politically with white minority colonial regimes in Rhodesia and Mozambique. As a consequence, Malawi did not offer material support to African liberation movements such as Frelimo of Mozambique and the Patriotic Front of Rhodesia. When Mozambique attained its independence, the image of Malawi was further damaged by allegations that, in collaboration with South Africa, it was giving support to the Renamo rebels who were fighting against the Frelimo government (Hedges 1989). In 1984, Malawi and Mozambique established a Joint Permanent Commission to regulate their relations. Naturally, matters of defence and security were high on thc commission's agenda. Despite the existence of this commission, allegations over Malawi's support for Renamo continued to be voiced by Mozambique. Relations between Malawi and Mozambique came to a low ebb in 1986 when the latter threatened to close the borders, a move that would have cut off Malawi's access to the seaports. In October 1986, President Machel of Mozambique died in a plane crash. The South African government alleged that documents found at the scene of the accident contained a plan by Mozambique and Zimbabwe to overthrow the Banda regime, further aggravating a sense of mutual distrust. To repair its damaged political image, in 1987 Malawi sent troops to Mozambique to safeguard the safety of the Nacala rail route that links Malawi to the Mozambican seaports. This move drove Malawian troops into direct confrontation with the RENAMO rebels.

The situation has now changed for the better due to an alteration in the political landscape in both countries. First, the civil war in Mozambique ended following a peace accord between RENAMO and FRELIMO in 1992. Genuine peace has now returned to Mozambique and RENAMO is playing the role of an opposition party in a multiparty dispensation. In Malawi too, the political scene has changed. Multipartyism was legalised in 1993 and, in the following year, Banda lost the presidency through the ballot box. The end of the war in Mozambique and the demise of the Banda regime in Malawi have created an atmosphere of more trust and genuine relationship between the neighbouring countries. This new political climate is conducive to enhanced bilateral collaboration.

The question worth asking at this point is: what are some of the benefits for the management of cross-border languages that can come out of the collaboration? One of the gains to be made out of this type of a venture is that cross-border languages offer collaborating countries the opportunities for sharing both human and material resources. In addition, it has been argued by Elugbe (1998) that cross-border languages offer an opportunity to share the cost of language development. With enhanced cooperation between countries, the standardisation and harmonisation of orthographies is one of the joint tasks that could be pursued. By using a single spelling system across several countries that share a common language, the market for publications in that language is enlarged. Another benefit that can be realised from cross-border cooperation is joint research in areas such as dialectology.

4.0 Towards a SWOT analysis

My tool for analysing the existing cooperation between Malawi and Mozambique is what is known as SWOT. The acronym SWOT stands for Strengths, Weaknesses, Opportunities and Threats. In other words, this paper intends to identify the strengths of Malawi's and Mozambique's cooperation and the weaknesses that exist. The paper will also examine the opportunities that the two countries can exploit and consider potential threats; that is, issues that threaten the cooperation between the two countries. It has to be acknowledged that I do not treat the categories Strengths, Weaknesses, Opportunities, and Threats in a rigid manner. Some of the categories do actually overlap.

4.1 Strengths

The first strength behind any cross-border language cooperation between Malawi and Mozambique is the existence in both countries of personnel with advanced training in linguistics/language studies. The existence of such scholars can be noted from the works cited section of this paper. These scholars enjoy varying levels of expertise and experience; by pooling them together in joint projects, the two countries stand to benefit immensely from shared expertise. The existence of well-established language research and curriculum development centres in both Malawi and Mozambique is another strength. In terms of language research, the University of Malawi has a Centre for Language Studies, which was established in 1996 to fulfil the following aims:

i. to establish orthographic principles of Malawian languages;
ii. to develop descriptive grammars of Malawian languages;
iii. to compile lexicons of Malawian languages;
iv. to provide translation and interpretation services;
iv. to teach various local and foreign languages that are deemed to be of socio-economic and political relevance to Malawi;
v. to promote research in language studies.

On the side of Mozambique, language research is well served by the Unit for the Study of Mozambican Languages, commonly known as NELIMO. On the curriculum-development side, Malawi has the Malawi Institute for Education whilst the National Institute for Educational Development (INDE) is its counterpart in Mozambique. These are well-experienced institutions and, through cross-border cooperation between these institutions, the two countries stand to learn from what they have in common.

4.2 Weaknesses

Cross-border collaborative activities involve money. The governments of Malawi and Mozambique and their institutions on their own cannot fully finance the language development activities already mentioned. A weakness of most African governments is their over-reliance on donor support for development projects. One of the sour realities of donor support is that it often comes with conditionalities. Often donors have their own research agenda. For example, after the demise of the Banda administration in Malawi in 1994, it was necessary to conduct a nationwide language survey in order to provide an accurate and up-to-date linguistic profile of the country. When this proposal was sent to a number of donors, the majority's response was that the subject of the survey was not within their areas of interest. On a positive note, the German Technical Cooperation Agency known as GTZ, said it was willing to go into this area of research. GTZ, however, made it clear that it could only fund sociolinguistic surveys that had a special focus on the use of local languages as media of instruction in primary schools. To avoid having research projects whose agenda is set by donors, Malawi and Mozambique need to tap internal sources of funding to support language research. One way of doing this is to increase government subvention given to language research institutions such as the Centre for Language Studies in Malawi and NELIMO in Mozambique. These institutions also need to explore means of generating their own funds in order to improve their financial bases. This scenario can lead to cross-border research projects that could be self-financed jointly by the two countries. By pooling their financial resources together, the two countries could reduce their reliance on donor support. The advantage of having locally financed research projects is that there is no external (donor) influence on the research agenda.

Another weakness is the absence of formal links of collaboration among the language research and language teaching institutions of Malawi and Mozambique. It is normal that when two or more institutions establish links, they spell out the terms and conditions under which they will collaborate. Without such formal links, cross-border collaboration will not be realised to any meaningful extent. In the concluding section, I suggest the forms that this collaboration on cross-border languages could take.

Whilst Malawi and Mozambique have a joint Permanent Commission of Cooperation at the governmental level, the commission has mainly focused on defence, security and economic matters. This commission has not expressed interest in language matters, which is a weakness on the part of the commission. The omission of language issues reflects the tendency in many African countries to give lukewarm support to language issues. Whilst many declarations on African languages have spelt out the importance of cross-border language collaboration, there is often a lack of political will to translate declarations and resolutions into practice. There is need, therefore, for language activists in both Malawi and Mozambique to lobby for more active government support towards language matters.

4.3 Threats

A possible threat to cross-border collaboration can be the obsession with what are seen as national symbols or national interests. Languages have the potential to fall into this category. For example, in 1968, a Malawi Congress Party convention resolved to make Chinyanja its national language and proceeded to change the name of the language to Chichewa (the name of president Banda's dialect). Kishindo (1998: 225) observes: "by giving the language a name which immediately identifies it with a particular ethnic group, Chichewa was robbed of its status as an appropriate lingua franca for the people whose countries border Malawi. It is not surprising, therefore, that countries such as Zambia, Mozambique and Zimbabwe, which use the language, retained the former name since they did not want to be associated with Dr. Banda's language." So, Chichewa became the symbol of national identity in Malawi. After the demise of the Banda regime, there have been attempts in Malawi to revert to the name Chinyanja. These attempts have attracted mixed reactions. Whilst some quarters have welcomed the name Chinyanja, others have argued that the name Chichewa gives the language a clear Malawian identity; hence, calling the language Chinyanja is tantamount to losing part of the national identity. Therefore, Malawi continues to use the name Chichewa whilst the same language continues to be officially known as Chinyanja outside Malawi.

The post-Banda government in Malawi has been an active advocate of regional cooperation by the Southern African Development Council (SADC). Given that Chichewa/Chinyanja is one of SADC's major cross-border languages, the continued use of the name Chichewa isolates the country. The name Chichewa does not faithfully reflect the regional identity of the language. The name mainly links the language with one country, Malawi. The name is also a reminder of the dictator Banda, who changed the name of the language from Chinyanja to Chichewa. On the other hand, the name Chinyanja gives the language a regional identity. The second possible reason why the post-Banda government has been trying to drop the name Chichewa is probably the desire to be different from the Banda regime. As already mentioned, the Banda regime was largely condemned by other Southern African States for its political isolation and active collaboration with the white colonial powers of Mozambique, the then Rhodesia and the apartheid regime in South Africa. By proposing to revert to the regional name Chinyanja, the post-Banda government in Malawi is attempting to use the name of the language as one way of aligning itself more closely with its neighbours than was the case during the Banda era. As we have seen here, Banda's political agenda stood in the way of regional cooperation in general. We can say, therefore, that some unfavourable political agendas do act as threats to cross-border collaboration.

The harmonisation of orthographies of cross-border languages is an area in which national pride or national interest can threaten regional collaboration. Given that on each side of the border the same language has different orthographic traditions in use, it sometimes becomes difficult for the language-users to accept a harmonised orthography that is a product of cross-border collaboration. One country may feel that it has lost its national identity and pride through the adoption of elements of another country's orthography. Resistance to changes in the orthography can sometimes simply be a matter of the desire to be seen to be different from others. Furthermore, it has been argued that having different orthographies for the same language is perfectly normal: if the Americans and the British can do it with English, why should we worry about harmonisation of orthographies? A good example of the slippery politics of orthography harmonisation comes from Lesotho and South Africa. The two countries share a cross-border language, Sesotho. On the Lesotho side, various governments have not been receptive to the idea of harmonisation for fear that such harmonisation could easily be interpreted as a sign of political subjugation (Machobane and Mokitimi 1998). The case of Lesotho raises fears about the acceptability of the unified standard orthography for the languages of Malawi, Mozambique and Zambia that has been proposed under the sponsorship of the South-African-based Centre for the Advanced Study of African Society. This unified orthography (Banda et al. 2002) has not yet been tried in the three countries, so there is currently no documented reaction.

4.4 Opportunities

As mentioned earlier, strengths also can act as opportunities. For example, the existence of language research centres and well-established curriculum development institutes can be viewed as both strengths and opportunities. The general mood for regional cooperation and integration, which is at the core of the Southern African Development Council, needs to be taken as an opportunity that can support regional collaboration in language issues. The desire for regional cooperation has the backing of the political leaders of the region. For example, Pandor, a South African member of parliament, had this to say at Namibia's workshop on cross-border languages: "South Africa has indicated that regional links are a high priority and we anticipate such links going beyond trade and focusing on language and culture" (Pandor 1998: 20). Similar sentiments were voiced at Malawi's second national symposium on language policy in education, where the country's Minister of Education said: "The development of these cross-border languages calls for cross-border collaboration. Harmonisation of orthographies is one example of such collaborative tasks. To this end, I call upon the SADC region to put its intellectual and research resources together to deal with these cross-border languages" (Pfaffe 2000: 13). At this same symposium, one of the fifteen resolutions passed was specifically about cooperation with other countries: "Efforts be made to increase regional cooperation with neighbouring countries regarding mother tongue education issues" (Pfaffe 2000: 269).

In line with the desire to forge cross-border collaboration in the field of mother-tongue education, Malawi has invited speakers from other countries to two of its national symposia on language in education. The idea is to learn from other countries as far as their successes and failures are concerned. To this end, at the 2000 symposium, keynote speakers were invited from Kenya (Okoth Okombo), Botswana/Tanzania[1] (Herman Batibo), South Africa (Neville Alexander), and Germany (H. E. Wolff) (see Pfaffe 2000). At the 2001 symposium, foreign speakers came from the Curriculum Development Centre of Zambia and the University of Eduardo Mondlane (Armindo Ngunga). There was no symposium in 2002 but one is expected to take place in 2003.

Another opportunity that should be exploited is the existence of some donor agencies that are willing to support local language-in-education programmes. The leading donor in Malawi is the German Technical Agency, GTZ, which since 1996 has been funding mother-tongue-related activities. Such activities include a sociolinguistic study of four Malawian languages (Centre for Language Studies 1999); Chiyao and Chitumbuka orthography reviews; four national symposia on language policy for education (Pfaffe 2000); the feasibility and acceptability of using Chitumbuka as a medium of instruction in Northern Malawi. In Mozambique, the Swedish Development Agency (SIDA) has been involved in supporting the use of local languages in education. The experimental bilingual education launched in Tete and Gaza provinces in 1992 is one example (Benson 2001), and the experiences of these projects in the neighbouring countries could and should be directly pooled and harnessed in bilateral cooperation. A favourable by-product beyond the sharing of expertise would be an increased political understanding between the former rivals and a reduction in the neo-colonial mediating role of European aid agencies.

At the regional level, an opportunity worth appreciating is the provision of financial and technical support towards language development made available by the Centre for Advanced Study of African Society (CASAS). As part of its orthography development project, CASAS has been able to pool together linguists from Malawi, Mozambique and Zambia to formulate a unified orthography for all the languages of these countries. This unified orthography (Banda et al. 2002) will make it easy for printed materials to cross the borders for use in education and other sectors. Currently, publications made in one country are hard to accept in another country due to the fact that a common language is spelt differently in each nation.

5.0 The way forward

Malawi and Mozambique share a number of common challenges and problems related to languages. It is therefore suggested that through collaboration and joint efforts, some of these challenges could be overcome. Before mapping out the way forward for the proposed collaboration, it is imperative that I mention some of the common challenges that Malawi and Mozambique face. The first challenge is that in both countries, only a tiny minority of the citizens are able to speak and write the official language. This means that English in Malawi and Portuguese in Mozambique are not the common languages of the masses. The reality is that the majority of the citizens are denied access to socio-political and economic activities that take place within and through the ex-colonial languages. The label Lusophone (or Portuguese-speaking) for Mozambique and Anglophone (or English-speaking) for Malawi are misleading in the sense that they do not faithfully capture the linguistic capabilities of the majority. Given this state of affairs, there is a need to elevate the status of local languages so that they can also perform some of the functions that at the moment can only be conducted through either Portuguese or English. It has been argued that if meaningful development is to take root in Africa, the use and over-dependence on foreign languages (mainly ex-colonial languages) has to be minimised. This, of course, does not mean having a revolution that would result in the removal of the ex-colonial languages. Rather, it means giving African languages a more robust and meaningful role in national development whilst at the same time maintaining a healthy and non-adversarial relationship between Portuguese and English on the one hand, and the local languages on the other.

There are certain institutions in Malawi and Mozambique that could benefit from collaboration in language-related matters. On the language research side, there is the Centre for Language Studies in Malawi and NELIMO in Mozambique. On the language curriculum side, there is the Malawi Institute of Education and INDE in Mozambique. In terms of mass media, the Malawi Broadcasting Corporation and Radio Mozambique have a language dimension that could be enriched through cross-border collaboration. Radio Mozambique has vast experience in broadcasting in at least twelve Bantu languages (Lopes 1998), some of which are also broadcast on the Malawian national radio. As Lopes remarks: "radio Mozambique is undoubtedly the national institution that has contributed most to the development and dissemination of the various Bantu languages" (1998: 457). Malawi could learn from and take more advantage of the increasing political will in Mozambique to nurture radiographically local languages.

Malawi and Mozambique have some common challenges. This situation then makes cross-border collaboration in language matters more relevant. As already mentioned, the first common challenge for the two countries is that only a small minority of their populations are competent users of their official languages. The challenge for the two countries is to incorporate local languages (which the majority know and use) into the official domains such the media, justice, health and politics.

The second common challenge for the two countries is the provision of literacy and basic education through the commonly used languages. In Mozambique, for instance, several authors (e.g., Benson 2001, Månsson 1995, Palme 1993, Ngunga 2001) have claimed that the use of Portuguese as a medium of instruction is one of the principal causes of low pass rates, grade repetition and high dropout rates. To this end, bilingual education (involving Portuguese and a Bantu language) has been proposed as a possible solution. In 1992, an experimental project on bilingual education known as PEBIMO started in Tete Province (using Chinyanja) and Gaza province (using Changana) (Benson 2001). PEBIMO arranged visits to neighbouring countries to learn from their experiences. Given Malawi's current interest in mother-tongue instruction, the two countries could learn from each other's successes and failures in the use of local languages in education.

The third common challenge is democracy and access to information. Today, the two countries have the large task of disseminating various types of information on health (e.g., reproductive health and HIV/AIDS), agriculture, the environment and human rights through languages that the people understand. The end of the war in Mozambique and the multiparty political dispensation in both Malawi and Mozambique have increased the importance and relevance of using local language as tools for national development (see Langa and Chambale-Mshotola). In a democracy, citizens have the right to all information that is useful for their well-being. Citizens are also supposed to have unlimited access to all the information they need. Due to language barriers, some citizens may not access certain kinds of information. To increase access to information, the use of local languages becomes necessary. To this end, community radios and newspapers that employ local languages become effective channels of communication. Given that the bulk of the information needed is in either English or Portuguese, there is a need to translate such information into cross-border languages. The two countries could collaborate in the development and standardization of translation terminologies.

In this paper, I have argued that cross-border language cooperation between Malawi and Mozambique is largely lacking. Whilst there have been contacts between the two countries in the past, there has not been any formalised link. There is a need, therefore, to set up mechanisms that would look into matters affecting the cross-border languages. One proposal is the creation of a cross-border language commission whose mandate would be to monitor and coordinate collaboration. The commission, for example, could organise regular interactions between the two countries in the form of visits, symposia, workshops and conferences. The commission would also coordinate corpus-planning activities such as orthography reviews and lexicographical projects. At the institutional level, there is a need to establish official links between institutions that have similar goals and interests. For example, NELIMO in Mozambique could establish a formal link with the Centre for Language Studies in Malawi. At a higher level, the University of Malawi and the University of Eduardo Mondlane could establish links between their language/linguistics and language education departments and research units. Through these links, joint research projects could be done. In addition, staff and student exchange programmes could be set up for the mutual benefit of the two countries. The links could also facilitate the regular exchange of ideas as well as the exchange of literature and other relevant resources. In terms of language curricula, it may not be possible to have them harmonised due to differences in the two countries' educational plans. However, regular and active interaction between curriculum specialists from the two countries is one way of learning from each other's experiences.

My final word is that cross-border languages between Malawi and Mozambique offer the two countries an avenue through which collaboration can take place as far as language management and language development are concerned. This spirit of collaboration is part and parcel of the aspirations of the Southern African Development Community and the African Union to which the two countries belong. Whilst talking about the gains that can be made out of cross-border collaboration, we also need to be fully aware of some factors that can work against this goal. But the potential benefits are enormous. Cross-border languages should be able to work as magnets that bring countries together into meaningful collaboration.

Notes

[1] Professor Batibo is a Tanzanian national working in the Department of African Languages at the University of Botswana.

Works Cited

Asiwaju, A. I., ed. *Partitioned Africans: Ethnic Relations Across Africa's International Boundaries 1884-1984.* London: Christopher Hurst, 1985.

Banda, F., et al. *A Unified Standard Orthography for South Central African Languages: Malawi, Mozambique and Zambia.* Cape Town: CASAS, 2002.

Benson, C. J. *Final Report on Bilingual Education: Results of the External Evaluation of the Experiment in Bilingual Schooling in Mozambique.* Stockholm: Swedish International Development Agency (SIDA), 2001.

Centre for Language Studies. *A Sociolinguistic Study of Four Malawian Languages: With Special Reference to Education.* N.p.:University of Malawi/GTZ, 1999.

Chumbow, B. S. "Transborder Languages of Africa." *Social Dynamics* 25.1 (1999): 51-69.

Chumbow, B. S. & P. N. Tamanji. "Linguistic Identity across the Borders of the Cameroon Triangle." *Between Distinction and Extinction: The Harmonisation and Standardisation of African Languages.* Ed. K. K. Prah. Johannesburg: Wits UP, 1998. 53-74.

Elugbe, B. "Cross-border and Major Languages of Africa." *Cross-border Languages: Reports and Studies: Regional Workshop on Cross-border Languages.* Ed. K. Legere. Windhoek: Gamsberg Macmillan, 1998. 22-39.

Gadelii, K. E. "Languages in Mozambique." *Africa and Asia* 1 (2001): 6-12.

Hedges, S. D. "Some Notes on Malawi-Mozambique Relations 1961-87." *Journal of Southern African Studies* 15 (1989): 617-644.

Katupha, J. M. M. "The Language Situation and Language Use in Mozambique." *African Languages, Development and the State.* Eds. R. Fardon and G. Furniss. London: Routledge, 1994. 89-96.

Kayambazinthu, E. "The Language Situation in Malawi." *Journal of Multilingual and Multicultural Development* 19.5-6 (1998): 369-439.

Kishindo, P. J. "Politics of Language in Contemporary Malawi." *Democratization in Malawi: A Stocktaking.* Eds. K. M. Phiri & K. R. Ross. Blantyre: CLAIM, 1998. 252-280.

Langa, L. and S. Chamabale-Mshotola. "The Status of Mozambique Languages." *Between Distinction and Extinction: The Harmonisation and Standardisation of African Languages.* Ed. K. K. Prah. Johannesburg: Wits UP, 1998. 213-221.

Legere, K., ed. *Cross-border Languages: Reports and Studies: Regional Workshop on Cross-border Languages.* Windhoek: Gamsberg Macmillan, 1998.

———. "The Languages of Tanzania Project: Background, Resources and Perspectives." *Africa and Asia.* 2 (2002): 163-186.

Lopes, A. J. "Language Policy in Mozambique: A Taboo?" *African Linguistics at the Crossroads: Papers from Kwaluseni.* Ed. K. R. Herbert. Köln: Rudiger Kööpe Verlag, 1997. 485-500.

———. "The Language Situation in Mozambique." *Journal of Multilingual and Multicultural Development* 19.5-6 (1998): 440-486.

Machobane, M. and M. Mokitimi. "Problems in the Development of Sesotho Orthography." *Between Distinction and Extinction: The Harmonisation and Standardisation of African Languages.* Ed. K. K. Prah. Johannesburg: Wits UP, 1998. 203-212.

Månsson, A. B. *Women's Literacy and the Question of Dropout: Two Mozambican Case Studies.* Master Degree Studies. Stockholm: Stockholm University, Institute of International Development, 1995.

Matusse, R . "The Future of Portuguese in Mozambique." *African Linguistics at the Crossroads: Papers from Kwaluseni.* Ed. R. K. Herbert. Köln: Rudiger Koope Verlag, 1997. 541-554.

McMaster, C. *Malawi: Foreign Policy and Development.* London: Julian Friedmann, 1974.

Ngunga, A. "Language Policy for Education and the Media in Mozambique: An Alternative Perspective." *Language and Development in Southern Africa: Making the Right Choices.* Eds. R. Trewby and S. Fitchat. Windhoek: Gamsberg Macmillan, 2001. 94-108.

Palme, M. *The Meaning of School Repetition and Dropout in the Mozambican Primary Schools.* Stockholm: SIDA Education Division, 1993.

Pandor, N. "National Languages and Constitutional Development." *Cross-border Languages: Reports and Studies: Regional Workshop on Cross-border Languages.* Ed. K. Legere. Windhoek: Gamsberg Macmillan, 1998. 13-21.

Pfaffe, J. F., ed. *Local Languages in Education, Science and Technology: Proceedings of the Second National Symposium on Language Policy Formulation.* Centre for Language Studies, University of Malawi/GTZ, 2000.

Short, P. *Banda.* London: Kegan Paul and Routledge, 1974.

Stroud, C. "Framing Bourdieu Socioculturally: Alternative Forms of Linguistic Legitimacy in Post Colonial Mozambique." *Multilingua* 21 (2002): 247-273.

UNESCO. *Language Policies in Africa: Final Report on the Intergovernmental Conference on Language Policies in Africa.* Web version, 2002. www.african.gu.se/lasu/papers.html.

Gregory Kamwendo is a Senior Lecturer in the Department of English at Chancellor College, University of Malawi. His area of specialisation is sociolinguistics; his research interests cover language policy and language planning; the language/politics interface; and language use in the delivery of health services. Apart from contributing to edited books, Kamwendo has also published in journals such as *Nordic Journal of African Studies; Language Matters; English Teaching Forum; Alternation;* and *Malilime: Malawian Journal of Linguistics.* Currently, Gregory Kamwendo is pursuing doctoral studies at the University of Helsinki in Finland.

Mia Couto or the Art of Storytelling

Patrick Chabal

Abstract. Although a great deal has by now been written about Mia Couto, the key to his exceptional success remains largely unexplained. Why should he appeal so widely, especially to those readers who know little or nothing about Mozambique? What can such readership find in a prose so replete with "Mozambicanisms" and so heavily accented by an invented language? Couto started his literary journey as a poet and he has written novels as well as a number of plays, but this article focuses on his short stories, or *contos*, for it is in the short stories that Couto achieves the greatest degree of literary originality, exhibits the most notable poetry, creates the most imaginative language, and reveals the most acute psychological insights. The article examines in its appropriate chronology the whole of Mia Couto's corpus of short stories, with a view to assessing their literary qualities. The aim is both to explain why the author excels in a genre not so widely practised and to illustrate the manner in which language is related to theme within a very specific African context.

In 1999, the Mozambican writer Mia Couto was awarded the Prémio Vergílio Ferreira. This was a great honour for someone only 43 years old, and whose oeuvre consists largely of short stories. By then, however, Couto was not only an established writer in his own country but he was well known throughout the Portuguese-speaking world, where his books sell in large numbers. Although a great deal by now has been written about him, the key to his exceptional success remains largely unexplained. Why should Mia Couto appeal so widely, especially to those readers who know little or nothing about Mozambique? What can such readership find in a prose so replete with "Mozambicanisms" and so heavily accented by an invented language?

Couto started his literary journey as a poet and he has written novels as well as a number of plays, but I want here to focus on his short stories, or *contos*, for they represent in my view the essence his work. It is in the short stories that Couto achieves the greatest degree of literary originality, exhibits the most notable poetry, creates the most imaginative language, and reveals the most acute psychological insights. It is also in the *contos* that he develops a body of writing chronicling the evolution of the country in which he lives. Finally, it is plain, as I shall explain later, that his novels are, in large measure at least, constructed according to a "short story" blueprint.

The writing of short stories has always been a most difficult art, which very few contemporary writers attempt. Among the present canon of twentieth century writers, only a small number are the crafters of short stories. Interestingly, it has been, in the recent past, a genre more widely essayed in non-European settings—whether in North or South America—than it is in the continent in which such writing flourished in the nineteenth century. Perhaps it is today a form of literary expression particularly well suited to the new world, frontier spaces, the far reaches of empire, or even more, to the postcolonial experience. Perhaps it is a type of writing that remains closer to the orality of everyday life, and such orality is often the mark of "new" or "marginal" areas.

Whatever the reasons for Mia Couto's inclination to compose short stories, and I shall explore them in detail in this article, it is important to discuss the personal and historical context within which he has been writing. Mia Couto was born in 1955 in the Mozambican city of Beira, where his parents had settled. His father was a journalist, a writer of poetry, who was both an opponent of the Salazar regime and someone with a great interest in the lives of Africans in the midst of whom he lived.

> O meu pai era jornalista e era poeta. Ele publicou cinco ou seis títulos em Moçambique, uma poesia pouca íntima, mas também dois dos livros foram livros que tentaram ser livros de preocupação social, em relação ao conflito da situção existente em Moçambique. Mas eram livros em que a consciência política era mais antifascista, liberal, democrática, mas não questionando ainda a questão colonial.[1]

His mother knows little about her own origins, since she was an orphan, but what Mia Couto mentions in the same interview is, in my view, significant: "Ela ficou órfã, abandonada [...] até o nome dela foi reescrito, foi inventado para ela não ter uma ligação com a sua mãe—uma 'senhora do pecado.'"

Two features of his early life are particularly important. The first is that his parents were not typical Portuguese settlers in that they did not seek merely to live a "colonial" existence, insulated from the local population. Beira was notoriously a socially and politically conservative city, where race relations were not good, and the Coutos' ways set them aside from the bulk of the local white community. The second aspect of his childhood that is relevant, therefore, is that right from the beginning he lived and interacted with peers from different racial and social backgrounds, particularly black and *mestiço* children. Although in the formal sphere of school and home, he largely lived the life of the typical European youth, the rest of his time was spent with boys and girls from all horizons. The fact that his parents, unlike most other settlers, did not object to such a lifestyle enabled the young Mia to grow up in close proximity to Africans and to absorb their language and traditions.

Couto, consequently, is a Mozambican, not just in the sense that he was born in that territory but in the more significant way that he partook of the whole of its (at least urban) diversity when he was a child. Crucially, he also understands the African languages most commonly used in southern Mozambique. What matters for the understanding of his work, however, is what this complex, and somewhat contradictory, Beira childhood meant to him.

> Eu guardo da minha infância, assim, uma coisa muito esbatida, um ponto de referência, as histórias que eram contadas, dos velhos que moravam perto, vizinhos do outro lado da rua, de um outro mundo, e eu recordo desse mundo encantado até algumas histórias, sobretudo como eles me deixaram uma marca.[2]

> [R]ecordo-me das histórias que me eram contadas—quer em português, quer em chissena—pelos velhos e pelas pessoas que pertenciam a esse mundo, que transportavam esse outro imaginário. [...] [E]u ainda hoje volto muito a histórias que me foram contadas há muitos, muitos anos, das quais só me lembro de pedaços, de coisas que me assustavam, que me tiravam o sono como criança.[3]

Couto went to Lourenço Marques, the capital, for his secondary and university education and it is there that he became a supporter of FRELIMO, the anti-colonial movement, which came to power in 1975, following a ten-year armed struggle and the return of democracy in Portugal. At that time, he was one of a number of young white Mozambicans to join the nationalists and to commit himself to the socialist politics that they advocated. He interrupted his medical studies after the 25th of April 1974 when he was asked by FRELIMO to become active in journalism. He worked successively for *Tribuna* (with Rui Knopfli), the *Agência de Informação Nacional*, the review *Tempo* and finally the newspaper *Notícias.* He resigned from this last post in 1985, partly because he was dissatisfied with the lack of professionalism in his work and partly because he no longer wanted to be a "functionary" of the state. He resumed university, this time in biology, and started working in environmental studies, chiefly in research and mostly on NGO contracts.

In 1983, he published his first book, a volume of poetry—*Raiz de Orvalho*, one of the early collection of poems in the country that moved away from the militant and political towards the personal, intimate and subjective. The book was well received, as were others, in the same literary vein, among those issued by the Association of Mozambican Writers, at the time one of the few outlets for home-grown literature.[4] Couto and his fellow versifiers (Patraquim, Viegas, White, Baptista, Artur, Bucuane, Muteia and Saúte) followed in the footsteps of a generation of strikingly original Mozambican poets, of whom the most influential undoubtedly were José Craveirinha and Rui Knopfli. Naturally, they all wanted to make their mark in ways that differed from those of their elders.

Couto, however, had already started writing brief prose pieces, *contos* or short stories, based on his interest in the life histories, fantasies or rumours that he uncovered as a working journalist, and influenced by memories of storytelling harking back to his childhood. His first volume, *Vozes Anoitecidas*, was published in Mozambique in 1986. In 1988, he put out a collection of the weekly *crónicas* he had written for the newspaper *Notícias* in the previous two years. Both books were immensely successful in Mozambique and were reprinted by the Portuguese publisher *Caminho*, who has now not only brought out all of his work but has published other Mozambican writers like Suleiman Cassamo, Eduardo White, Ungulani Ba Ka Khosa and Paulina Chiziane. Couto has received prizes for *Vozes Anoitecidas*, *Cronicando*, and his first novel, *Terra Sonâmbula*. His literary fame has grown steadily and it has undoubtedly helped raise the status of Mozambican writing in the Portuguese-speaking world.[5]

Mia Couto has published five novels, to which I will refer briefly, but it is as a writer of short stories that I should like to approach his work, for I am convinced that this is the medium through which he has succeeded in creating a new (Mozambican) form of prose writing that will endure.[6] Although *Vozes Anoitecidas* was the first book of short stories Couto published, partly (I suspect) because it is more "literary," the roots of his writing is to be found in his journalistic work. In this respect, then, the collection of *contos* that came out in *Cronicando* is a useful starting point for the study of his very unusual writing. Three features of the *crónicas* immediately stand out, and all three are at the heart of all of his subsequent prose. They have to do with the choice of character, the way in which the story is recounted and the highly unexpected, unreal or discordant development of events.

The first is the ability to focus on highly distinctive characters, a (real or invented) person, or animal, either because of who they are, or because of the situation in which they find themselves, or, finally, because of their behaviour. All three aspects are important and may well overlap, for the point is to bring to the attention of the reader a type, or range, of characters that are often not just strange, different, but also behave in a highly unusual fashion. The key is that they may appear normal, and then reveal themselves to be odd, or they may be distinctly bizarre, unreal, right from the start and yet behave in straightforward and sensible ways. Whatever the situation, the characters are inevitably bound up in events, incidents, or actions that are simultaneously within *and* outside the common range of human experience, beyond the pale of everyday life. The hallmark of Couto's writing, then, is the ability to present these characters, *as though* they were perfectly ordinary, *as though* what they were doing, what was happening to them, was in every respect logical. In other words, the characters chosen serve not just to illustrate the point that the tale will make, as they would in all short stories, but also, and maybe more importantly, to challenge, or interrogate, the reader's assumptions and expectations. The great originality of characterisation, therefore, is the ability to portray seemingly normal personages involved in plausibly fantastic situations.

The second trait of Couto's prose writing is the manner in which the story is told. The strict discipline involved in having to write newspaper *crónicas* to a set limit has influenced or, better, conditioned the author's style from the outset. For Couto, implicitly or explicitly, a *conto* is in practice a piece that is limited to a very small number of words indeed. Whilst other short story writers have also published brief prose fiction, they have most often written at different length. What is noteworthy in Couto's work is the virtually standard size of all his short stories. Although this may seem a relatively trivial point, I believe it is in fact crucial, for in this case writing to length is one of the main reasons why the *contos* work so well. The very brevity of the piece brings out in the writer a conciseness of expression, both in the text and in the dialogue, which sharpens inventiveness and heightens imagination.

The third attribute of the *crónicas* is the unexpected ending, or the twist at the conclusion of the tale. To some extent, this is a feature of all good short story writing and it is commonly found in authors as far apart as Somerset Maugham and Richard Carver. Nevertheless, Mia Couto has perfected the art to a degree simply unknown in contemporary Western literature, and even unusual in the so-called "magic realism" from Latin America. Indeed, it might even be said that it is the way in which the Mozambican writer wraps up his stories that is their most original aspect. What is undeniable is that Couto constructs the *contos* around the finale, aiming always to close them in a strikingly unexpected manner. This is achieved in many different ways, depending on who the characters are and what has happened to them, but the key is the element of surprise. Couto's stories are very largely revealed for what they truly are at the very last moment—and sometimes not even then.

Let me illustrate what I mean by means of a closer look at the first *crónica* published in the Mozambican version of *Cronicando*.[7] The piece, "A Velha e a Aranha," is apparently about a mother waiting for her son to come back from the army. The first sentence encapsulates the way in which Couto creates a fundamental disjuncture, a juxtaposition of real and unreal, of fact and fiction, within an apparently banal setting:

> Deu-se em época onde o tempo nunca chegou. Está-se escrevendo, ainda por mostrar a verdade caligrafada [...]. Uma mulher, oculta de face, entretinha suas vidas numa casinha tão pequena, tão mínima que se ouvia o roçar das paredes umas de encontro às outras. O antigamente ali se arrumava [...]. Sentada, imovente, a mulher presenciava-se sonhar. Naquela inteira solidão, ela via seu filho regressando.[8]

This opening is not only a model of brevity but it sets the tone: an ordinary person in ordinary circumstances is about to live through an extra-ordinary event.

The old woman, sensing that her son is about to return, prepares for this happy event by donning her best outfit. She then notices a cobweb under the roof. Intrigued, she waits (a long time) for its creator—it turns out to be a small green spider—to appear. The spider requests silence, so as not to be disturbed. The two talk and agree that they are both waiting. The old woman settles in for the (long) haul. Finally, she hears the sounds of boot steps. The story, in other words, unfolds "normally." However, this is how it ends:

> Encontraram a velha em estado de retrato, ao dispor da poeira. Em todo o seu redor, envolvente, uma espessa teia. Era como um cacimbo, a memória de um fumo. Ao seu lado, sem que se vislumbrasse entendimento, estava um par de botas negras, lustradas, sem gota de poeira.[9]

The force of the story lies, as I indicated above, in the way in which the three aspects of the telling intermingle. What Couto likes best, when he can, is to leave a *conto* without obvious resolution, without simple closure. For him, a short story is not a fable; it is not edifying but symbolic. And it is in this respect that his writing, though influenced by local oral culture, is not really derivative of the African tradition of orature, which is almost always didactic.

In order to demonstrate how Couto's technique is consistent over time, I now turn to the first story of his most recent collection: "O menino no sapatinho."[10] Here too the tale is of the relationship between identity, loss, time and space; here too the focus is on the relationship between mother and son. Again, the account is plausibly simple, if entirely fantastic: a child was born unusually small:

> Era uma vez o menino pequenito, tão minimozito que todos seus dedos eram mindinhos. Dito assim, fino modo, ele, quando nasceu, nem foi dado à luz mas a uma simples fresta de claridade.[11]

The mother rejoices in the fact that her son is undemanding, either in food or affection. He is so slight that even his tears float up to the ceiling. Because he is small she uses one of her husband's shoes as a cradle, but he is angry at the undignified use of his footwear and threatens forcibly to empty it. She now bemoans her child's size and, come Christmas, begs that he be returned to a normal dimension. Following the Western tradition she places the shoe, with the child, under the improvised Christmas tree. She worries all night. On Christmas morning she rushes to see what has happened:

> Dentro do sapato, porém, só o vago vazio, a redonda da concavidade do nada. O

> filho desaparecera? Não para os olhos da mãe. Que ele tinha sido levado por Jesus, rumo aos ceus, onde há um mundo apto para crianças [...]. De relance, ainda notou que lá o tecto já não brilhavam as lágrimas do seu menino. Mas ela desviou o olhar, que essa é a competência de mãe: o não enxurgar nunca a curva onde o escura faz extinguir o mundo.[12]

Although perhaps slightly less unexpected an ending than the first story, there is nevertheless an absence of closure, or rather a closing that does not "resolve" the riddle of the tale itself. Here too, therefore, the *conto*'s freshness lies in the juxtaposition of the improbable with the poetic. The author himself wants to express nothing more than a light whisper, the shadow of a sentiment, as it might have emerged in the heart of a sad mother.

Across the decade and a half that spans these two stories, Couto has remained true to his vision of the short story. We have seen how these tales are constructed. Let us now look more closely at the style and language in which they are written. The author is famous for his inventiveness with the Portuguese he uses. He is often compared with that other well-known creator of "African" Portuguese, the Angolan Luandino Vieira. Yet, above and beyond the fact that they both, writing over thirty years apart, have fashioned what is recognisably a different literary language from that used in Portugal, there is little in common between the two. Perhaps the only link is the homage they pay to the Brazilian writer, Guimarães Rosa, who was at once a very fine writer and a pioneer in the invention of a locally based version of Portuguese, one that integrated the language spoken in its local setting.[13]

I do not intend here to give a linguistic analysis of Couto's writing, an enterprise that would require a much more systematic study of the current Mozambican Portuguese language than is possible in an article.[14] I should like instead to make a little clearer how the author fashions his prose and give a brief assessment of its undoubted qualities. It is relevant at this stage to distinguish between the short stories and the novels, as indeed there are differences in style between the two. Nor should these differences be glossed over. Nevertheless, what, from my point of view, is most noticeable is how much the novels are written like short stories. Indeed, a study of the longer prose work would only highlight the linguistic characteristics of the *contos*.

The novels are divided into a large number of (usually) short chapters. Each chapter exhibits some or all of the features discussed above—particularly as concerns the openings—even if, naturally, their ending must allow for some continuity. But since the short stories, as I have shown, are themselves never properly "closed," the parallel with the novels' chapters is quite clear. Moreover, the construction of the novels is not so much cumulative, or even linear, as it is circular—by which I mean that there is no standard plot development as such but rather a series of events, or accounts, which may or may not be resolved at the end. What matters, and in *this* way Couto's novels are very African, is the road travelled rather than the point of arrival. This is best demonstrated in the author's main novel, *Terra Sonâmbula*,[15] undoubtedly the emblematic prose work of postcolonial Mozambique at the height of the civil war.[16] Nevertheless, it is equally noticeable in his two other main novels, *A Varanda do Frangipani*[17] and *O Último Voo do Flamingo*,[18] where the endings, again, fail to bring a sense of closure.[19]

Terra Sonâmbula opens thus:

> Naquele lugar, a guerra tinha morto a estrada [...]. A estrada que agora se abre a nossos olhos não se entrecruza com outra nenhuma. Está mais deitada que os séculos, suportando sozinha toda a distância [...].[20]

The first paragraph of the second chapter is even clearer, from the point of view of the link with short story writing:

> Quero pôr os tempos, em sua mansa ordem, conforme esperas e sofrências. Mas a lembranças desobedecem, entre a vontade de serem nada e o gosto de me roubarem do presente. Acendo a estória, me apago a mim. No fim destes escritos, serei de novo uma sombra sem voz.[21]

And the book's last sentences are as follows:

> Me apetece deitar, me anichar na terra morna [...]. Mais adiante segue um miúdo com passo lento. Nas suas mãos estão papéis que me parecem familiares. Me aproximo e, com sobressalto, confirmo: são os meus cadernos [...]. Movidas por um vento que nascia não do ar mas do próprio chão, as folhas se espalham pela estrada. Então, as letras, uma por uma, se vão convertendo em grãos de areia e, aos poucos, todos meus escritos se vão transformando em páginas de terra.[22]

What is interesting about the ending of *Terra Sonâmbula* is how similar it is to that of most of his short stories. Not only is it not "possible" from the perspective of what has been happening to the main characters in the novel, but also it is fantastic in the sense that it transmutes the fictitious into the factual. Above all, like his *contos*, it fails to conclude. The last few lines serve only to close the circle in the sense that they suggest a continuation of that elusive dialectic between the words that produce an account of events and the soil that holds the country's cultural heritage. The novel is a chronicle of a tragedy unfolding. It serves to impart a sense of the mindless journey on which the inhabitants of this cursed land are embarked. Like the short stories, therefore, *Terra Sonâmbula* allows us to feel, rather than comprehend, what is taking place.

Of course, Couto's novels are much more explicitly about the history of independent Mozambique, and in this way touch much more directly than the short stories on the question of the country's identity and the calamity of its postcolonial condition. Nevertheless, it is clear that they are also, and, I would argue, are primarily, about constructing a literary language that can account for such a history in what might be termed culturally indigenous writing. For this reason, they are not simply an expression of the complexity of the experience of the country since independence, but they are above all an attempt to root that experience in a locally meaningful context—that is, one that is in consonance with the traditions and beliefs of the majority of its inhabitants. Thus, the novels are more overtly ambitious. They aim to create a body of culturally significant prose writing that bridges the gap between the modern, even post-modern, circumstances in which the country finds itself and the "traditional" foundations from which the ruling elites all too often want to dissociate themselves.

Here, *A Varanda do Frangipani* is quite unambiguous. Ostensibly about an enquiry into the death of the governor of an old people's home, the novel is in fact a disquisition on how the country's modernity is at the expense of its cultural roots. The frangipani tree is the link with the past and the enquiry, predictably, does not achieve its aims. Here, again, I can do no better than quote the last paragraph of the novel:

> Aos poucos, vou perdendo a língua dos homens, tomado pelo sotaque do chão. Na luminosa varanda deixo meu último sonho, a árvore do frangipani. Vou ficando do som das pedras. Me deito mais antigo que a terra. Daqui em diante, vou dormir mais quieto que a morte.[23]

The inmates, among whom is an old Portuguese man, decide to return to the roots of the frangipani tree rather than suffer the madness of the "real" world. Tradition overcomes the blindness and futility of modernity. As in *Terra Sonâmbula*, the concluding sentences bring together the words with the soil, as though it is truly the earth that shelters the "reality" worth preserving.

A Varanda do Frangipani, however, also illustrates my point about the genesis of Couto's novels, for it undoubtedly is a novel that is most obviously constructed as a succession of chapters closely following the patterns of his short story writing style. It is in this respect, therefore, quite literally a collection of connected *contos* about the characters that appear, in the tale, either as residents or outsiders. Although the novel is evidently more than the mere appending of separate accounts, what makes it so attractive is the quite unique (in terms of contemporary literature) way in which it constructs the narrative by way of self-contained and finely rounded sections. The device is the apparently straightforward report given by each character of the death of the director. In reality, each chapter is the story of one life as recounted, in fact as in fantasy, by those who reject an objective, modern, and "external" explanation of their lives.

This brings us back to the short stories. If in the novels Mia Couto is concerned to bear testimony to the history of Mozambique as it is unfolding, in the *contos* he allows himself complete freedom. As he himself says, he does not seek the stories out; they come at him: "Olha, as pessoas que convivem comigo, *constroem* as histórias que me vêm contar. Episódios que vêem no meio da rua e me vêm dar o instrumento que é o material para fazer depois um trabalho que é um trabalho de artesanato."[24] This point is critical, for it explains why the short stories have such a distinct edge. It is the fact that they issue from the "real" world as it touches the author that makes them both original and arresting. It is almost as though they could not be invented. Reality is much stranger than fiction. The novels, by contrast, are, in my view, more deliberately constructed for the purpose of rendering into literature the more general narrative of the country. And, while they follow the same style as the short stories, both their ambition and their length make them far less "spontaneous," or fresh.

Thus, one undoubted quality of the short stories is their instant quirkiness, this powerful sense that they have materialised "out-of-nowhere." Not because they have not been chosen and crafted meticulously, since they quite clearly have been, but simply because they usually manage to confound utterly the quiet, implicit, and perhaps lazy, expectations of the reader. A second aspect of their originality is the absolute coherence with which fact and fiction, reality and fantasy, are woven together. This is not achieved, as with other writing (for instance, in some magic realist or even postmodernist literature), in the all-too-deliberate overlay of the actual and the invented, so that the two are still recognisably distinct. Rather, it comes about through the exposition of an apparently quite "objective" reality that only incidentally happens to be an admixture of the factual and fictive.

Moreover, the importance of such a literary construct does not simply lie in the exploitation of the effects achieved by such disparity. Quite the reverse: the originality of Couto's writing is that it is precisely this blend that makes up the "authentic" life of the stories. Whereas in contemporary "postmodern" writers like Rushdie, for example, the contrast is often played for effect, for Mia Couto there is no such (crude) undertaking: it is quite simply objectively the case that life is an unexplainable combination of fact and fantasy. He writes, pointedly, in the epigraph to *Vozes Anoitecidas:*

> O que mais dói na miséria é a ignorância que ela tem de si mesma. Confrontado com a ausência de tudo, homens abstêm-se do sonho, desarmando-se do desejo de serem outros. Existe no nada essa ilusão de plenitude que faz parar a vida e anoitecer as vozes.[25]

Hence, what makes his stories so vivid is the way in which they draw the reader into a world, as real as any, where all boundaries are put into question, when not completely erased.[26]

Almost every story demonstrates this characteristic but, in order to clarify more fully what I mean, I shall refer to one that Couto himself has identified as triggering in him the wish to write in this way. It is the *conto* that appears in *Vozes Anoitecidas* as "As baleias de Quissico." He says:

> Depois, em 1985, comecei a ouvir umas histórias que vinham ligadas à guerra, como aquela história da baleia [...]. e pensei que havia de haver uma maneira de contar aquelas histórias, mantendo a *graça* e a *agilidade* das pessoas que mas contavam [...]. [27] (my italics)

The *conto* refers to a man who hears about a whale, near Quissico, that disgorges bounties at night. The event, connected to the very real delivery of supplies by South African submarines to the armed opposition, Renamo, is transmuted into a rumour about fantastic black beasts landing on the beach, and induces in the main character a dream of easy opulence. He goes to Quissico and, having witnessed a storm, which, he believes, announces the arrival of the whale, he enters the waters to retrieve the goods. The story ends with the discovery of his clothes on the beach, evidence for some that there has indeed been a distribution of goods "out of the seas."

Paradoxically, but bearing out my argument, "As baleias de Quissico" is not one of the most effective, or suggestive, short stories. This, I would venture, is because, like the novels, it is a trifle didactic. Such rumours may have been an inspiration to the writer, but he is at his best when the idea germinating in his mind is not capable of a straightforward "explanation." It is as though what most inspires him is the experience of a tale that can only be revealed, rather than made "clear," by means of the literary creation it triggers in the author's imagination.

What is plain, however, is that it is in the local tradition of storytelling that Couto originally found inspiration. Recounting his first attempt to write the story of the "baleias de Quissico," he says:

> E, à medida que eu ia fazendo, eu me apercebi que não podia usar o português clássico, a norma portuguesa, para contar a história com toda a *carga poética* que ela tinha. Era preciso recriar uma linguagem que trouxesse aquele ambiente de magia em que a história me foi contada. E aí começa essa experiência e, interessantemente, eu fui de repente projectado para a infância, para os tais momentos de que falo, em que os tais velhos contavam as tais histórias [...].
> E isso [story telling] só é possível através de, numéro um, a *poesia* e, numéro dois, uma linguagem que utilize este jogo de dança e de teatro que eles faziam. Então foi aí que eu comecei, de facto, a experimentar os limites da própria língua e a transgredir no sentido de criar um espaço de magia.[28] (my italics)

The key to the origins of his stylistic quest, therefore, lies in the search for a way of conveying the magical by way of "poetic" prose. There is, as he himself has said, no valid distinction in his mind between the two forms of literary expression:

> A única coisa que eu posso dizer é que eu estou tentando criar [...]. beleza, mostrar um pouco o que é a possibilidade de alguém fazer uma língua sua. De criar a partir da desarrumação daquilo que é o primeiro instrumento de criação, que seria a

> língua, a linguagem, e os modelos de uma narrativa. Por exemplo, abolir esta fronteira entre poesia e prosa. Porque é que a coisa tem que estar arrumada, porque é que é preciso haver esta categorização de géneros literários [...]. o realismo mágico, o realismo neo-realista? Nos podemos talvez criar à margem disso [...]. [29]

While it is often the case that writers' pronouncements on their own work are not enlightening, I believe that here Mia Couto is providing us with a genuine insight into his writing—as is easily validated by a sensitive reading (rather than simply a linguistic analysis) of his short stories.

I propose to illustrate the texture of poetry in Couto's prose by discussing one short story from each of his volumes. Not because there are only a limited number of such "poetic" *contos*—though they are obviously not all equally successful in this respect—but simply because there would be too many to choose from and my point here is to show the thread that runs through his writing over time. Admittedly, this is a somewhat contrived approach but it is the only one that makes it possible to be wide-ranging without becoming tediously repetitive.[30]

From *Vozes Anoitecidas*, I should like to offer "Afinal, Carlota Gentina não chegou de voar." The main character sits in prison, accused of having killed his wife. He tries to explain to the authorities what has happened. The point, as always with Couto, is both straightforward and fantastic. The man, convinced that his wife had become a bird, resolved that the only way to find out was to pour boiling water on her. If she screamed she would be human. But she did not utter a sound, even as she died, which confirms the husband's suspicion that she is in fact a bird. This is how the account opens:

> Eu somos tristes. Não me engano, digo bem. Ou talvez: nos sou triste? Porque dentro de mim, não sou sozinho. Sou muitos. E esses todos disputam minha única vida. Vamos tendo nossas mortes. Mas parto foi só um. Aí, o problema. Por isso, quando conto a minha história me misturo, mulato não das raças, mas de existências. A minha mulher matei, dizem. Na vida real, matei uma que não existia. Era um pássaro. Soltei-lhe quando vi que ela não tinha voz, morria sem queixar. Que bicho saiu dela, mudo, através do intervalo do corpo?[31]

What is enchanting in the writing here is the juxtaposition of, on the one hand, verisimilitude of expression, as though this was the speech of a most ordinary man in the most ordinary circumstance and, on the other, the simultaneous deployment of arresting images. Indeed, these few lines demonstrate the freshness of Couto's prose: its poetic quality is a blend of "common sense," apparently mundane statements and a pungent, unexpected, quasi-naïve, expression. In this story, the explanation given of the man's behaviour is rational: he was led to believe that his wife, like her sister, might have been a "witch." His action, though reprehensible, is at least explainable.

At the end, the man demands, without much hope, to be judged by those who share his faith in witchcraft. The story, however, would easily have become merely edifying, were it not for the writing. The concluding paragraph casts the whole episode into a mournful, yet moving, light:

> Agora já é tarde. Só reparo o tempo quando já passou. Sou um cego que vê muitas portas. Abro aquela que está mais perto. Não escolho, tropeço a mão no fecho. Minha vida não é um caminho. É uma pedra fechada à espera de ser areia. Vou entrando nos grãos do chão, devagarinho. Quando me quiserem enterrar já eu serei terra. Já que não tive vantagem na vida, esse será o privilégio da minha vida.[32]

From Mia Couto's second, and very successful, collection of short stories, *Cada Homem é uma Raça*, I should like to discuss another astonishing story, "O Pescador cego." This *conto*, like the previous one, touches on what is a fairly consistent thread throughout the author's work: the account of acute, and apparently gratuitous, violence in the life of humble people. Whilst the first story turned around beliefs in the occult, which remain as strong today as they were a century ago, "O Pescador cego" takes place within the context of a period of war and famine. The fisherman is desperate to bring provisions to his family. After days at sea without success, mad with hunger, and bereft of food, he uses his eyes as bait. He comes home with fish but without the means to continue his profession. The narrator introduces the story, as he is wont to do, in a discursive, but stylistically accomplished, manner:

> Vivemos longe de nós, em distante fingimento. Desaparecemo-nos. Porque nos preferimos nessa escuridão interior? Talvez porque a escura junta as coisas, costura os fios do disperso. No aconchego da noite, o impossível ganha a suposição do visível. Nessa ilusão descansam os nossos fantasmas.[33]

The fisherman's wife, even more desperate now than before, wants herself to go to sea in the hope of bringing fish back. Her husband cannot accept what would be tantamount to his total social disgrace. Having already rejected his wife's affection out of humiliated pride, he finally burns the boat rather than let her use it. His life now becomes a long tortured stay on the beach, prey to the elements and to the wanderings of his mind. Until one day a woman he cannot identify comes and provides him with food and affection. Is it his wife? A changed man, he builds a new boat, and invites the unknown woman to go out to sea, to find the eyes he has lost. The story ebbs away with these somewhat wistful lines:

> Desde então, todas as infalíveis manhãs, se viu o pescador cego vagandeando pela praia, remexendo a espuma que o mar soletra na areia. Assim, em passos líquidos, ele aparentava buscar seu completo rosto, gerações e gerações de ondas.[34]

For the sake of continuity, but also to illustrate the change in Couto from a concern with the tragic fate of his country during the civil war to a more hopeful look into the future after peace returned, I should like to present another story about blindness—"O cego Estrelinho"—from *Estórias Absensonhadas*, the author's third collection of *contos*:

> O cego Estrelinho era pessoa de nenhuma vez: sua história poderia ser contada e descontada não fosse seu guia, Gigito Efraim. A mão de Gigito conduziu o desvistado por tempos e idades. Aquela mão era repartidamente comum, extensão de um no outro, siamensal. E assim era quase de nascença. Memória de Estrelinho tinha cinco dedos e eram os de Gigito postos, em aperto, na sua própria mão.[35]

Gigito is a dreamer, conveying to his blind friend a wonderful world of fantasy, so that the blind man lives an enchanted life. When Gigito is drafted into the army and Estrelinho is left to his own device, his life turns upside down. He lapses into great sadness until, one day, a friendly hand, that of Gigito's sister, takes charge of him. She, however, is down to earth and her factual account of the world fails to remind Estrelinho of what her brother had invented for him. Yet, they fall in love. Gigito is killed. His sister now sinks into depression.

> A moça, essa, deixou de falar, orfã de seu irmão. A partir dessa morte ela so tristonhava, definhada. E assim ficou, sem competência para reviver. Até que a ela se chegou o cego e lhe conduziu para a varanda da casa. Então, iniciou de descrever o mundo,

> indo além dos vários firmamentos. Aos poucos foi despontando um sorriso: a menina se sarava da alma. Estrelinho miraginava terras e territórios. Sim, a moça se concordava. Tinha sido em tais paisagens que ela dormira antes de ter nascido [...].[36]

Here, the poetry of the author's language is expressed more through the invention of words than the display of striking images. This in itself is noteworthy, for there is in Couto's writing a steady development of a new form of linguistic expression, of which one of the most notable features is the creation of an entirely fictional, but exceedingly plausible, construction of words.[37] There is in the above paragraphs quite a selection of such verbal imaginings, all of which manage to communicate a precise meaning and bring aesthetic pleasure. Expressions such as "desvistado," "tristonhava," or "miraginava" are not just an original way of conveying the type of Portuguese spoken in Mozambique; they are also music to the ear—in short, utterly poetic.[38]

Couto's third collection, *Contos do Nascer da Terra*, was published on the morrow of the peace agreement and within a perspective of renewed hopefulness. Perhaps for this reason it is a volume of miniatures focused on the subjective, the intimate, and the emotional. The author seems to have responded to the country's changed circumstances by prying even deeper into ordinary humanity, as though it was that quality that was most needed at the time. As ever, the book's epigraph provides a most valuable handle on what follows. I quote it in full here, because it is relevant to most of Couto's recent work, not just to the particular book it prefaces:

> Não é da luz do sol que carecemos. Milenarmente a grande estrela iluminou a terra e, afinal, nós pouco aprendemos a ver. O mundo necessita ser visto sob outra luz: a luz do luar, essa claridade que cai com respeito e delicadeza. Só o luar revela o lado feminino dos seres. Só a lua revela intimidade da nossa morada terrestre. Necessitamos não do nascer do Sol. Carecemos do nascer da Terra.[39]

I have picked in this volume a tale that is perhaps more hermetic than the previous ones, but I believe it is quite representative of much of the author's work—and this for two reasons. Firstly, it belongs to a strange and disquieting streak in his writing, much of which goes against the grain of our Western sensibilities. The second is that it appears to be even more thematically "African" than most. "O ultimo voo do tucuano" is at first a weird, but still understandable, story. A pregnant woman begins to behave oddly:

> Ela estava grávida, em meio de gestação. Faltavam dois meses para ela se proceder a fonte. O que fazia nessa demora? Deitava-se de ventre para baixo e ficava ali, imóvel, quase se arriscando a coisa. Que fazia ela assim, barriga na barriga do mundo?
> *–Ensino o futuro menino a ser da terra, estou-lhe a dar pés de longe.*[40]

The husband is intrigued but puts it down to the foibles of a pregnant woman. Then the story takes a most fascinating turn. His wife tells him that she wants to prepare for the birth like the bird "tucuano,"[41] entirely walled inside her house (nest), with a small hole through which he is to deliver food. He acquiesces reluctantly and thus begins a long wait. The woman gives birth silently and refuses her husband access. Eventually, she hands him the delicate bundle inside which she claims the offspring lies. As he attempts to lift the extraordinarily insubstantial cloth, it falls to the ground:

> Foi quando, de dentro dos panos, se soltou um pássaro, muito verdadeiro. Levantou voo, desajeitoso, as encontrões com nada.
> O homem ficou a ver as asas se longeando, voadeiras. Depois, ergueu-se e se arremessou contra a parede da casa. Tombaram paus, desabaram matopes, despertaram poeiras. Agachada num conto estava a mulher, de ventre liso. Junto dela a capulana ainda guardava sangues. Areias revolvidas mostravam que ela já escavara o chão, encerrando a cerimónia. Ele se ajoelhou e acariciou a terra.[42]

The latest collection of short stories, *Na Berma de Nenhuma Estrada*, displays a very assured hand. All the tales are of similar length and format. All touch on the question of identity within a world with shifting boundaries and unformed future. They are written within the context of Mozambique's post-conflict, but ruthlessly unequal, development. Times change but does it really matter to the ordinary men and women who continue to struggle in their daily existence and still largely fail to make sense of what is happening to them? The violence of war is gone but the arbitrariness of the present is even now at hand. Reality continues to be odder than fantasy. Identities dissolve: who is a man, who is a child, who is human? What does it mean? I have opted this time for a common tale, found throughout the ages and across the world, about the bond between a child and her grandmother.

In "A adivinha," the child, Mimirosa, is very fond of her ailing granny, an old woman with a lively imagination, and whose influence the parents fear.

The girl, after all, ought to concentrate on her schoolwork. The *conto*, like most of Couto's others, is at once a fairy tale and the account of an ordinary situation. It is the language that turns it into the wonderfully whimsical story it becomes. As ever, and this is his trademark, the author encapsulates the essence of the tale in the first few sentences:

> Há o homem, isso é facto. Custa é haver o humano. A vida rasga, o homem passa a linha, a costurar os panos do tempo. Mimirosa, a menina, nada sabia desses acertos. Nem sabia que tudo é um jogo, passatemporário. Acreditava ser a vida simples como molhado e água, poeira e chão. E assim, em tamanho não aparado: os seres em infância, as coisas sem consequência.[43]

The grandmother's riddle to Mimirosa is the question of which river has only one bank. The prize for guessing right is the power to arrest time. The girl is hooked but does not find the answer immediately. Granny becomes ill and bed-ridden. Mimirosa finally escapes school to see her again but finds her apparently lifeless. She deposits her precious notebook by the grandmother and announces, triumphantly, that she has solved the riddle:

> *–É o mar, avó. Esse cujo rio: é o mar.*
> Se retiravam daquele luto, todos mais Mimirosa, quando os dedos da avó tactearam o ar e, cegos, chegaram até ao caderno. Suaves, acarariciaram o azul da imagem. E o caderno começou a pingar. Primeiro gotas, depois água gorda e cheia. E o caderninho se estuou como um rio. Como se o papel não mais contivesse aquela toda imensa água.[44]

Here, as in other stories, inanimate objects acquire life and soul. The poetry, the rhythm and music, of the prose makes it possible for the author to give substance and emotion to the slightest event and the most banal of items. Water is, of course, central to Couto's fiction and is found, both in short stories and novels, to provide the gateway between the world of reality and fantasy, and to free the characters from the mere contingencies of everyday existence.[45] But my point here is not primarily to "explain" Couto's images, metaphors or similes—a useful but limited type of literary analysis. It is, more exactly, to suggest how the writing achieves so much by mere evocation. The greatest quality of the prose is undoubtedly the economy of means and the simplicity of expression, both of which are, plainly, central features of poetry. In the end, therefore, it is the tone of the short story that makes it so luminous.

Although the tenor of this tale, as that of most of those included in the collection, has shifted markedly from that of the earlier volumes, the style and language have continued to evolve coherently. Mia Couto is today a quintessential writer of short stories and these have acquired an entirely distinct identity, recognisably his but also recognisably of his time and place. Yet, how "African" is his style, and is it that which makes his writing so telling? There has been debate about the extent to which Couto's writing has been influenced by "traditional" oral literature. I have already hinted that this is a more complex issue than at first appears. There is a view that the author's eccentric construction and his idiosyncratic language are in fact derived from indigenous roots. Mia Couto himself has helped buttress that opinion by resorting in the epigraph of many of his books to (invented) African sayings or proverbs, as though the inspiration for the writing drew from a well-established corpus of "customary" wisdom.

However, a moment's reflection would show that such sayings are but a convenient way of distilling the spirit of the text that follows. Far from deriving the story from the adage, it is the story that brings about its creation. I use as illustration, one of the three aphorisms offered at the beginning of *Terra Sonâmbula*:

> Se dizia daquela terra que era sonâmbula. Porque enquanto os homens dormian, a terra se movia espaços e tempos afora. Quando despertavam, os habitantes olhavam o novo rosto da paisagem e sabiam que, naquele noite, eles tinham sido visitados pela fantasia do sonho. (Crença dos habitantes de Matimati)[46]

Here, as elsewhere, Couto is laying down on paper the kernel of his book, drawing our attention to what matters, at least to him. His use of a (fictional) African citation is not directly relevant to the question of whether he has been "influenced" by African literature, as should be made clear by the fact that on the same page, he offers a delightfully "traditional" aphorism from Plato: "Há três espécies de homens: os vivos, os mortos e os que andam no mar."[47]

However, there are a number of very subtle ways in which his prose writing is rooted in the culture within which he lives. Of these, I would want to highlight only three: language, character and construction. Couto is (quite rightly) famous for having created a linguistic space in which he manages both to render in literary form the tone, cadence and composition of the language that is spoken in (at least urban) Mozambique. It is not that he reproduces the way(s) in which people actually express themselves, as Suleiman Cassamo does to a much greater extent. It is, to be more precise, that he evokes the music and theatre attached to such characteristics as are found in the Portuguese language spoken by ordinary people. His prose is acutely attuned to what I would call the "mannerisms" of that living form of expression that makes communication, but also misunderstanding, between Mozambicans possible. Mia Couto has an extraordinarily sharp ear, not just for the concrete expressions heard every day on the streets of Maputo, but also for the linguistic eccentricities of a language that is made of an unexpected blend of colonial Portuguese and the local vernacular(s). It is in this respect only, I believe, that he can be said to have followed Guimarães Rosa's example.[48]

The second feature of his writing I would highlight concerns his characters. As is obvious to those who are familiar with his books, Couto inhabits a world of wonderfully "simple" but extremely evocative creatures. None is recognisable as someone anyone might actually know but all are immediately familiar—as though we had been living alongside them without noticing them properly. The point, of course, is not that any one of us, in Mozambique or elsewhere, might in reality have met, or known, any such person. It is that these characters are notable for their humanity, a feature relevant to all of us and which makes them all so palpable. What links such characterisation to the local milieu is Couto's unfailing eye for their demeanour. Like a painter, he captures what is essential in such minor personages and in the tableaux he offers us, for this is what they really are; they make us feel, rather than understand, how people in Mozambique might experience the life they lead but which they fail fully to grasp. That the writer should have evolved such perceptive characterisation in part because of his assimilation of African culture is unquestionably true. Yet, it would be considerably to reduce his art to argue that his prose simply follows the models of oral literature.

The one area where perhaps the author has been most strongly influenced by African literature is in the architecture of his storytelling. The environment the author inhabits is one that is predominantly oral—even if ever larger number of Mozambicans can now read and write—not just because it is African, but because he has chosen to engage characters who live in just such a milieu. His interest does not lie with the educated, literate, middle classes but with the ordinary men and women whose existence is more seldom captured by writers of fiction. Couto has acknowledged his debt to the

African storytelling tradition and it is clear that he has continued to entertain the greatest interest in the ways in which people account for their lives, in fact as in fiction. His claim that he draws for his stories on what he has heard might be seen as contrived modesty but it should merely be understood as a statement of the obvious. Inspiration is not the same as imitation. Insofar as Mia Couto is intent on "telling" stories, it is clear that the construction of his writing draws inspiration from the craft of storytelling with which he is most familiar—that of Africa.

In the end, however, it is pointless to seek to establish the degree to which the author's work is or is not African, and, if it is, how. The question itself is redundant. Mia Couto is a Mozambican and there is no reason to presume, other than out of racism, that the colour of his skin, or his Portuguese ancestry, should make it more difficult for him to draw on the culture within which he has grown up. As he himself says: "O que eu escrevo é moçambicano, digamos inconscientemente, involuntariamente. Eu não faço nenhuma coisa para que seja. É uma maneira, simplesmente, entre mil outras."[49] The author is demonstrably writing about the country, the people and the society he knows best—as all writers do. Whatever influence African literary traditions may have had upon him do not explain why his books are so successful. They merely help place them in the appropriate historical and cultural context.[50]

What makes Mia Couto an innovative writer is that he has managed to blend a unique perception of the ordinary people of his country with an imaginative narrative style. His achievement does not lie in his linguistic contrivances or the sources of his inspiration but in a finely attuned sense of poetry dedicated to the revelation of the sheer humanity of people whose lives he has shared since he was child. His is truly an original art of storytelling.

Notes

[1] Interview with Mia Couto, in Patrick Chabal, *Vozes Moçambicanas: literatura e nacionalidade*, 274.

[2] Ibid., 286.

[3] "Encontro com Mia Couto," in Michel Laban, *Moçambique: Encontro com Escritores*, 3.1011.

[4] See here Patrick Chabal, "Mozambique," in Patrick Chabal, *The Postcolonial Literature of Lusophone Africa*.

[5] For an early study of Mia Couto, see David Brookshaw, "Mia Couto: a new voice from Mozambique." For a more recent analysis by the same scholar, see Brookshaw's "Mia Couto."

[6] It is fair to say, however, that Mia Couto rejects such a division of his writings. He says: "Da mesma maneira que me atrai estar a trabalhar na desobediência da norma, também, even-

tualmente, me atrai trabalhar na desobediência dos géneros literários," in Laban, 1021.

[7] Mia Couto, *Cronicando*. I choose this story because it is the first one and we might well presume that the author's choice to place it there is not irrelevant.

[8] Ibid., 5.

[9] Ibid., 6.

[10] Mia Couto, *Na Berma de Nenhuma Estrada*, 13-16.

[11] Ibid., 13

[12] Ibid., 16.

[13] Mia Couto in the interview cited above, says: "Quando li o Luandino, em 1977, 1978, isso foi importante para mim. Depois, lendo o Guimarães Rosa, senti que afinal há maneiras de fazer este trabalho de recriação da língua. O Brasil consegiu com o brasileiro e eu pensei que é possível fazer isto em Moçambique, com um sabor moçambicano. Eu penso que faço uma coisa bastante diferente do Luandino. Ele tem outro tipo de ambiente, tem outro tipo de imagens, tem outro tipo de recriação" (289).

[14] On the Mozambican Portuguese language, see Perpétua Gonçalves, *Português de Moçambique: Uma Variedade em Formação.*

[15] Mia Couto, *Terra Sonâmbula.*

[16] For one discussion of this important novel, see Fiona Gonçalves, "Narrative Strategies in Mia Couto's *Terra Sonâmbula.*"

[17] Mia Couto, *A Varanda do Frangipani.*

[18] Mia Couto, *O Último Voo do Flamingo.*

[19] I devote less attention here to the commissioned novel, *Vinte e Zinco*, because it appears to me to have suffered in some respects, and not least stylistically, from its programmatic origins. His latest novel, *Mar me Quer*, is in my view, best seen as an extended short story. It is otherwise, in construction, style and characterisation most similar to *A Varanda do Frangipani.*

[20] *Terra Sonâmbula*, 9.

[21] Ibid., 15.

[22] Ibid., 218.

[23] *A Varanda do Frangipani*, 152.

[24] *Vozes Moçambicanas*, 290 [italics in the original].

[25] *Vozes Anoitecidas*, 19.

[26] For a discussion of Mia Couto as a postmodern writer, see Phillip Rothwell, *A Postmodern Nationalist: Truth, Orality and Gender in the Work of Mia Couto*; and Maria Manuela Lisboa, "Colonial Crosswords: (in)voicing the gap in Mia Couto."

[27] *Vozes Moçambicanas*, 287.

[28] Laban, 1015-1016.

[29] *Vozes Moçambicanas*, 289.

[30] My choice is not an attempt to highlight the "best" stories, but is merely a device for comparison over time. In any event, it would be quite futile to try to rank Couto's stories in such a fashion. For the sake of contrast, and also because it matters greatly in terms of how a *short story* is constructed, I shall cite, as I have already done, the beginning and end of each *conto.*

[31] *Vozes Anoitecidas*, 85.

[32] Ibid., 95.

[33] *Cada Homem é uma Raça*, 93.

[34] Ibid., 100.

[35] *Estórias Abensonhadas*, 29.

[36] Ibid., 33.

[37] Whether such constructions are derived from African languages or not is to my mind irrelevant to the very effective result achieved.

[38] On Mia Couto's linguistic innovations, see Fernanda Cavacas, *Mia Couto: Brincriação Vocabular*.

[39] *Contos do Nascer da Terra*, 7.

[40] Ibid., 61.

[41] A "tucuano" is a bird.

[42] Ibid., 64.

[43] *Na Berma de Nenhuma Estrada e outros contos*, 155.

[44] Ibid., 158.

[45] On the most important theme of the "sea," both in general and in the case of Mia Couto, see Ana Mafalda Leite, "Os Temas do Mar em Algumas Narrativas Africanas de Língua Portuguesa: insularidade e viagem."

[46] *Terra Sonâmbula*, 7.

[47] Ibidem.

[48] Here, see Mary Daniel, "Mia Couto: Guimarães Rosa's newest literary heir in Africa."

[49] *Vozes Moçambicanas*, 290.

[50] On the much-debated issue of "moçambicanidade," see Gilberto Matusse, *A Construção da Imagem de Moçambicanidade em José Craveirinha, Mia Couto e Ungulani Ba Ka Khosa*.

Works Cited

Brookshaw, David. "Mia Couto: a new voice from Mozambique." *Portuguese Studies* 5 (1989): 188-189.

———. "Mia Couto." *African Writers*. 2 vols. Ed. C. Brian Cox. New York: Charles Scribner, 1997. I.185-197.

Cavacas, Fernanda. *Mia Couto: Brincriação Vocabular*. Lisbon: Mar Além, 1999.

Chabal, Patrick. *Vozes Moçambicanas: literatura e nacionalidade*. Lisbon: Vega, 1994.

———. *The Postcolonial Literature of Lusophone Africa*. London: Hurst, 1996.

Couto, Mia. *Vozes Anoitecidas*. Maputo: AEMO, 1986.

———. *Cronicando*. Maputo: Publicações Notícias, 1988.

———. *Terra Sonâmbula*. Lisbon: Caminho, 1992.

———. *A Varanda do Frangipani*. Lisbon: Caminho, 1996.

———. *Vinte e Zinco*. Lisbon: Caminho, 1999.

———. *Mar me Quer*. Lisbon: Caminho, 2000.

———. *O Último Voo do Flamingo*. Lisbon: Caminho, 2000.

———. *Na Berma de Nenhuma Estrada*. Lisbon: Caminho, 2001.

Daniel, Mary. "Mia Couto: Guimarães Rosa's newest literary heir in Africa." *Luso-Brazilian Review* 32.1 (Summer 1995): 1-16.

Gonçalves, Fiona. "Narrative Strategies in Mia Couto's *Terra Sonâmbula*." *Current Writing: Text and Reception in Southern Africa* 7.1 (1995): 60-69.

Gonçalves, Perpétua. *Português de Moçambique: Uma Variedade em Formação.* Maputo: Universidade Eduardo Mondlane, 1996.

Laban, Michel. *Moçambique: Encontro com Escritores.* Vol. 3. Porto: Fundação Eng. António de Almeida, 1998.

Leite, Ana Mafalda. "Os Temas do Mar em Algumas Narrativas Africanas de Língua Portuguesa: insularidade e viagem." *La Lusophonie: voies/voix océaniques.* Eds. Anne Quataert and Maria Fernandes Afonso. Lisbon: Lidel, 2000. 251-256.

Lisboa, Maria Manuela. "Colonial Crosswords: (in)voicing the gap in Mia Couto." *Postcolonial Perspectives on the Cultures of Latin America and Lusophone Africa.* Ed. Robin Fiddian. Liverpool: Liverpool UP, 2000. 190-212.

Matusse, Gilberto. *A Construção da Imagem de Moçambicanidade em José Craveirinha, Mia Couto e Ungulani Ba Ka Khosa.* Maputo: Universidade Eduardo Mondlane, 1998.

Rothwell, Phillip. *A Postmodern Nationalist: Truth, Orality and Gender in the Work of Mia Couto.* Lewisburg: Bucknell UP, forthcoming.

Patrick Chabal is Professor of Lusophone African Studies at King's College London, University of London. He has lived and worked in many parts of Africa and has written a large number of articles on its history, politics, and literature. His books include *Amílcar Cabral* (1983 & 2002), *The Postcolonial Literature of Lusophone Africa* (1996), *A History of Postcolonial Lusophone Africa* (2002). He is currently working on culture and politics.

Terra Sonâmbula: Manifestações de uma 'Odisséia' Africana no Moçambique Pós-Independência

Robert H. Moser

Abstract. This essay focuses on Mia Couto's first novel, *Terra Sonâmbula* (1992) and, specifically, his incorporation of the epic genre from Western literature into the cultural milieu of post-colonial Mozambique. Ana Mafalda Leite, in her study of epic discursivity in African literature, *A Modalização Épica nas Literaturas Africanas*, establishes significant structural parallels between the orality of Homer's epics and the predominant oral tradition to be found in pre-independence Lusophone African literature. The cornerstone of her thesis lies in her argument that the epic model functioned as an important paradigm in the literature of such Portuguese colonies as Angola and Mozambique which, in their struggle for autonomy, were necessarily engaged in the process of constructing a national identity. Since its independence in 1975 until 1992, Mozambique was mired in a drawn-out civil war that drained the natural and human resources of that country. It is within this context that Mia Couto introduces his protagonists in *Terra Sonâmbula*, portraying the journey of an elderly man and a young boy fleeing from a refugee camp in Mozambique. By utilizing parallel episodes of Homer's *Odyssey* this study illustrates those epic characteristics in *Terra Sonâmbula* that reveal the ongoing search for both a cultural and a national identity in war-torn, post-colonial Mozambique.

> Há três espécies de homens: os vivos, os mortos e os que andam no mar.

É com estas palavras provocantes de Platão que o escritor moçambicano Mia Couto abre o seu primeiro romance, *Terra Sonâmbula*, publicado em 1992.

Das inúmeras leituras possíveis desta citação do filósofo grego, duas se destacam, em particular, quando são lidas no contexto desse romance. Primeiramente, "os que andam no mar" significa aqueles que pertencem ao mar, fazem dele a sua vida: portanto, os marinheiros perpétuos e descobridores de terras e oceanos distantes. Contudo, essa primeira leitura não explica a designação de uma categoria aplicável nem aos mortos nem aos vivos. Aliás, a terceira espécie identificada por Platão implica um ser com qualidades senão divinas, pelo menos sobre-humanas. Em termos literários, esta espécie de homem super-humano que oscila entre os vivos e os mortos, e que ultrapassa o mundo comum, está colocada em dimensões heróicas.

De uma forma semelhante, a combinação destes dois elementos, o da viagem e o dos atributos heróicos, impregna a citação de uma forte insinuação sobre o gênero épico. Não é por acaso que Mia Couto escolhe uma nota introdutória que exibe conotações deste gênero. Será, precisamente, a proposta deste ensaio a de investigar as diversas formas e motivações do gênero épico que se manifestam em *Terra Sonâmbula*. Nesta linha, proponho utilizar a *Odisséia* de Homero como instrumento de comparação, não simplesmente por ser ela (juntamente com a *Ilíada*) o modelo definitivo da epopéia clássica, mas em função dos paralelos iluminadores que podem ser delineados entre ela e a obra de Mia Couto.

Obviamente não é possível comparar diretamente, nem linearmente, as manifestações épicas da prosa contemporânea de Mia Couto com as do poema clássico da *Odisséia*. Em vez de utilizar este método, a minha análise focalizará os atributos épicos encontrados em *Terra Sonâmbula* e considerados como fragmentos de qualidades permanentes do gênero épico. É justamente o significado destes fragmentos na realidade sócio-política africana que constitui a tese de Ana Mafalda Leite no seu estudo, *A Modalização Épica nas Literaturas Africanas*, onde considera a função de componentes épicos na literatura moderna da África lusófona, componentes que, segundo esta, surgiram justamente *durante* as lutas de independência e construção simultânea de uma identidade nacional nestes países.

Contudo, neste ensaio, adotaremos a noção de modalização épica na literatura africana, proposta por Ana Mafalda Leite, no âmbito da realidade moçambicana *depois* da sua independência, pois é neste contexto histórico que podemos localizar a acção em *Terra Sonâmbula*. Embora Moçambique seja uma nação soberana desde 1975, a persistência da guerra civil até 1992 tem sido a expressão mais devastadora dos fortes conflitos e discordâncias etno-linguísticas e ideológicas que ainda existem hoje em dia nesse país. Portanto, esta investigação dos componentes épicos em *Terra Sonâmbula* considerará tanto o seu papel na construção de uma identidade nacional, como a sua força condutora na demanda de uma identidade *cultural* pelos povos denominados "moçambicanos." Como veremos, é na representação da mundividência cultural deste povo que encontramos o campo mais fértil do texto de Mia Couto.

O Gênero Épico: algumas considerações

Antes de fazer qualquer análise comparativa entre *Terra Sonâmbula* e a *Odisséia* é preciso primeiro salientar algumas feições básicas do gênero épico. O épico, como sabemos, é uma narrativa que conta as ações heróicas de um povo, (ou de um indivíduo que representa aquele povo), e que retrata como tais ações levam a uma nova ordem social. No seu modelo clássico, a epopéia era construida em verso, seguindo um plano bastante formal, e geralmente era acompanhada por música. O portador desta poesia era o bardo, um especialista que não apenas guardava na memória os longos poemas, mas também possuía um talento extraordinário para embelezar estas histórias, assim ganhando fama aos olhos de seus campatriotas.

O período histórico em que o mais famoso dos bardos gregos, Homero, contava a *Ilíada* e a *Odisséia*, situa-se aproximadamente em 1.000 A.C. entre os gregos jônicos da Ásia Menor, isto é, mais de dois séculos depois da acção destes poemas que se centraliza historicamente na tomada de Tróia pelos gregos, um evento que data mais ou menos de cerca de 1.250 A.C. (Hainsworth, "Ancient Greek" 22-23). Portanto, a *Ilíada* e a *Odisséia* são fundamentadas tanto na fábula como no conhecimento histórico. Embora estes poemas não passem de uma representação semi-histórica, o impacto que tinham na sociedade grega é inegável. O comentário de J.B. Hainsworth sobre a aceitação geral pelos gregos da historicidade dos poemas homéricos pode servir como um exemplo:

> The Archaic period was indeed the heyday of the hero-cult. Not all of these heroes were epic ones, but many were, and the cults, tombs, and the politically-inspired traffic in bones, could not have existed without a belief in the literal existence of the heroes and the historical reality of their deeds. Even the political geography of *Iliad,* Book Two was quoted in support of territorial claims ("Ancient Greek" 29).

Hainsworth nos oferece ainda uma ilustração do impacto que esta aceitação teve na visão global da sociedade grega:

> ...the epic was for several centuries the sole important art of its community. As such it inevitably incorporated and served to transmit the ideals and experience of the people. The epic poet was the custodian of the past. Even so it is something of a quirk of chance that throughout the archaic and well into the classical period Homer's poetry enjoyed an almost biblical reputation. It became the staple of education and shaper of opinion... (37).

Este impacto manteve-se durante o período helenístico e romano, assim espalhando a valorização do poema épico pela Europa.

Embora os poemas épicos homéricos sejam conhecidíssimos, vale a pena delinear os seus traços narrativos básicos. Na *Ilíada* Homero conta, em imagens altamente heróicas, as façanhas gloriosas dos aqueus na sua tomada da cidade de Tróia e o resgate de Helena. A história destaca, sobretudo, as figuras de Agamemnon, Aquiles e Ulisses, em cenas de batalha bastante descritivas, nas quais estes guerreiros lutam contra o exército do poderoso Heitor. A *Odisséia* começa onde a *Ilíada* termina, contando o regresso de Ulisses a Ítaca, sua terra natal, e todos os obstáculos que ele confronta durante a viagem. Explícita neste relato é a dinâmica conflituosa que existe entre Ulisses e os deuses do Olimpo, em que alguns, principalmente Atena, lutam para auxiliar Ulisses a regressar e a repor a ordem na sua casa, enquanto outros, como Poseidon e seu filho Polifemo, o ciclope, tentam impedir o sucesso do herói. Contudo, mesmo em Ítaca há perigo à espreita, pois enquanto Ulisses vagueava pelos mares, durante cerca de vinte anos, um bando de pretendentes explorava os recursos de sua casa na tentativa de pedir a mão de Penélope, sua fiel e paciente esposa. A história termina com o triunfo de Ulisses que, com a ajuda do filho Telémaco, consegue matar os pretendentes e restabelecer a ordem em sua terra.

Embora esta descrição da história corra de uma forma direta e linear, na realidade a narrativa da *Odisséia* desenrola-se através de uma rota multidimensional e cheia de circunvoluções. De fato, a história começa já quase dez anos depois do início da viagem de Ulisses, que se encontra prisioneiro na ilha da deusa-ninfa Calipso. Com a intervenção de Atena, Ulisses é libertado apenas para encalhar de novo na terra dos Feácios. Sobreposta a esta narrativa primária, está uma narrativa secundária, que conta a demanda de Telémaco por seu pai perdido. Além desta justaposição de narrativas, temos a parada de Ulisses com os Feácios, tempo durante o qual o herói conta aos seus hospedeiros a sua trajetória nos últimos dez anos. Esta trajetória costuma ser nomeada como os seus "wanderings" ou "vagueações." São as vagueações que incluem tão famosos episódios como o encontro de Ulisses com os Ciclopes e as Seréias.

Como vemos, a *Odisséia* constitui uma multiplicidade de narrativas repletas de histórias dentro de histórias. Esta componente da epopéia de Homero será recuperada quando analisarmos um plano narrativo semelhante em *Terra Sonâmbula*. Os temas principais da *Odisséia*, além dos já mencionados como o do heroísmo e o da viagem, incluem a separação e a união da família, a prova da resistência tanto física como psicológica do herói perante obstáculos aparentamente insuperáveis, e a dicotomia entre ordem/desordem no nível socio-político da história. Revisitaremos também estes temas quando considerarmos os paralelos temáticos que existem entre as duas obras.

Manifestações Épicas na Literatura Moderna

Até agora consideramos o gênero épico exclusivamente na sua forma e contexto clássicos. Sabemos, porém, que a epopéia tem passado por uma evolução constante desde os tempos antigos. Obras como a *Divina Comédia* de Dante e o *Paraíso Perdido* de Milton, produzidas durante a Idade Média e começo da Modernidade, e, mais contemporaneamente, *Moby Dick* de Herman Melville e *Ulisses* de James Joyce, servem como testemunho da continuidade do gênero, se bem que em formas diversas. À procura de algumas explicações para esta continuidade, e utilizando as teorias sobre gêneros literários formulados por Gérard Genette e Alistair Fowler, Ana Mafalda Leite aponta a distinção entre os elementos formais e temáticos de uma obra e o seu *modo* inerente. Enquanto questões de forma e tema são sujeitas aos fatores históricos que existem exteriores a um determinado gênero, o *modo* permanece como elemento intrínseco àquele gênero. É esta noção trans-histórica do modo que Fowler adianta no seu livro *Kinds of Literature - An Introduction to the theorie of genres and modes*:

> External forms rapidly change. And kinds have also been linked to social institutions, along with which they have become obsolete – or, as we say – 'outmoded.' The modes however appear to be distillations, from these relatively evanescent forms, of the permanently valuable features. Thus, they have achieved indepen-

> dence of contingent embodiments and may continue to all ages incorporated in almost any external form, long after the antecedent kind has passed away. (111)

É neste sentido perserverante do modo que Ana Mafalda Leite considera a presença do gênero épico na literatura africana moderna. Como Leite menciona, a modernidade é caracterizada pela extrema multiplicidade de traços genéricos e pela sua "dimensão plural" de formas, temas e modos (35). As modalizações épicas que ela encontra, portanto, na literatura angolana e cabo-verdiana escrita antes da independência, conformam-se a esta dimensão plural. A citação seguinte, retirada da sua análise sobre a literatura contemporânea destes países, serve como um exemplo nítido deste processo.

Verifica que a dessacralização efectuada no seio da comunidade tradicional, no decorrer dos últimos anos, levou a uma separação entre a criação poética e a vida. A narrativa épica, tal como outro texto oral, deslocada do seu contexto ritual, ganha um cariz mais abstrato e perde a sua funcionalidade.

Por estas razões, a atitude do escritor moderno não se pode limitar à imitação ou recolha dos textos antigos, mas tem de ser criativa, no sentido de adaptar o mito ao *logos,* de o repensar, actualizando-o, integrando-o numa dimensão, neste caso, romanesca:

> Segundo este ponto de vista o romance recupera apenas parcialmente aspectos do mito; no caso da epopeia oral, um deles é do herói, que poderá ser encarado criticamente e retrabalhado de forma paródica. (81)

Certamente, o mesmo argumento pode ser aplicado às comunidades modernas e menos tradicionais, onde o processo de "dessacralização" e deslocamento de contextos rituais tem ocorrido em um ritmo acelerado. É precisamente o deslocamento de contextos rituais que Mia Couto frequentemente tenta mostrar tanto nas situações rurais e tradicionais como nos ambientes urbanos e modernos. As páginas seguintes deste ensaio têm por missiva evidenciar como Mia Couto actualiza o gênero épico na sua obra e como esta actualização funciona dentro da realidade moçambicana após a sua independência.

Terra Sonâmbula

É necessário dizer desde já que, embora sejam as modalizações épicas da tradição especificamente clássica o objeto da minha análise de *Terra Sonâmbula,* isto não sugere que não existam traços épicos de outras tradições no romance. A mais óbvia omissão, portanto, é a presença da tradição épica africana e, sobretudo, aquela que surge dos costumes e crenças moçambicanos. Certamente, manifestações destas tradições estão patentes no livro inteiro e são essenciais para o seu desenvolvimento. Tais características 'africanas' incluem aspectos folclóricos, mitos tanto antigos quanto populares, e, com toda a probabilidade, histórias épicas com origem na tradição africana.

Porém, é importante lembrar que a presença de tradições africanas inerentes a este romance, não nega o significado de temas épicos advindos da tradição ocidental. Sabemos que Mia Couto, como a grande maioria dos autores africanos da sua geração, recebeu sua formação através da literatura ocidental e, portanto, a sua interação com a mundividência africana acaba sendo filtrada pela lente da literatura européia. Por esta razão, é essencial não ignorar as consequências, na sua complexidade, de tal interação.

A história contada em *Terra Sonâmbula*, como na *Odisséia*, só pode ser compreendida na sua duplicidade. Primeiro temos a história dos dois deslocados, o órfão Muindinga e seu companheiro, o velho Tuahir, que andam à procura de refúgio da violência da guerra civil que devasta a terra. Contudo, justapostos a esta primeira narrativa escrita na terceira pessoa estão os cadernos lidos por Muidinga, que contam na primeira pessoa a viagem feita por Kindzu, essa figura enigmática que se retrata igualmente como "órfão da família e da amizade" (29). Estes dois planos narrativos desenvolvem-se simultaneamente durante o percurso do livro. Notamos que, além desta construção dupla da narrativa, existe uma multiplicidade de histórias narradas pelas diversas personagens encontradas no livro, o que acaba por criar uma sobreposição de histórias semelhante à que apontamos na narrativa da *Odisséia*. Mais à frente esta comparação tornar-se-á mais clara.

No primeiro capítulo de *Terra Sonâmbula* encontramos as duas personagens principais, Muidinga e Tuahir, na estrada, ou mais precisamente na "estrada morta," o caminho que os leva para o exterior de um campo de refugiados em Moçambique, em direção a um novo destino (9). Logo aparece um "machimbombo" ou "autocarro" incendiado ao lado da estrada e Tuahir resolve fazer dele a sua casa. Mesmo que esteja coberto de corpos também queimados e apesar de outros sinais horríveis da guerra, os dois conseguem arrumar o espaço da melhor forma possível, e assim, trocam a estrada pelo autocarro.

Ao enterrar os cadáveres retirados do autocarro, eles encontram um outro lá fora, embora este tivesse sido morto a tiro. Os deslocados então notam que junto dele está uma mala que contém as cartas autobiográficas de Kindzu. As histórias de Kindzu, lidas por Muidinga, captam imediatamente a imaginação dos dois refugiados e, consequentamente, integram-se intimamente na sua paisagem psicológica. A leitura, cumprida por Muidinga (Tuahir é analfabeto) durante toda a noite antes deles adormecerem, assume uma função ritualista. Esta forte presença dos cadernos nas suas vidas revela-se quando Tuahir, ao sentir a sua falta, exclama: "Esse fidamãe desse Kindzu já vive quase connosco" (99).

A familiaridade que os refugiados sentem em relação a Kindzu não é surpreendente, pois, em muitos aspectos, a história dele serve como um espelho que reflete as suas próprias vidas. Com a morte do pai (aquele que recebia sonhos/profecias na família), o desaparecimento do irmão, e a saída do amigo, Surendra, indiano dono da loja onde o menino partilhou a sua amizade, Kindzu percebe que não há nada para si mesmo em sua aldeia e resolve fugir da brutalidade da guerra. Levando a canoa do pai, Kindzu parte com a idéia de entregar-se aos Naparamas, guerreiros de uma tribo mística, situada no interior, que lutava contra os instigadores da guerra naquela terra. A canoa de Kindzu o leva para encontros tanto com os vivos da terra, pessoas com quem ele interage, quanto com os mortos, como, por exemplo, o espírito caprichoso de seu pai, cujo papel oscila entre perseguidor e protetor do filho durante a viagem. A verossimilhança do pai é necessariamente ambígua, pois há fortes insinuações de que Kindzu sofre de sentimentos de culpa por abandonar sua tarefa de levar oferendas ao pai morto. Seu pai aqui, por exemplo, surge em seu sonho, para lhe dar advertências e mostrar desprazer para com ele: "Se tu saíres terás que me ver a mim: hei-de-te perseguir, vais sofrer para sempre as minhas visões..." (30). Embora esta dinâmica agonística entre pai e filho mude na evolução do livro, ela é simbólica da ruptura que existe entre os vivos da terra e os seus antepassados. Verificaremos que este tema ocupa um lugar extremamente importante no decorrer do livro.

Manifestações Épicas em *Terra Sonâmbula*

1) Viagem e Regresso

Um dos temas essenciais da *Odisséia*, como já foi apontado, é o da viagem. O próprio título o demonstra. Certamente, uma leitura cuidadosa do poema revela uma preponderância de comentários, da parte de mortais e de deuses, que ligam o destino de Ulisses com a sua viagem, aparentemente, perpétua. A entidade que mais se opõe ao regresso de Ulisses é Poseidon, deus englobante da terra e do mar. Enfurecido por Ulisses ter cegado Polifemo, seu filho ciclope, ele desencadeia os elementos contra o herói grego, como podemos ver, por exemplo, nesta exclamação, enquanto Ulisses está nadando para a terra dos Feácios: "The proud Earth-shaker saw him, wagged his head and gloated to himself thus: 'Everywhere in trouble, all over the seas, wherever you go!' (80)" E mesmo depois, quando Poseidon reclama a Zeus, dominador dos céus, sobre a chegada de Ulisses a Ítaca: "The Earth-shaker had not yet forgotten his fateful word against great Odysseus long ago. Wherefore he began to sound the mind of Zeus, saying,'...I did announce that Odysseus should not get home before he had exhausted the sum of miseries' (185)." Portanto, antes de poder voltar ao conforto de sua casa, Ulisses é obrigado a cumprir o seu destino como um náufrago errante por terras estranhas.

Notamos que em *Terra Sonâmbula* o tema da viagem ocupa igualmente um lugar central. Quando Kindzu pede conselho ao "nganga," o "adivinhador" da sua aldeia, os ossos divinatórios anunciam-lhe: "você é um homem de viagem. E aqui vejo água, vejo o mar" (33). Quer dizer, a sua decisão de pegar a canoa de seu pai e embarcar para terras desconhecidas estava já escrita no seu destino. Verificamos que o destino de Tuahir, ao morrer deitado numa jangada na praia esperando que a maré o leve, segue um semelhante caminho marinheiro.

Implícita no tema da viagem, porém, está a esperança do regresso. Esta esperança funciona como preocupação subjacente nas personagens de Muidinga, Kindzu, e Farida, todos motivados, de um modo ou de outro, por um desejo de recuperar laços familiares da sua vida anterior. Encontramos este desejo na sua forma mais intensa nos sentimentos saudosos da portuguesa Dona Virgínia, mãe adotiva de Farida, e, semelhantemente, na esposa de Surendra, Assma, que imaginava por trás do mero barulho emitido por seu rádio "melodias de sarar saudades do Oriente" (24). Vemos que o tema do regresso está vinculado com o da coesão da família, um ponto que ficará mais claro na sequência desta exposição.

Talvez, o melhor exemplo de uma manifestação épica em *Terra Sonâmbula,* acerca do tema da viagem, suceda não na terra dos vivos, mas no reino dos mortos. Logo no início da sua viagem, Kindzu chega às areias de Tandissico, onde os "psipocos," fantasmas que habitam o mundo subterrâneo dos mortos, assombram quem passa. Uma aparição o manda entrar em uma das covas e lhe dá o seguinte conselho: "Fica saber: o chão deste mundo é o tecto de um mundo mais por baixo. E sucessivamente, até ao centro, onde mora o primeiro dos mortos" (43). Esta descrição dos níveis sucessivos do mundo dos mortos manifesta fortes ecos dos círculos de inferno descritos por

Dante na primeira parte da sua *Divina Comédia.* Notamos, porém, que no caso da história de Kindzu, as particularidades deste mundo estão enraizadas na linguagem e na cosmologia africana.

Cabe, também, chamar a atenção para um episódio semelhante na *Odisséia*, em que Ulisses estende sua viagem a um tributário do rio de Styx e faz oferendas para contactar os habitantes do Hades. Vem então uma série de guerreiros mortos que contam cada um a sua história, a aparição de sua mãe morta, e, finalmente, o espírito profético, Tirésias, que vai contar ao guerreiro o caminho que ele precisa tomar para regressar a sua casa. Assim, a viagem de Ulisses para o reino dos mortos representa uma prova essencial para o herói grego, uma vez que contribui para a formação de seu carácter e lhe fornece uma sabedoria maior, por ter ido às fontes da Verdade.

É de salientar que a outra personagem principal em *Terra Sonâmbula*, Muidinga, também passa, temporariamente, pelo reino da morte, só para depois emergir com uma perspectiva renascida. Sabemos que Muidinga foi quase enterrado vivo, enquanto sofria por ter consumido "maquela," a mandioca venenosa. É Tuahir quem o salva, mas só depois do menino passar pelo estado de quase morto:

> — Dobra as pernas, depressa. Não podes morrer de pernas esticadas.
>
> E o velho ajudou o miúdo a dobrar as pernas. Ficou à espera que a morte viesse. Passou-se tempo sem que o moço se tornasse em pessoa conluída. E se passou ao inverso do esperado. No dia seguinte, já Muidinga despertava, fortelecido. Era uma criança a nascer, quase em estado de saúde. (57)

2) As Provações

A viagem para a morte representa apenas uma de várias provas de resistência que os protagonistas hão-de confrontar no decorrer de *Terra Sonâmbula.* Como já foi mencionado, a prova de resistência tanto física como psicológica perante grandes obstáculos constitui um tema fundamental na poesia épica. O primeiro tipo de prova que podemos identificar é o "trial by terror," ou a prova por terror. Encontramos um bom exemplo deste tipo no "Livro Oitavo" da *Odisséia*, quando Ulisses e seus companheiros desembarcam na terra dos ciclopes, sem saber do perigo terrível que habita aquele lugar. Uma combinação de curiosidade e de fome os leva até a uma grande caverna, onde decidem esperar até que alguém volte. Infelizmente, o dono desta casa de pedra é o próprio Polifemo, o Ciclope gigantesco e filho de Poseidon, que, ao trazer suas cabras para dentro da caverna, descobre os aventureiros inesperados. Embora Ciclope seja parente de um deus, os seus atributos culturais e intelectuais são retratados em termos bastante depreciativos, como vemos neste trecho narrado por Ulisses:

> We left in low spirits and later came to the land of the arrogant iniquitous Cyclopes who so leave all things to the Gods that they neither plant nor till: yet does plenty spring up unsown and unploughed, of corn and barley and even vines with heavy clusters: which the rains of Zeus fatten for them. They have no government nor councils nor courts of justice: but live in caves on mountain tops, each ruling his wives and children and a law unto himself, regardless. (123)

Desgovernado e de temperamento vicioso, Ciclope recusa obedecer às regras da hospitalidade, e opta por aprisionar Ulisses e seus companheiros, comendo-os um de cada vez. Ulisses chama a atenção do Ciclope para sua posição de suplicante e para a proteção que Zeus acostuma dar aos convidados. No final, é o desdém de Ciclope para com tais regras universais que traz o seu castigo, ou seja, nas palavras de Ulisses: "fit punishment for the impiety that had dared eat the guests in your house" (133).

Faltando a força física para dominar Ciclope, Ulisses é forçado a contar com seus recursos intelectuais. Depois de seduzir o monstro com vinho, ele e seus companheiros enfiam uma lança no único olho do gigante adormecido. Enfurecido por sua dor inexplicável, Ciclope procura cegamente vingar-se de Ulisses. Ainda preso na caverna, Ulisses então leva a cabo a segunda parte do seu plano de fuga, quando ele e seus amigos se escondem em baixo da pele das cabras e, assim, passam pelos dedos do Ciclope, enquanto ele conta o seu rebanho. Verificamos que a prova que Ulisses enfrenta no seu combate com o Ciclope pertence à categoria do terror, ainda que, seu sucesso seja atribuído à superioridade intelectual do herói grego.

Como já foi dito, tais provas de resistência também permeiam as histórias de *Terra Sonâmbula*, embora com diferenças e particularidades determinadas pela própria natureza do livro. Talvez o paralelo mais direto em termos temáticos entre as duas obras se manifeste no quarto capítulo, quando Muidinga e Tuahir caem na armadilha de Siqueleto. Andando pelo mato, os dois pisam numa cova coberta de folhagem e ficam presos em um buraco enorme. Quando Muidinga pergunta: "Estamos onde, Tuahir?" a resposta do seu amigo sugere o mau presságio da situação: "Nem fale. Deve ser morada do sapo gigante, o tal comedor de escuro" (70). A confirmação deste presságio se completa quando vem o dono da armadilha, Siqueleto, que, invés de os salvar, os deixa na rede, como animais presos. Convencidos de que ele os vai comer, começam a vomitar, como se eles próprios estivessem estragados.

Uma leitura comparada revela que a figura de Siqueleto compartilha abundantes características com o monstro ciclópico na *Odisséia*. Descrito como "um velho alto, torto" (71) ele fala um idioma estranho, compreendido só por Tuahir, e mesmo assim com dificuldade, por causa da "ausência de dentes" que deformava "as palavras do solitário aldeão" (72). Contudo, a característica mais marcante do Siqueleto é, certamente, o seu uso de apenas um olho. Há várias referências dadas pelo narrador: "Um dos olhos permanece fechado enquanto o outro está aberto. O olho de serviço reveza-se, ora um ora outro" (71) e "Encara os prisioneiros com um só olho enquanto fala na língua local" (71). É quando Tuahir pergunta se ele estaria triste, que Siqueleto oferece a explicação seguinte: " 'Já não fico triste, só cansado.' Era por causa do cansaço que ele não abria os dois olhos de uma só vez" (72). Percebemos aqui um exemplo nítido de uma manifestação da epopéia clássica surgindo no texto moderno com uma clareza indubitável. Em outras palavras, a condição ciclópica do Siqueleto siginifica uma cristalização do processo delineado por Ana Mafalda Leite como uma "recriação" ou "actualização" do mito no contexto romanesco.

Verificamos que algumas das mesmas preocupações vistas no episódio do Ciclope, na *Odisséia*, também estão presentes neste capítulo de *Terra Sonâmbula*. A noção da generosidade perante os convidados surge quando, por exemplo, Muidinga exclama nervosamente, "Por que motivo ele não recebia bem os visitantes como ordenavam as velhas leis hospitaleiras?" (73). O destino dos dois prisioneiros "abichados" mantém-se duvidoso até que, por acaso, Siqueleto vê Muidinga escrevendo palavras na poeira:

> — Que desenhos são esses? pergunta Siqueleto.
> — É o teu nome, responde Tuahir.
> — Esse é o meu nome? (75)

O fascínio que Siqueleto experimenta perante seu nome escrito, identidade apresentada numa forma tangível, o leva a soltar os dois, sob a condição de que o menino desempenhe mais uma façanha. Todavia quando Muidinga escreve seu nome no tronco de uma árvore Siqueleto é transformado no tamanho de uma semente, e se sente seguro de que seu "nome está no sangue da árvore" (75). Então a resistência de Muidinga em passar por esta prova é baseada na sua capacidade intelectual, ou mais precisamente, no poder quase mágico e rejuvenescedor da sua alfabetização. Neste sentido, podemos interpretar o título do capítulo, "A Lição de Siqueleto," de duas maneiras: primeiro, como a lição de sobrevivência que os dois prisioneiros aprendem de Siqueleto; e, segundo, como a aprendizagem através das letras escritas, que Siqueleto ganha a respeito da sua própria identidade.

Os exemplos de paralelismos temáticos nas duas obras são, como já se torna óbvio, abundantes. Apenas quero chamar a atenção para alguns outros casos que servem para ilustrar a ampla criatividade que Mia Couto utiliza na sua actualização do gênero épico. O segundo tipo de prova que surge com uma grande frequência na epopéia clássica é o "trial by temptation" ou a prova por tentação. Na *Odisséia,* descobrimos talvez a mais conhecida expressão deste tipo de prova no encontro de Ulisses com as Sereias encantadoras, que seduzem marinheiros incautos com seu fatal canto. A solução de Ulisses, de se amarrar ao mastro do barco, incorpora a combinação de ingenuidade e ambição que conjuntamente forma o carácter extremamente humano do herói grego. Embora esta cena seja a mais conhecida, há outras provas por tentação que se destacam na *Odisséia*, como, por exemplo, a detenção de Ulisses por Circe, a deusa sedenta, que transforma viajantes desprevenidos em porcos, e, sobretudo, a ninfa-deusa, Calypso, que cobiça o herói para seu companheiro de cama por dez longos anos.

Logo no "Primeiro caderno de Kindzu" o jovem protagonista dialoga com o velho adivinho, antes da sua viagem, que oferece o seguinte conselho:

> O mar será tua cura, continuou o velho. A terra está carregada das leis, mandos e desmandos. O mar não tem governador. Mas cuidado, filho, a pessoa não mora no mar. Mesmo teu pai que sempre andou no mar: a casa onde o espírito dele vem descansar fica em terra. Vais encontrar alguém que te vai convidar para morar no mar. Cuidado, meu filho, só mora no mar quem é o mar. (33)

A profecia do feiticeiro cumpre-se, quando no final do "Terceiro caderno," Kindzu encontra aquela que "mora no mar." Logo, a relação de Kindzu com Farida, a gémea fragmentada e sonhadora, assume as dimensões de uma prova de tentação. A cena surrealista no navio encalhado, quando ele a vê pela primeira vez, reforça as qualidades fantásticas e encantadoras da mulher:

> De repente, a âncora tombou com enorme estrondo. Por momento me pareceu que, em seu lugar, jazia estendido um corpo humano. Pés-pós-pé, me afastei. Fosse coisa ou gente aquilo era assunto da minha incompetência...
> Foi então que encontrei a mulher. No princípio, era só um vulto no meio das cordas. Seria mais um fantasma? Depois seu rosto apareceu mais claro. Estremeci. Me cheguei mais, espreitando na penumbra. A lua me ajudava, enxotando as brumas.
> — Não tenha medo, lhe disse. (66)

E depois a descrição da sua beleza semelhante à de uma deusa:

> Suas roupas molhadas ofegavam de encontro à pele. A beleza daquela mulher era de fazer fugir o nome das coisas. Olhando o seu corpo se acreditava que nunca nele a velhice haveria de morar. Corpo sedento, olhos sedentários. Sua voz saía sem vestes, nua como se dispensasse palavras.
> — Me chamo Farida, disse. (66)

Como no caso das sereias, o lugar de Farida era o mar. Embora a atração de Kindzu por Farida não chegue a ser fatal, ele reconhece o perigo de ficar no barco com esta mulher: "Farida me roubava coragem do caminho, me roubava força de decidir" (105). Quando o jovem resolve deixá-la no barco, para sair à procura de seu filho, Gaspar, está sem consciência de que seus destinos nunca mais irão se cruzar. A prova de tentação que Farida simboliza para Kindzu também se manifesta nas suas relações sexuais com outras personagens secundárias, como Carolinda, esposa do administrador em Matimati, e Jotinha, a jovem do campo dos refugiados que é descrita como "dona de poderes" feiticeiros. (199)

Vale a pena aqui fazer um breve comentário sobre a evolução da personagem de Kindzu durante o percurso do livro, sobretudo, perante a sua capacidade crescente de ultrapassar provas. Ainda no amanhecer da sua viagem, Kindzu escuta as palavras ameaçadoras de seu pai: "Já que eu tanto queria a viagem, num dado entardecer, me haveria de aparecer o mampfana, a ave que mata as viagens. Estará de asas abertas, pousando sobre uma grandíssima árvore, disse ele" (46). Porém, sabemos que o pai, mesmo na sua raiva, desempenhará o papel de guia de seu filho errante: "Quando encontrar o mampfana me chame, então. Talvez eu lhe escute, nesse momento. Mas não esqueça de trazer boa sura. Não vou fazer cerimónia sem ela" (46).

Na figura do "mampfana," "ave que mata as viagens" descobrimos vestígios sugestivos da *Odisséia,* na forma do monstro Scylla, que guarda a passagem estreita entre o caminho de regresso e Erebus, a terra da morte. Circe descreve a Ulisses este monstro apavorante, como tendo seis cabeças, cada uma com dentes compridos que apanham marinheiros incautos nesta passagem traiçoeira. Daí, o seu aviso para Ulisses:

> I tell you, Scylla is not mortal, to be fought off, but an immortal blain, unpitying, fierce, fiendish, invincible...Your best course is to push hard past her, invoking Crataiis, Scylla's dam, who whelped this curse of humanity. Crataiis, if called upon, will keep Scylla from a second plunge. (172)

Como todas as profecias divinas na *Odisséia*, o encontro de Ulisses com Scylla passa a acontecer, e é somente depois de chamar a Crataiis e de perder uma parte da sua tripulação que Ulisses consegue passar.

De uma forma semelhante, descobrimos Kindzu no crepúsculo da sua viagem entrando no "Campo da Morte," onde ele encontra "a árvore do demónio," e, como foi previsto, o temível "mampfana, a ave matadora de viagens" (194) pousada nos seus ramos negros. Kindzu então chama do fundo da sua alma por seu pai, cuja ajuda demora a vir. De súbito, o pássaro se rasga ao meio e uma voz sai do tronco da árvore assombrada, a voz de Taímo, o pai de Kindzu:

> — O que aprendeste debaixo da casca desse mundo?
> — Eu quero voltar, estou cansado. Eu agora sei quem és, me ajude a voltar...
> — O que andas a fazer com um caderno, escreves o quê?
> — Nem sei, pai. Escrevo conforme vou sonhando.
> — E alguém vai ler isso?
> — Talvez.
> — É bom assim: ensinar alguém a sonhar. (195)

Pela primeira vez no percurso de sua viagem, Kindzu ouve o louvor de seu pai falecido. Contudo, e ainda mais significativamente, a derrota de mampfana representa para Kindzu o seu domínio sob os medos e a realização do seu papel como contador de histórias. E como nos guerreiros gregos que incorporam as virtudes do seu tempo, a função barda de Kindzu, de "ensinar alguém a sonhar," ganha proporções heróicas nesta terra onde os sonhos são esmagados pela guerra perpétua.

3) Desordem e Ordem

A terceira categoria temática que consideraremos é a dicotomia entre desordem/ordem no campo sócio-político que permeia a estrutura do gênero épico. Neste aspecto, a *Odisséia* não é exceção. J.B. Hainsworth, por exemplo, no seu artigo mencionado acima, descreve o impacto da primeira passagem do poema: "[…] it stamps the Odyssey as a serious and moral work. It begins with chaos, it ends, under the guidance of heaven, with the restoration of the proper order of society" (42). Verificamos também que no gênero épico é o herói que funciona como o engenho principal desta restituição do equilíbrio social. A própria trajetória de Ulisses serve como exemplo deste processo. A sua partida de Ítaca para juntar-se à batalha de Tróia está marcada por glória e esperança, porém seu longo regresso caracteriza-se por uma desintegração gradual da ordem, tanto na sua casa, como nas etapas da sua viagem. Esta queda na desordem está exemplificada na destruição dos recursos de sua casa pelos pretendentes: nas palavras de Telémaco, "the grim, slow sack of my innocent house" (16). A respeito dos solicitadores, notamos um esforço retórico de Homero para lançar uma luz bastante negativa, e conseqüentemente, tirar qualquer vestígio de simpatia que uma platéia poderia sentir por eles: "these suitor-maggots who freely devour another man's livelihood. Freely indeed, without let or fine!" (5).

Lançado à costa na terra dos Feácios, Ulisses, naúfrago nu, com a ajuda deste povo consegue voltar a Ítaca, mas ainda aqui, na sua própria casa, o grande guerreiro deva sofrer a humilhação de andar como um vagabundo, pedindo esmolas dos pretendentes. Todavia, o clímax deste processo restituitivo vem, com força brutal, quando Ulisses e Telémaco massacram todos os pretendentes presos, como bichos, nos corredores da grande casa. Com a morte dos mesmos, símbolos de esbanjamento e exploração, a ordem é restaurada. Contudo, a história não termina aqui. Esperando a vingança dos seus vizinhos, familiares dos pretendentes mortos, o grande herói prepara-se de novo para a batalha. Atena, temendo a erupção de uma guerra civil, intervém pedindo a Ulisses: "Hold back. Cease this arbitrament of civil war" e depois na forma de mediador, "set a pact between them for ever and ever" (327), trazendo paz, finalmente, para a terra de Ítaca.

Em *Terra Sonâmbula* a guerra existe como uma entidade fora do controle das pessoas e, assim, toma a sua própria vida. Em todos os aspectos, é uma guerra que aparentamente não tem começo nem fim, mas sim uma existência inevitável e imutável. Também, e aqui se revela seu lado mais pernicioso, ela existe dentro de nós: "A guerra é uma cobra que usa os nossos próprios dentes para nos morder" (17). O enlouquecimento, o suicídio e a violência dirigida contra os nossos familiares, todos constituem sinais de uma guerra civil que divide ao meio não só a nação, mas também a paz interior de cada pessoa que a habita.

Segundo o pai de Kindzu, a guerra "era confusão vinda de fora, trazida por aqueles que tinham perdido seus privilégios" (17). Na realidade, ela ganhava força tanto de dentro quanto de fora das fronteiras do país. A imagem de Vinticinco de Junho, irmão de Kindzu e símbolo da esperança perante a independência de Moçambique, tornando-se bicho dentro de uma capoeira e, finalmente, dentro de um tanque de guerra, exprime mais nitidamente a desilusão que permeia todo o país. Quando Farida pergunta a Kindzu sobre os motivos daquela guerra, ele responde:

> Lembrei as palavras de Surendra: tinha que haver guerra, tinha que haver morte. E tudo era para que? Para autorizar o roubo. Porque hoje nenhuma riqueza podia nascer do trabalho. Só o saque dava acesso às propriedades. Era preciso haver morte para que as leis fossem esquecidas. Agora que a desordem era total, tudo estava autorizado. Os culpados seriam sempre os outros.
> — Pode acabar no país, Kindzu. Mas para nós, dentro de nós essa guerra nunca mais vai terminar. (114)

A lei do saque ganhava a sua expressão mais aguda na cidade de Matimati e, em particular, nas acções corruptas de alguns dos seus cidadãos. Encontramos, por exemplo, a figura do Assane, que alugava "cadeiras de rodas" para "divertir o pessoal" e ganhar algum dinheirinho à custa do povo (116). Também, sócio de Surendra, Assne explorava a sua amizade com o indiano para depois "nacionalizar," a loja e chutar "o baniane no rabo" (123). Esta peculiaridade semântica de "nacionalizar" que acaba sendo um sinónimo de roubar, também se apresenta na história de Quintino:

> Aconteceu quando Quintino decidiu visitar a velha casa onde trabalhara como empregado doméstico. Ia ver se ainda sobravam os valiosos bens dos patrões. Não usaria a palavra roubar. Talvez nacionalizar. *Nacionalizar* uns bens a favor do povo original. (154)

O patrão da casa é o ex-colono português, Romão Pinto, que morreu (de causas supersticiosas) por dormir com a sua empregada mulata, enquanto ela menstruava. Descobrimos depois que o espírito do ex-colono branco está de pacto com o admininstrador de Matimati, Estêvão Jonas, para reestabelecer, clandestinamente, o negócio do português falecido. Por isso, e também por seu tratamento corrupto das "calamidades," as quais deveriam ser entregues aos refugiados esfomeados, que a sua esposa lhe chama "*administraidor*" (181).

Este conjunto de personagens que aproveitam da desordem causada pela guerra para se enriquecer assume um papel semelhante aos pretendentes na *Odisséia.* São parasitas que se alimentam da miséria dos outros, enquanto que a justiça está ausente. E, no final das contas, é o país que acaba sendo a vítima desta violação, como "uma dessas baleias que vêm agonizar na praia" e que ainda viva, "já as facas lhe roubavam pedaços, cada um tentando o mais para si" (23). A crítica sócio-política que o autor evoca nesta metáfora é transparente.

Na épica clássica, a retribuição dada pelo herói às forças do mal e, conseqüentemente, a restituição da ordem, são sempre garantidas. Contudo, no mundo moderno as coisas são menos certas. No fim de *Terra Sonâmbula,* os corruptos ainda exploram os bens da terra e a guerra continua como sempre. Mesmo assim, há sinais de que a vingança do povo não está tão longe assim. Evidentemente, em *Terra Sonâmbula* geralmente tais sinais são comunicados por meios fantásticos. Quase na última cena do "Último Caderno de Kinzu" encontramos Kindzu sonhando que seu irmão, Junhito, símbolo de independência, voltava já um tanto humanizado. De súbito, aparecem os instigadores da guerra:

O que sucedeu, seguidamente, foi que surgiram o colono Romão Pinto junto com o administrador Estêvão, Shetani, Assane, Antoninho e milicianos. Vinham armados e se dirigiram para Junhito, com ganas de lhe depenar o pescoço. Cercaram o manito, dizendo:

> — Teu pai tinha razão: sempre te viemos buscar.
>
> Então Junhito me chamou. Eu me olhei, sem confiança. Mas o que em mim foi de dar surpresa, mesmo em sonho: porque em meus braços se exibiam lenços e enfeites. Minhas mãos seguravam uma zagaia. Me certifiquei: eu era um naparama! Ao me verem, em minha nova figura, aqueles que maltratavam o meu irmão se extinguiram num fechar de olhos. Mas Junhito ainda lutava para se desbichar, desembaraçar-se da condenação. (217)

Depois, Kindzu, como guerreiro naparama, canta as músicas da infância deles e, através destes "embalos," seu irmão volta a ser "completamente

Junhito" (217). A coragem desempenhada aqui por Kindzu ganha dimensões altamente heróicas, do tipo que Ulisses manifesta na sua luta final com os pretendentes. Embora a desordem não esteja totalmente vencida neste ato, torna-se claro que as sementes de uma nova ordem foram semeadas.

Mas que forma tomam estas sementes rejuvenescedoras? Verificamos que a canção de infância que Kindzu canta para seu irmão, na verdade, ecoa a canção profetizada pelo adivinho no final do livro. Depois de descrever o futuro da terra e do seu povo em termos apocalípticos, o adivinho prevê que:

> ...surgirão os doces acordes de uma canção, o terno embalo da primeira mãe. Este canto, sim, será nosso, a lembrança de uma raiz profunda que não foram capazes de nos arrancar. Essa voz nos dará a força de um novo princípio e, ao escutá-la, os cadáveres sossegarão nas covas e os sobreviventes abraçarão a vida com o ingénuo entusiasmo dos namorados. (216)

Pois, sabemos que as causas da guerra e do sofrimento vão mais fundo do que as intrigas políticas e os burocratas corruptos. Na verdade, é a ruptura que ocorreu entre os vivos da terra e seus antepassados o que provoca a guerra, e só a reconciliação desta relação trará paz ao país.

Neste sentido, a voz que o adivinho descreve é a voz do bardo, ou seja, o contador de histórias. O heroísmo de Kindzu não se manifesta na sua demanda de justiça neste mundo (ele perdeu Gaspar e Farida), mas na sua decisão de escrever suas memórias nos cadernos. É na palavra, ora contada, ora escrita, que vive a esperança de um novo mundo. É justamente esta idéia que é confirmada por Leonor Simas-Almeida no seu artigo, "A Redenção pela Palavra em *Terra Sonâmbula* de Mia Couto":

> Num presente em apocalíptica decomposição insere-se — é a tese aqui defendida — a esperança no futuro, subtilmente entretecida em todos os fios da narração, já que a omnipresença das 'costuradas histórias' por si só representa a reinvenção de uma realidade potencialmente letal quando desprovida de alternativas imaginadas. Afirmava T.S. Eliot que 'o género humano não suporta muito a realidade,' decerto por isso dispõem as criaturas humanas da linguagem e da sua função poética que lhes permitem toda a sorte de ficções capazes de minorar, e às vezes redimir, a tragédia da vida. (160)

A redenção para Kindzu reside na sua capacidade de transmitir sua história para um outro, neste caso Muidinga. E, assim, na criação de uma memória não apenas pessoal mas coletiva, começa a costurar-se a linha que se havia rompido entre o futuro e o passado. Sabemos que, além de encontrar Gaspar, o destino de Kindzu era o de "ensinar alguém a sonhar." Porém, podemos dizer que, embora eles não se reúnam fisicamente, uma conexão profunda e permanente se estabelece entre eles através dos cadernos.

Conclusão

Na parte introdutória deste ensaio chamei a atenção para a multiplicidade narrativa que organiza a *Odisséia* de Homero e a *Terra Sonâmbula*, de Mia Couto. Considerei também a diversidade dos paralelismos temáticos que existem entre as duas obras, examinando, em pormenor, as dicotomias entre viagem/regresso, ordem/desordem, e a preponderância da prova de resistência nestes textos. Também procurei dar continuidade ao diálogo que se tem desenvolvido na crítica sobre a existência de modalizações épicas nas obras de literatura africana moderna. É notável que tais modalizações, ou seja, recriações de características trans-históricas, encontrem lugar auspicioso na imaginação de Mia Couto.

Em última análise, os dois textos contam as histórias de famílias separadas e a força requerida para reatar tais laços familiares. O gênero épico, historicamente tem servido como um repositório importante da memória coletiva de cada povo, que vê nas suas histórias os traços espalhados da sua própria vida. Como para os heróis que habitam estas histórias, o ato de contar fornece uma conexão psicológica para os interlocutores, um elo narrativo que dá significado a uma viagem aparentemente interminável e fútil. Pois o ato de contar, quando bem realizado, transforma-se em componente indispensável desta própria viagem.

Podemos afirmar também que esse ato de contar histórias cumpre um papel fundamental na narrativa de Mia Couto, na medida em que funciona como veículo da memória coletiva popular em Moçambique. E é justamente nessa memória coletiva que encontramos as fontes de uma identidade cultural nesse país. Historicamente, a epopéia constituiu um gênero que exprime com exímia não somente a fundação de uma nação, mas também a construção de uma memória coletiva. É nestes dois sentidos que Ana Mafalda Leite considera a modalização épica na literatura angolana e cabo-verdiana, e o seu papel na construção de uma identidade nacional durante as lutas de independência.

Entretanto, a função desse gênero no período de pós-independência, sobretudo em Moçambique onde as divisões etno-linguísticas e políticas conduziram ao extremo de guerra civil, tem que ser reconsiderada. Como as questões de identidade não são necessariamente as mesmas depois da independência, é preciso modificar o gênero épico para acompanhar essas mudanças. As modificações significativas que encontramos em *Terra Sonâmbula* sugerem que a epopéia, como gênero literário, terá no futuro nova relevância na demanda de uma identidade tanto cultural como nacional em Moçambique.

Bibliografia

Couto, Mia. *Terra Sonâmbula.* Lisboa: Caminho, 1992.

Fowler, Alistair. *Kinds of Literature - An Introduction to the Theory of Genres andModes.* Oxford: Oxford UP, 1982.

Genette, Gérard. "Introduction à l'Architexte." *Théorie des Genres.* Paris: Seuil, 1986.

Hainsworth, J.B. "Ancient Greek." *Traditions of Heroic and Epic Poetry.* (Ed. A.T.Hatto). London: The Modern Humanities Research Association, 1980. 22-23.

Homer. *The Odyssey of Homer.* (trans. T.E. Shaw). New York: Oxford UP,1932.

Leite, Ana Mafalda. *A Modalização Épica nas Literaturas Africanas.* Lisboa: Vega,1995.

Simas-Almeida, Leonor. "A Redenção pela Palavra em *Terra Sonâmbula* de Mia Couto."*Revista da Faculdade de Letras* No. 19-20, 5ª Série, 1996: 159-168.

Robert H. Moser is Assistant Professor of Portuguese at the University of Georgia. He completed his doctoral thesis, *The Carnivalesque Defunto: Death and the Dead in Modern Brazilian Literature* in the Spring of 2002 at Brown University's Department of Portuguese and Brazilian Studies. He also taught Portuguese at Harvard University during the 2001-2002 academic year. He has published on 20th century Brazilian literature in *Brasil/Brazil, Hispania* and the forthcoming volume of *Representations of the Dead.* His work on the Portuguese historian Jaime Cortesão was published in *Leituras: Revista da Biblioteca Nacional.* His current research is focused on the figure of the dead, posthumous narration, and related expressions of haunting and mourning in Luso-Brazilian literature, as well as Lusophone African writers Germano Almeida and Mia Couto.

A Feminist Dance of Love, Eroticism, and Life: Paulina Chiziane's Novelistic Recreation of Tradition and Language in Postcolonial Mozambique

Russell G. Hamilton

Abstract. This article analyses the form and content of *Niketche: Uma História de Poligamia (Niketche: A Story of Polygamy)*, the most recent work by Paulina Chiziane, Mozambique's first female novelist. A brief introduction offers some considerations of Chiziane's latest work as an aesthetic object and a literary product, published in Lisbon and intended for readers from all seven of the countries, on three continents, whose official language is Portuguese. The article analyses relevant aspects of the novel's imaginative portrayal and reformulation of traditional social and cultural institutions, especially polygamy, and how these practices continue to affect gender relationships in postcolonial Mozambique. With respect to how female and male characters inter-relate in the story that unfolds, the novel can legitimately be labelled "feminist." Basically, the article seeks to reveal how this literary work, composed from a female perspective and infused with a storyteller's "orature," constitutes a linguistic and artistic achievement of international appeal in its African recreation of Portuguese expression and of traditional social and cultural themes.

With the publication, in 1990, of *Balada de Amor ao Vento* (*Love Ballad on the Wind*), Paulina Chiziane gained renown as Mozambique's first female novelist. On a number of occasions, in print and orally, Chiziane has asserted, however, that she is not a novelist. She refers to herself as a teller of stories, some short and others long. Although in much of the world, and certainly in the West, a citizen who writes a novel that gains recognition normally receives special praise in his or her home country for having reached the pinnacle of national literary grandeur. That this form of literary expression is the quintessential genre of the modern nation-state is captured in such laudatory acclamations as "the great American novel." Chiziane, by insisting that she is a storyteller, is asserting her roots in an African and, specifically, a Mozambican tradition. She is, in effect, following, *mutatis mutandis*, the ancient tradition of the caste of hereditary storytellers, commonly known in parts of Africa as griots.[1]

As a storyteller who transmits her artistic orality as "literature," the latter being a term that by definition refers to pencraft and the printed word, Paulina Chiziane is indeed a writer.[2] Most readers of Chiziane's works can readily appreciate the degree to which the storytelling tradition has influenced the language, technique, and style of her, to date, four published novels. The author herself has stated the extent to which orality drives her writing.[3] Despite her self-characterization as a storyteller and not a writer of novels, Chiziane presumably accepts that the volumes bearing her name be marketed abroad, specifically in Portugal, as novels. Thus, on the front cover of each of her three most recent works, *Ventos do Apocalipse*, *O Sétimo Juramento*, and *Niketche: Uma História de Poligamia*, directly under the title is printed the word *romance*. These three works, all published in Lisbon by Editorial Caminho, are intended for a Portuguese-speaking audience that goes beyond readers from the author's native land. *Niketche*, the novel under consideration in the present article, was published in a Caminho series called "Outras Margens: Autores Estrangeiros de Língua Portuguesa." With respect to "marginality," the series is an attempt to bring literary works by African authors to prospective readers from the periphery (i.e., the five Lusophone African countries) as well as to those at the center (i.e., Portugal and Brazil) of the Portuguese-speaking world.

Quite naturally, vocabulary and language usage in general have special significance with respect to works from the margins of the Portuguese-speaking world. In this regard, it may first strike some readers as curious that on the front cover of Chiziane's recently published novel the main title, *NIKETCHE*, which appears in large capitalized letters, is not a Portuguese word. Readers unfamiliar with the indigenous languages of Mozambique may be intrigued by the exotic but unfamiliar word, which is followed, in smaller letters by the explanatory subtitle: *Uma História de Poligamia*. This clarification notwithstanding, most prospective readers will want to consult the volume's glossary, containing a total of forty-four terms, to discover that *niketche*, a word from an indigenous language of northern Mozambique, is the designation for a "dança de amor."[4]

It is worth noting that *Balada de Amor ao Vento,* Chiziane's first novel, published in Maputo by the Associação dos Escritores Moçambicanos, does not include a glossary. Although this relatively short novel has fewer indigenous language terms than do Chiziane's three works published in Portugal, the author does use a number of Bantu words in the narrative and dialogues. Among the words of Bantu origin found in *Balada de Amor ao Vento* are *machamba* (garden plot or small farm) and *lobolo* (bride price or dowry). These two nouns, along with other indigenous terms used in the novel, are part of the active vocabulary of most of contemporary Mozambique's citizens and other residents, regardless of their race or ethnicity. Chiziane presumably wrote her first novel, published and mainly distributed in Mozambique, for literate Mozambicans as well as for those non-Mozambican readers who are familiar with the more or less standard dialect of the Portuguese spoken in that southern African country.

In our consideration of the form and content of *Niketche* we shall have occasion to return to the matter of the social, cultural, and aesthetic roles of language in the story. At this juncture, we offer a brief appraisal of the book's graphic design. Although by no means a mere marketing ploy, the volume's cover illustration does catch one's attention because of its exoticism and what some might view as its eroticism. On the volume's cover appears the frontal depiction of a naked female figure and to either side of her a large bird, two snake-like creatures, and a peripheral and partial view of a clothed male figure clutching one of the reptiles. This archetypal, totemic painting, of unquestionable aesthetic appeal, is the work of Malangatana, unquestionably modern-day Mozambique's most celebrated graphic artist.

Niketche's intriguing hybrid title and the volume's captivating graphic design indeed prepare the reader for the main story and complimentary tales that unfold in the text. Also intriguing is the story's epigraph: *Mulher é terra. Sem semear, sem regar, nada produz.* A proverb of the northern Zambezia province, the epigraph prepares the reader for the role of women in the story about to unfold.[5] The proverb also sets the tone for the orature and traditionalism that permeate the story's language and its social and cultural themes.

Rami, the first-person narrator and protagonist of the forty-three untitled chapters in the volume, recounts a story of polygamy and, indeed, aspects of the history of that traditional multi-conjugal practice in Mozambique. From her perspective as the first of the five wives of Tony, as well as the mother of five of his sixteen children, Rami tells what comes to be an uncomplicated but thematically multifaceted story line with a complex plot. Briefly stated, the story depicts events, over a period of several months, in the daily lives of women as they relate to their polygamist mate, other men, their nuclear and extended families, and to each other. The plot is made complex by a set of factors having to do with several interrelated, far-reaching, and often engagingly contradictory subjects and themes. Moreover, the language and style of the narrative and dialogues are infused with the obliqueness of a poetic prose style that frequently simulates symphonic crescendos and reaches dramatic heights of magic realism.

Niketche's narrator, as the voice of the story's implied author, appears to be ambivalent, if not overtly contradictory, with respect to polygamy as a social institution in postcolonial Mozambique. In the interview published, in 1994, in Chabal's *Vozes Moçambicanas*, Chiziane rather sets the stage for the attitudes of *Niketche*'s implied author and narrator with regard to polygamy and other traditional social practices as they relate to the status of women. Chiziane asserts that what she calls "hidden polygamy" constitutes a major problem in a monogamous society:

> Porque hoje, de facto, é o que se diz: "A poligamia mudou de vestido." Porque esses homens todos têm quatro, cinco, dez mulheres em qualquer canto por aí. Têm filhos com duas, três, quatro mulheres todas juntas. São filhos que, porque crescem numa sociedade de monogamia, não se podem reconhecer. São crianças fruto de uma situação como a que vivemos hoje, uma situação de adultério. Mas numa sociedade de poligamia já não acontece isso, as coisas são mais abertas. A situação de adultério que vivemos hoje é muito pior que a poligamia. (299)

Chiziane's interview elucidates much of what Rami, the narrator, other female characters, and, by implication, the implied author express in the fictional account of polygamy. Of fundamental significance with respect to the story are Chiziane's above-quoted assertions in reference to what polygamy was traditionally and what it has become—i.e., a "hidden practice" tantamount to adultery. In a later interview published in Laban's *Moçambique: Encontro com Escritores*, Chiziane emphatically states that "[...] é claro que não concordo com a poligamia" (976).[6] As she does in her earlier interview,

Chiziane makes a distinction between contemporary adulterous polygamy and the traditional practice, which she sees as having provided a firm familial context for the multiple wives and their offspring. In *Niketche* the dichotomy between the traditional and the contemporary plays itself out poetically and often dramatically. The stories that make up *Niketche* not only focus on polygamy and other traditional practices, they also feature such correlatives as love, eroticism, religion, sorcery, magic, ethnicity, race, parenthood, and the social and economic status of women.

Chapter 11 is an especially striking example of how throughout the work the storyteller effectively combines form and content. With colourful images, striking metaphors, and rhythmic phrasing Rami delivers a dramatic soliloquy on polygamy. Four consecutive paragraphs, in response to the rhetorical question "O que é poligamia?," begin with the words "Poligamia é [...]." The first of these paragraphs reads: "Poligamia é uma rede de pesca lançada ao mar. Para pescar mulheres de todos os tipos. Já fui pescada. As minhas rivais, minhas irmãs, todas, já fomos pescadas. Afiar os dentes, roer a rede e fugir, ou retirar a rede e pescar o pescador? Qual a melhor solução?" (93). In what comes to be something of a transitional point in the story, Rami indulges in a kind of regional and gender power reconstruction with respect to polygamy as it exists in her country. Instead of seeing polygamy as a traditionally *matriarchal* practice of northern Mozambique, she considers it to be based on *patriarchal* power and domination that men of the northern Macua ethnic group embraced when they became Islamized. On the other hand, Rami contends that her own southern-based ethnic group has roots in the tradition of polygamy. With the arrival of Christianity, brought by the European colonizers, Rami declares, however, that her people "[...] jurou deixar os costumes bárbaros de casar com muitas mulheres para tornar-se monógamo ou celibatário" (94). This view runs contrary to the belief held by many of the women in the story that traditional polygamy was a northern, matriarchal practice predicated on the willingness to share. Rami herself originally held that belief as well as the conviction that such southern traditions as *lobolo* ("bride price") are patriarchal in nature.

Chapter 11 thus marks a turning point at which Rami resolves to seek a solution by uniting Tony's women in a conspiracy against non-traditional polygamy, a practice steeped in male power and tantamount to adultery and concubinage. Rami does not seek to flee from the net of polygamy but rather to exercise the authority inherent in her status as *nkosikosi*, a Bantu title for the first of the wives to enter into the conjugal relationship. When, as an act of vengeance, Tony seeks to divorce Rami, whom he correctly recognizes as the chief conspirator, she refuses to comply. Pursuant to her decision to lead a conspiracy Rami had already engaged in some liberating activities with respect to sharing and sexual rituals. She had slept with Vito, the lover of Lu (Luísa), one of Tony's other wives. Besides sharing her man with other women, by having taken a lover Lu also is engaging in what might be termed adulterous polyandry.

With the encouragement of Lu, Ju (Julieta), Saly, and Mauá, Tony's four other wives, Rami seeks to reaffirm and enhance her femininity, physical attractiveness, and sexuality. At the beginning of the novel, the fear of losing Tony leads Rami to enrol in a course taught by a woman whom she identifies as a very famous love counsellor. During one of the first of a total of fifteen private tutorials, the love counsellor, who is part professor and part sorceress, assures Rami of her womanliness: "Tu és feitiço por excelência e não deves procurar mais magia nenhuma. Corpo de mulher é magia. Força. Fraqueza. Salvação. Perdição. O universo cabe nas curvas de uma mulher" (44).

Initiation rites and erotic enhancements redefine and regenerate traditional practices in this quintessentially postcolonialist work of fiction. Female genital circumcision is a traditional initiation rite, still practiced in a number of African countries, that has incurred considerable condemnation in today's world.[7] Rami, in reporting on the classes she attended, including those on matters one normally does not discuss, makes the following observation: "Enquanto noutras partes de África se faz a famosa excisão feminina, aqui os genitais se alongam. Nesses lugares o prazer é reprimindo, aqui é estimulado" (46). The foregoing may well lead some readers, who before they perused the passage were unaware that such a practice existed, to take another look at the illustration on the volume's front cover. Those readers will verify that Malangatana's totemic painting does indeed depict a female who has undergone elongation of the vaginal labia majora. Later on in the story, Mauá, Tony's youngest wife, encourages Rami to undergo the procedure as a means of enhancing her sexual attractiveness.

The portrayal of erotica, while by no means pornographic, does represent a rather audacious undertaking on the part of an increasing number of the postcolonial writers of Lusophone African. That several of such writers are women is seen as especially audacious, but also as a liberating gesture on their part. To cite an example, the Angolan Ana Paula Tavares's "O Mamão" is a sensual poem that uses fruit imagery to celebrate the female genitalia. In a way, this imagery recalls the sea creature vaginal allusions that appear in *Niketche.* Another relevant example occurs in the young Angolan writer Rosária's *Totonya,* a novel that depicts explicit sex scenes. Postcolonial audaciousness on the part of female African writers is, in effect, a form of "womanist" (to use the term coined by Alice Walker, the African American writer) liberation.

In Paulina Chiziane's novelistic works, particularly *Niketche,* this liberation applies, somewhat paradoxically, to certain traditional practices that might be considered at best outmoded and at worst reprehensible. What constitutes the most imaginative, if somewhat bizarre, episode in a series of unusual occurrences in this story of polygamy comes to pass when Tony is reported to have died in an automobile accident. Rami herself had passed the scene of the accident and noted that the victim was a man around fifty, which is indeed Tony's age. What is even more bizarre is that Tony's relatives identify the body. Consistent with the magic realism that permeates the story, Rami herself does not contest the family's verification of the death of their beloved Tony, who is a high-ranking police official. Rami goes along with the validity of the occurrence even though Eva, Tony's newest lover, has assured her that he was alive and well in Paris at the time of his alleged demise in Maputo.

In the following passage Rami reveals her thoughts as the funeral ends: "A multidão lança gritos de bradar aos céus. É um oceano de desespero. Quem quer que seja o morto enterrado, teve um funeral condigno, com lágrimas que não eram suas. Eu estou serena, derramo uma lágrima apenas, para não estragar a minha pose. Olho para o Levy com olhos gulosos. Ele será o meu purificador sexual, a decisão já foi tomada e ele acatou-a com prazer. Dentro de pouco tempo estarei nos seus braços, na cerimónia de kutchinga" (220). *Kutchinga* is a Bantu word that refers to levirate, the custom whereby a brother of the deceased inherits the latter's widow.[8] Levy, Tony's brother, accepts Rami as his wife on the eighth day after the funeral. Rami looks forward to the consummation of the union as her sexual liberation and her dance of love: "Daqui a oito dias vou-me despir. Dançar niketche só para ele, enquanto a esposa legítima morre de ciúmes lá fora. Vou pedir a Mauá para me iniciar nos passos desta dança, ah, que o tempo demora a passar! Deus queira que o Tony só regresse a casa depois deste acto consumado" (220). Recognizing what some may think of her, Rami then exclaims: "Chamem-me desavergonhada. Dêem-me todos os nomes feios que quiserem. Sou mulher e basta. Estou a cumprir à risca a tradição ditada pela família do meu marido"

(220). Within the context of this magical realist story of reinvented customs and practices, the episodes are natural.

Within the dictates of the tradition, Rami's in-laws seize many of her worldly possessions, including furniture, and give her thirty days to vacate the house. Tony's four other consorts are spared this pillage and expulsion on the grounds that they are not really wives and are thus not true widows. Moreover, according to the in-laws, who are from southern Mozambique, these women are northerners and thus have another culture. Northerners do not use the southern tradition whereby the groom pays a bride price (*lobolo*) to his future wife's parents. Moreover, the pillaging in-laws allege that these *xingondos*, a name by which southerners refer to northerners, "[...] são unidos e provocar um é provocar todos" (221).

On the eighth day after the funeral, Levy and Tony's pseudo-widow consummate the *kutchinga* and symbolically Rami dances the *niketche*. Later that very day Tony returns home to his widow's nearly empty house. Rami tells her resurrected husband why the house is empty of furniture, and she reports that "(a)té o kutchinga, ceremônia de purificação sexual aconteceu" (226). In effect, the events surrounding Tony's supposed death, his funeral, the *kutchinga*, his return home, and Rami's sexual fulfilment, as well as the latter's sense of having avenged herself, are climatic. The denouement, albeit replete with dramatic episodes and stories, essentially plays out Rami's, Ju's, Lu's, Saly's, and Mauá's vengeful reinvention of their polygamous relationship with Tony. As a final result of their having come to terms with a disarranged tradition, Ju, Lu, Saly, and Mauá enter into monogamous marriages (on the other hand, Rami's union with Levy is, in effect, annulled). All five women, including Rami, feel vindicated, however, in having gained emotional peace and economic independence along with a sense of having engaged in a conspiratorial, shared experience that has revindicated the traditional practice of polygamy.

The novel ends with Tony's discovery that Rami is pregnant. As Rami and Tony embrace, she reveals, however, that the father of the child is Levy, and then narrates the story's descriptive closing and her polygamous husband's dramatic if uncertain fate: "Os seus braços caem como um fardo. As três trovoadas que um dia tentou encomendar contra o noivo da Lu hoje atacam-lhe o cérebro, o coração e o sexo e fazem dele um super-homem calcificado no éden da praça. Ele só vê o escuro e a chuva. Fica uns minutos intermináveis a contemplar o vazio. Era uma ilha de fogo no meio da água. Solto-o. Não cai, mas voa no abismo, em direcção do coração do deserto, ao inferno sem fim" (332). Words flow poetically, and as poetry often does, they convey an obliqueness that may appeal more to readers' aesthetic appreciation than contribute to an understanding of the story's outcome, which might be termed open-ended. The open-ended story, in a postcolonial sense, can be defined as providing no fixed answers or offering any definitive conclusions. *Niketche*'s open-ended conclusion invites the sort of speculation about Mozambique's future and, indeed, the futures of all of the relatively new Lusophone African nations so intricately tied to the colonial past. In other words, an author's postcolonial perspective inevitably means that the characters, story line, and themes of his or her works deal with much of the legacy of the political social, economic, and cultural past of a given nation-state. As it does in *Niketche*, this perspective may also reflect the pre-colonial past of indigenous beliefs, customs, practices, and native languages.

One legacy of colonialism in Paulina Chiziane's story of polygamy is the matter of race, skin color, and ethnicity in post-independence Mozambique. When Tony's wives learn that he has taken a bi-racial, light-skinned lover, named Eva, the narrator is moved to exclaim: "Uma mulata é uma rival a sério. Os homens negros são obcecados pelas peles claras, como os brancos são obcecados pelas cabeças loiras. Mas na verdade as escuras têm mais calor, eles sabem disso" (133). In an attempt to determine the degree to which Eva poses a threat to their relationship with Tony, the black wives discuss such matters as the *mulata*'s physical attractiveness and her social status. Lu remarks that Eva is a "third-class *mulata*," whose father is most likely a Portuguese of low socio-economic standing in the settler community. Rami admonishes the black wives not to be racist, because, after all, "—Mulata não é mulher?" (133). The question at the end of Rami's admonishment elicits a quick response from Mauá: "—Mulatas são mulheres e mais: são especialistas em magias de amor. Elas são a tentação no paraíso" (133). Mauá's mention of witchcraft and magic brings to mind the Luso-tropicalist cult of the *mulata* enchantress. Moreover, Mauá's allusion to "paradise" is in keeping with the mulatto woman's name—Eve in the Garden of Eden. As a young traditionalist from the north, Mauá further defends her racialism, if not racism, by asserting that polygamy is for black women, not *mulatas*. Lu then contributes to the discussion by assuring her "sisters" that "—[a]s mulatas de terceira são pretas e não se importam com a poligamia [...]" (133). She argues that what women like Eva want "...é um poiso, para que o mundo diga: ela tem marido" (133). When Tony's wives confront him about his choice of a mixed-race lover, he reacts with an explanation that supports a prior contention that he is the quintessential national husband: "—Vontade de variar, meninas. Desejo de tocar numa pele mais clara. Vocês são todas escuras, uma cambada de pretas" (140). Tony's apparent need for variation leads him, while in Paris, to become involved with a French woman named Gaby. He thus becomes an internationalist lover in the eyes of the indigenous traditionalists back home in Mozambique. After Tony's pseudo demise, the matter of Eva's identity gets an ethnic/regionalist twist when at a meeting of members of his family and his wives and lovers someone asks the *mulata* where she is from. Without hesitation Eva replies: "—Sou de Palma, lá do canto norte desta terra, a beira do mar, de onde ninguém fala. Sou maconde" (215). A collective gasp of surprise is issued when the group learns that Eva is a member of a Mozambican ethnic group that is well known for having retained its traditional ethnic purity and cultural identity. Eva also contends that she and Tony are just friends, with no amorous involvement.

The novel also delves into the matter of sexual encounters, both intra- and inter-racial, during and after colonial rule. While holding forth about the fate of women with respect to sexual exploitation, Rami offers a compellingly ironic example to make her point:

> Há dias conheci uma mulher do interior da Zambézia. Tem cinco filhos, já crescidos. O primeiro, um mulato esbelto, é dos portugueses que a violaram durante a guerra colonial. O segundo, um preto, elegante e forte como um guerreiro, é fruto de outra violação dos guerrilheiros de libertação da mesma guerra colonial. O terceiro, outro mulato, mimoso como um gato, é dos comandos rodesianos brancos, que arrasaram esta terra para aniquilar as bases dos guerrilheiros do Zimbabwe. O quarto é dos rebeldes que fizeram a guerra civil no interior do país. A primeira e a segunda vez foi violada, mas à terceira e à quarta entregou-se de livre vontade, porque se sentia especializada em violação sexual. O quinto é de um homem com quem se deitou por amor pela primeira vez. (277)

Rami declares that this particular woman has carried in her womb the history of all of Mozambique's wars, but that she laughs, sings, and tells her story to anyone who will listen because she is happy to have only given birth to males who will not know the pain of being sexually violated.

As noted above, Rami's four "rivals" in the polygamous relationship with Tony all embrace monogamy. In a kind of postcolonial defiance of the exploitative sexual encounters between the dominant colonizing male and the subjugated native female, Ju holds forth about her newly acquired husband. The usually silent Ju speaks out during the special session of the polygamous spouses' conjugal parliament: "Tony, os teus filhos pretos têm um padrasto branco, subiram de categoria. O teu filho de dezanove anos cavalga um mercedes que o padrasto ofereceu no dia dos anos. O meu novo marido é um português. Nós nos amamos, muito, muito, muito. É muito meiguinho, aquele meu velhinho. É viúvo, esse meu homem. E tem dinheiro. Muito dinheiro" (325).

Rami regales Tony with a summary of the breakup of his polygamous family. She gives a rundown of her fellow wives' new relationships, at least two, and possibly three, of which are interracial: "A Lu, a desejada, partiu para os braços de outro com véu e grinalda. A Ju, a enganada, está loucamente apaixonada por um velho português cheio de dinheiro. A Saly, a apetecida, enfeitiçou o padre italiano até que deixou a batina só por amor a ela. A Mauá, a amada, ama outro alguém" (331). A combination of vengeance, self-serving economic interests and motherly concerns, but also a "womanish" self-esteem, feelings of amorous passion, and, in the case of Rami, the *niketche* dance of life and love, underlie the dismantling of a polygamous configuration based on adultery, concubinage, and patriarchal exploitation. Judging by the implied author's perspective, the tradition of polygamy appears to be vindicated, however, as a social and emotional source of sisterhood, family, and a means of sharing in Mozambique's evolving postcolonial condition in Africa and among the family of nations in the world beyond.

Internationalism and cultural globalization in the former colony are reflected in the language and style of Paulina Chiziane's story of polygamy and other reinvented traditional patterns. The derivation and symbolism of a number of the characters' names reflect aspects of cultural hybridity. Rami, which derives from an apocopated combination of Rosa Maria, two common European names, has an African ring to it, and thus captures a kind of redefined measure of the traditional. On the other hand, Tony, the sobriquet of António Tomás, is a recognizable Euro-American appellation that labels the womaniser whose promiscuity extends from trans-regional, national multi-ethnicity and mixed-race fixation to an international, inter-racial affair. Levy also stands out in the story as not being a traditional Mozambican or otherwise African name. Readers of the novel might assume that the name is of Biblical, specifically Old Testament or Hebrew Bible origin. In view of the fact that Levy is the brother who "inherits" Rami, his name is most likely based on *levirato* (levirate), the equivalent of *kutchinga*, which, of course, refers to the practice of inheriting a wife.

The matter of characters' names leads to a consideration of the language question in Mozambique and language usage in Chiziane's literary expression. First, it should be noted that in interviews and other published statements, Paulina Chiziane makes some relevant observations on the language question in general as well as her literary expression (see Chabal and Laban). The author reveals that she grew up speaking Chope, a Bantu language of southern Mozambique, where she was born. When her Chope parents moved the family from their hometown of Manjacaze, in Gaza province, to the suburbs of Lourenço Marques (today, Maputo), Paulina Chiziane also learned to speak Ronga, a local language, and in grade school she began to acquire a spoken and written knowledge of Portuguese. In an interview, Chiziane insists, however, that despite her formal schooling she neither knows nor wants to know standard Portuguese (Laban 981). She also notes that she studied linguistics at Eduardo Mondlane University in Maputo. After then telling the interviewer that she would like to be able to write in her first language, Chiziane admits that even if she could compose literary works in Chope and Ronga, it would not be practical to do so because of a relatively small number of prospective readers of works composed in any of Mozambique's indigenous languages.

To a certain extent, Chiziane displays the same ambivalence about language usage that she seems to feel with respect to traditional social practices such as polygamy. The following rather lengthy passage is worth quoting because it puts into context the stylistic hybridity, rhetorical devices, and simulated orality that dominate the language and style of her imaginative writing:

> Para mim, a utilização da lingua portuguesa na escrita é um grande dilema. Na própria *Balada* há uma série de termos que eu uso, que eu não sei se deviam ficar de uma maneira ou de outra. Por exemplo, quando se fala de amor: bem, em português, porque eu ouvi—os meus namorados, pelo menos—, diziam: "Eu amo-te", enfim, com uma voz mais bonita ou menos bonita, mas é nesses termos. Na minha aldeia, a declaração de amor é diferente, é: "*Na kurandza, na kurandza, na kurandza,*" mil vezes [...]. Então, há uma frase que eu ponho ali: "Eu amo-te, amo-te, amo-te mil vezes amo-te." Quer dizer, isso é, mais ou menos, uma tradução daquilo que o povo sente, daquilo que o povo diz. E, ao fim e ao cabo, está escrito em português mas não é português, não é nada, é uma coisa qualquer. (Laban 981-982)

The above-quoted passage also illustrates what Chiziane may be getting at in an earlier published interview in which she makes what might be construed as a somewhat surprising declaration of intent when at the end of her statement she poses an intriguing question:

> Eu não quero escrever em português, não estou interessada em ser uma escritora de língua portuguesa. Estou interessada em ser uma escritora africana de expressão portuguesa. Ao querer ser uma escritora africana de expressão portuguesa eu tenho esses problemas, porque eu não consigo traduzir directamente as coisas como elas são para uma outra língua sem ser a minha. Tenho que recriar a língua, e neste processo de recriação muitos valores se perdem. Mas o que é que eu posso fazer?" (Chabal 300)

Some might argue that Chiziane and her fellow Mozambican authors are indeed Portuguese-language *African* writers. In fact, some Lusophone African writers and critics now reject the once commonly used label of African literature of Portuguese expression. Those who instead prefer African literature in Portuguese agree that the older label might convey a sense of "expressing" a Portuguese rather than an, Angolan, Cape Verdean, Guinean, Mozambican, or São Tomean perspective or ethos. In the context of Chiziane's afore-quoted statement, however, and in keeping with the ambivalence and poetic obliqueness that characterizes much of her prose fiction, her declaration of a recreated Portuguese expression, rather than the use of the Portuguese language, is indeed convincing. As to the question she poses about lost values, Chiziane's literary works, and particularly *Niketche: Uma História de Poligamia*, are perhaps themselves the answer to the question posed in the above-cited passage. Just as the reinvented traditional practices express refurbished values, so does the author's recreated Portuguese expression impart new aesthetic worth, with Mozambican, African, and universal meanings, to the novel.

Niketche abounds with imaginative examples of the use of indigenous words and phrases along with orality, trans-cultural hybridity, and rhetorical devices as evidence of the success of the author's attempts to recreate Portuguese expression. The novel is richly complex in theme and form and, simultaneously, its orality flows with an accessible comprehension for all readers of Portuguese expression. In conclusion, Paulina Chiziane, by virtue of *Niketche: Uma História de Poligamia* and her three earlier novels, assumes a well-deserved place among such innovative storytellers of postcolonial Mozambique as Mia Couto, Ungulani Ba Ka Khosa, and Lília Momplé.

Notes

[1] Germano Almeida, the prolific and highly regarded contemporary Cape Verdean author of long works of prose fiction, also identifies himself as a storyteller and not a novelist. Likewise of interest with regard to writers of the Portuguese-speaking world, João Ubaldo Ribeiro, one of contemporary Brazil's foremost novelists, also prefers to think of himself as a storyteller. All three writers no doubt consider themselves griots, or the relevant equivalent, who seek to weave tales that are culturally uplifting and aesthetically appealing.

[2] Although the term "oral literature" is still widely used by humanists and social scientists, many scholars, including Africanists, consider it to be something of an oxymoron. Increasingly, "orature" is the preferred label for literature that simulates or is influenced by orality.

[3] See the interviews of Paulina Chiziane published in Patrick Chabal's *Vozes Moçambicanas* and Michel Laban's *Moçambique: Encontros com Escritores.*

[4] *Ventos do Apocalipse*, Chiziane's second novel, also published in Lisbon by Caminho, includes a glossary consisting of fifty-one indigenous language terms. Originally, it was published in Maputo at the author's own expense and with no glossary. Not surprisingly, the Caminho edition, primarily directed at non-Mozambican readers, does include a glossary of indigenous words with Portuguese equivalents and/or definitions.

[5] On a number of occasions Paulina Chiziane, a southerner, has stated that Zambesia, where she has lived and worked, inspired her to write *Niketche.*

[6] While not widespread and although the country's ruling party disapproves of it, polygamy persists in Mozambique. Historically, polygamy has been more common among Muslims, who comprise about 10 percent of the population and are mainly in the country's northern regions. In the recent past, a group of women from the Muslim community in the capital city of Maputo, located in southern Mozambique, expressed their opposition to polygamy, which a number of Muslim men have claimed should be sanctioned by law.

[7] In March of 2003, several US newspapers carried a review of *The Day I Will Never Forget*, a film documentary produced and directed by Kim Longinotto. Shot in Kenya, the film is about female circumcision, also known as genital excision, widely practiced in that southeast African country as well as elsewhere on the continent. As "An Unblinking Eye on a Searing Topic," the title of Elvis Mitchell's review states, the practice, commonly referred to as female genital mutilation, has come under increasing condemnation around the world, including by many women and men in the African countries were it persists as a rite of initiation.

[8] "Rights Group Calls for an End to Inheriting African Wives," an item written by Marc Lacey and published in a recent edition of the *New York Times*, reports that Human Rights Watch has condemned the traditional practice in some African societies of wife inheritance. This condemnation is based on the fact that the practice permits that the brother or other in-laws take possession or control of the deceased man's property and finances. The widow is thus often left destitute. Some would argue, however, that traditionally the sibling who "inherits" his brother's widow is obligated to provide for her as a wife and to raise her children as if they were his own. This traditionalist, familial perspective, along with the stated "sexual purification," clearly drives Rami's acceptance of Levi as her "inheritor," even though, ironically, she is aware that her husband is not dead.

Works Cited

Chabal, Patrick. *Vozes Moçambicanas: Literatura e Nacionalidade.* Lisboa: Vega – Colecção Palavra Africana, 1994.

Chiziane, Paulina. *Balada de Amor ao Vento.* Maputo: Associação dos Escritores Moçambicanos – Colecção Karingana, 1990.

———. *Ventos do Apocalipse.* Lisboa: Editorial Caminho – Colecção Uma Terra sem Amos, 1999.

———. *O Sétimo Juramento.* Lisboa: Editorial Caminho – Colecção Uma Terra sem Amos, 2000.

———. *Niketche: Uma História de Poligamia.* Lisboa: Editorial Caminho – Outras Margens: Autores Estrangeiros de Língua Portuguesa, 2002.

Laban, Michel. *Moçambique: Encontro com Escritores.* Vol. III. Porto: Fundação Eng. António de Almeida, 1998.

Lacey, Marc. "Rights Group Calls for End to Inheriting African Wives." *New York Times* 5 March 2003, natl. ed.: A10.

Mitchell, Elvis. "An Unblinking Eye On a Searing Topic." *New York Times* 29 March 2003, natl. ed.: A1 & A20.

Silva, Rosária da. *Totonya.* Luanda: Brigada Jovem de Literatura de Angola, 1998.

Tavares, Ana Paula. "O Mamão." *Ritos de Passagem.* Luanda: União dos Escritores Angolanos, 1984. 15.

Russell G. Hamilton is Professor Emeritus of Lusophone African, Brazilian, and Portuguese Literatures at Vanderbilt University, Nashville, Tennessee. In 1978-79 he spent a sabbatical year in Cape Verde, Angola, and Mozambique. Over the ensuing decades he has had the opportunity to make frequent research trips in to all five Lusophone African countries, as well as Portugal and Brazil. The author of two books, *Voices from an Empire: A History of Afro-Portuguese Literature* and the two-volume *Literatura Africana, Literatura Necessária,* he also has published numerous chapters, articles, essays, and encyclopedia entries. One of several of his most recent articles is "Chronicling from the Center of the Periphery: *Estórias Contadas* by Germano Almeida," published in the recent issue of *Portuguese Literary & Cultural Studies* devoted to "Cape Verde: Language, Literature & Music."

The Serpent's Tongue: Gendering Autoethnography in Paulina Chiziane's *Balada de Amor ao Vento*[1]

Hilary Owen

Abstract. This article discusses the gendering of power and language in Paulina Chiziane's first novel *Balada de Amor ao Vento* (1990). Drawing on Cynthia Ward's analyses, informed by Bakhtin, I argue that Chiziane undoes the gender hierarchy implicit in constructing a dominant, national literary language in opposition to the naturalized feminine domestic realm associated with the "Mother Tongue." Exploring the gendering of poetic language in transcultural narratives such as auto-ethnography, I demonstrate that Chiziane's novel ironizes the pastoral mode that is central to colonial and anti-colonial (auto)ethnography, by positing a feminine pastoral subject of disillusion and displacement. Chiziane thus transposes onto African men the traditional culpability of Eve for Man's postlapsarian disillusion, colonially reiterated in representations of the conquest as the Fall. This appropriative move enables her to express the materiality of feminine desire through areas of miscommunication and untranslatability in traditionally male contact zones, so that she effectively disrupts any unitary, pastoral concept of a feminine "Mother Tongue" as the necessary, constitutive "other" to national literary language.

Paulina Chiziane has emerged in the last ten years as one of the most original and significant new voices in the contemporary Mozambican literary world. Like many Mozambican writers of her generation writing in Portuguese, her relationship to Portuguese as the official written language of the country exists in productive tension with a wealth of oral storytelling tradition. Born in Manjacaze, Gaza in 1955, she moved to Lourenço Marques in early childhood. Although her parents were Protestants, she was subsequently educated in a Portuguese Roman Catholic mission school in the capital city. Consequently, she was exposed early in life to four different languages. Chope was the first oral language she learned and spoke at home with her family in Gaza. Ronga was the oral language she had to speak with other Africans when she moved to the suburbs of the capital city at the age of six. Portuguese was acquired only in the context of literacy, by means of formal schooling and education in the Portuguese classics; her university degree studies at Eduardo Mondlane were in linguistics. In addition to this influential cultural heritage of Tsonga orature and Portuguese and Lusophone African literatures, her daily attendance at Catholic mass at her missionary school exposed her to spoken Latin (Laban 977). Not surprisingly, she has often described her background in inherently transcultural terms, resisting allegiance to any totalizing religious, class, or ethnic identification:

> Sou o resultado de duas culturas e não consigo delimitar em mim mesma as fronteiras entre uma e outra cultura. [...] Penso e falo numa língua europeia para retratar a minha vida de africana. Só pode ser assim e não de outro modo se quiser comunicar-me com outras fronteiras e mesmo dentro do meu país. (Laban 975)

If her race, class and language background is complex and nuanced, her gendered acceptance into the male-defined literacy canon of Mozambique is no less so. Chiziane has explicitly aligned herself with the expression of a gendered perspective on Mozambican history and society during the colonial period and post-Independence era. Indeed, she stated in a 1999 interview, "não sou capaz de ter uma visão assexuada da vida" (Sousa Guerreiro 1). However, this declaration in the negative is still far from arrogating a unitary viewpoint that could be pinned to any postcolonial, feminist or African womanist orthodoxy.[2] In fact, as will become evident, and on the principle that attack is the best form of defense, Chiziane's satirical critique of Mozambican masculinities is a defining element in all of her major published work to date.

Focusing on the cooperation between patriarchal systems of social organization under historically intersecting colonial, Marxist and post-colonial forms of rule, Chiziane necessarily complexifies the concept of a unitary feminist perspective in opposition to patriarchal control. At the same time, however, she clearly posits the need for a realignment of gendered power dynamics in southern Mozambican society, using a highly syncretic novelistic discourse in which communication between different languages and symbol systems metonymizes different social systems of material and economic exchange. As the critic Cynthia Ward indicates in a study of officialized literary languages and artificially engendered "vernaculars," which will underpin my analysis of Chiziane, the very idea of invoking a "woman's perspective" in African literature tends to cast perspective as masculine, and the woman's angle as different, partial, subjective, and, crucially for our purposes, materialized. According to Ward:

> Objectivity is constituted as precisely that which is not given to those whom it objectifies. The authority, the power, of objectivity finds its basis in the materiality of the thus embodied others [women as mothers] who are always subject to their physical condition. The 'silencing' of women is not merely a condition of limiting their access to means of education, but central to the giving 'voice' to the invisible author. (121)

Fundamental to Ward's Bakhtinian argument is the problematic of the feminized, materialized "Mother Tongue" as "primitive orality [reflecting] the dream of wholeness behind written language" (123). Taking issue with the gender blindness of Ngugi wa Thiongo's *Decolonizing the Mind* and its apparent unconcern with depatriarchizing as well as decolonizing the mind, Ward asserts that the pure African "Mother Tongue" is itself a necessary fiction, always required by and posited against the masculine pen. Thus, so-called "vernacular" languages are artificially feminized or more specifically maternalized, as the objectification of feminine "matter," in the monoglossic process whereby dominant literary (and written) languages appropriate oral (domestic) vernaculars as the knowledge they need to objectify in order to raise a literary language to the status of hegemonically national monoglossia.[3] Thus, as Ward puts it, the "'matrix-as-mother-of-all-mothers' does not appear outside of the monoglossic discourse that has been coded in advance" (120). Language becomes then a material thing, the objectifying panoptical standpoint associated with the white male gaze in European monoglossia not only, as theorists such as Walter Ong would have it, through being written down, but also when "national literatures [are] 'dialogically' engendered via the forcible appropriation of the feminized mother tongues by the father's pen" (121). Consequently, in Ward's view, the call for literature to be written in African vernacular languages that Ngugi wa Thiong'o makes would fail to avoid simply repeating this dialogic linguistic process, maintaining its hierarchical gender dynamic essentially in tact.

The gendered relationship between Tsonga orature and Portuguese writing has played a significant role in Chiziane's reception and status, particularly in the dominant metropolitan critical arena of Lisbon. Her acceptance into this normatively male-authored canon of marketable and exportable Mozambican literature over the last decade has been cautious and ambivalent. The following conditional acceptance from José da Silva Moreira is telling in this respect:

> Quando Paulina Chiziane se obrigar a um rigor maior junto ao seu talento indiscutível de contadora de histórias, facilmente ascenderá à qualidade de "terceira mosqueteira" da literatura moçambicana, a par de Mia Couto e Ungulani Ba Ka Khosa. (22)

The implications are clear. Chiziane will join the top-selling, marketable ranks more decisively if she disciplines her use of Portuguese literary language to the appropriate, predefined (written) standard. Validating written standardization and uniformity in Portuguese over her "talento indiscutível de contadora de histórias" (22) da Silva Moreira effectively reinforces a prioritization of writing over orature. He requires that Chiziane's implicitly feminized oral storytelling should play the role of a synthetic natural, spontaneous (though ultimately disciplined) other in relation to Portuguese literary writing. If we accept Ward's assertion that "a fully rationalized market language best fully rationalizes a market economy and vice versa" (120), the drive to regularize language through monoglossia has clear commercial as well as national payoffs. Conversely, then, and significantly for Chiziane, the diversification of language and symbol systems allows her to encode (women's) non-containment in the monoglossia upheld by dominant economic, sociocultural and national systems.

The dominant system under discussion in Chiziane's first novel *Balada de Amor ao Vento* (1990) is southern Mozambican polygamy. Refusing the centrifugal drive towards social conformity and linguistic monoglossia, Chiziane thematizes divorce in order to inscribe the taboo of women's non-maternal sexual desire into dominant discourses of material and economic exchange. Official opposition to polygamy was an important point of ideological continuity linking Christian colonial missions and post-independence marxism-leninism. Monogamy became a notorious source of hypocrisy and double-speak among FRELIMO men, who had much to gain from practicing public monogamy and clandestine polygamy. As Chiziane points out, it also licensed serial monogamy as a covert form of polygamy without providing the economic structures for maintaining more than one family. Chiziane consequently refuses to draw a neat defining line between polygamous forms of social organization and the institution of monogamy, which may be serialized into a form of *de facto*, non-simultaneous polygamy. Comparing the two marriage systems, the Christian lack of responsibility for abandoned children of former marriages, and the fierce rivalry between polygamous wives, Chiziane concludes "com a poligamia, com a monogamia ou mesmo solitária, a vida a mulher é sempre dura" (108). The episodic narration of events in the novel follows a dialectical format allowing for comparison and contrast between different forms of social organization and affording the main narrator/protagonist Sarnau opportunity to comment on her own changing fortunes.

Balada de Amor ao Vento describes the trials and tribulations in love of Sarnau, a young Tsonga woman in Inhambane province during the colonial period. Sarnau loves and loses Mwando several times. As an intending Catholic priest, Mwando breaks the rules of the seminary, makes love to Sarnau and gets her pregnant, only to abandon her with the pretext that a monogamous marriage has been arranged for him by his Christian family. Sarnau meanwhile makes a wealthy match becoming the number one wife and future queen in a polygamous union with the heir of the throne in Mambone. Abused by her husband she develops solidarity with her mother-in-law, the Queen, but suffers the rivalry and witchcraft of the other polygamous wives. Sarnau is supplanted in Nguila's affections, when she fails to produce an heir. She accepts Mwando back as her lover, when he returns to her after his Christian monogamous marriage has failed. Sarnau finally produces a son but through her relationship with Mwando, not with her husband. Unaware of the child's illegitimacy Nguila unwittingly accepts the child as heir to the throne but Sarnau and Mwando are forced to flee the kingdom when an embittered rival wife, Phati, betrays them to Nguila and the adulterous relationship is discovered. Mwando takes Sarnau to Vilankulos where he becomes a fisherman but his fear and guilt take over when he is pursued by a vengeful Nguila, and he abandons Sarnau again. The latter part of the novel switches its attention to Mwando for the space of three chapters, depicting the direct impact of the colonial regime on black African men, which Sarnau experiences only indirectly through Mwando and Nguila.

Mwando is arrested by the colonial authorities and deported for correctional labor on the Angolan plantations because he had an affair with a woman whose boyfriend turned out to be a *sipaio* who accused him of rape. The *sipaios* were colonial plantation foremen, usually Asian, whose job it was to oversee the workers for the white masters and whose mediatory position is often associated with betrayal, in anti- and post-colonial Mozambican texts. Despite the harsh conditions of the plantation, Mwando eventually makes good, using his seminarian skills in reciting Latin masses and funeral rituals to set up as a barefoot priest or "mafundisse," in league with the colonial authorities. Returning to Lourenço Marques at the end of the novel, Mwando finds Sarnau selling vegetables on a stall in Mafalala, where the story began. Reduced to prostitution to repay her "lobolo" to the king of Mambone, she demands the price of her honor or "resgate" from Mwando, in terms of the accumulated marriages her "lobolo" bought for her brothers, stating:

> Só as vacas do meu lobolo, fizeram outros vinte e quatro lobolos. Tiraste-me do lar, abandonaste-me, tive que lutar sozinha para devolver as trinta e seis vacas, pois se não o fizesse, todas seriam recolhidas em cada família, o que significa vinte e quatro divórcios. (113)[4]

Making her stand, symbolically in the market place, Sarnau creates a critical subtext on the gendered power structures that had always underwritten the narrative of the Mozambican revolution.[5] As Patrick Chabal has rightly noted, at the time of its publication the novel was "construed as an acid statement about the present" (92).

Balada was written in the late 1980s and published in 1990 when FRELIMO was experiencing a deepening crisis in state control. In their attempt to combat the growth of RENAMO's neo-traditionalist counter-insurgency, FRELIMO sought to increase the international standing and national membership of the FRELIMO party with a broadening of popular appeal and an extension of religious tolerance. One result of this was FRELIMO's controversial withdrawal at its Fifth Party Congress in 1989 of the official policy, which refused party membership to men who engaged in "traditional" religious practices such as polygamy and *lobolo*.[6] Not surprisingly in this context of incipient transition, then, Chiziane uses the highly topical polygamy/monogamy debate to frame a transcultural contact zone, which effectively connects three historical periods, the pre-colonial, the colonial and post-independence marxism-leninism. Read allegorically, the novel reveals the status of women being pressed into instrumentalist service as a symbolic and material bargaining chip in Frelimo's political transition from marxist-leninist state socialism to capitalism and liberal democracy.

Emphasizing the continuities linking colonial and pre-colonial hierarchies of gender in African societies, what Elleke Boehmer has termed the "history of intersecting patriarchies that was part of colonialism" (7), and extrapolating from this to contemporary post-colonial politics, Chiziane foregrounds the fact that women often figure the intersection point in male-authored (anti)colonial narratives.[7] As symbolic border guards of cultural tradition, women become the scapegoats for conflicted male identifications, embodying, mediating or absorbing the contradictions that the contact zone produces, doubly materially disadvantaged by the cultural transactions of the contact zone, losing one form of gender agency without acquiring another.[8]

Chiziane dramatizes this political *impasse* for women in terms of poetic language conflict as she rewrites and transforms the autoethnographic narrative, showing how it can operate as a medium of gender betrayal. As Pratt explains, "if ethnographic texts are a means by which Europeans represent to themselves their (usually subjugated) others, autoethnographic texts are those the others construct in response to or in dialogue with those metropolitan representations" (*Imperial Eyes* 7). However, colonial ethnography itself has a specifically gendered history, casting women as the object of study and traditionally over-relying on the greater accessibility (and conductibility) of male informants.[9] "Ethnographical objectification" by missionaries and anthropologists established a "fixed object of study that could be described, 'known,' and thus controlled" (Ward 124). This largely accounts for the counter-emphasis placed on sociology, anthropology and (auto)ethnography in the construction of the anti-colonial discourses that informed the consolidation of (masculine) national subjectivities.[10] How then do women, the sexual "others" of the colonized Other employ the (auto)ethnographic medium to enter into dialogue with *both* metropolitan representations of sexualized native otherness *and* the internalization and perpetuation of these sexualized representations by "Europe's subjugated other," the African male speaker of anti- and post-colonial discourses?

Chiziane engages with this in *Balada* by producing an ironic appropriation of the pastoral narrative on which Christian colonial ethnography relies.[11] As Sidonie Smith has noted, "there is a long history that conjoins pastoral visions and colonization" (171). The structure of the pastoral turns on the split between the rural idyll and the coming of commerce and war as the founding movements of urban civilization.[12] In this scenario, the objectification of the feminine is inherent to colonial ethnography because the pastoral imagination relies for its construction of eternally lost native innocence on the myth of Genesis and the doctrine of the Fall. Nostalgic for a lost world corrupted by the Fall from Grace, which may correspond to the coming of an Age of War, colonial conquest, or industrialization and the growth of money economies, the pastoral *topos* is equally available to colonial and anti-colonial ethnographic discourses of prelapsarian nostalgia.

In this context, African woman in particular is made to embody a pure, maternal and primitive essence, a hyper-materialized matrix or Mother Tongue "ahistorically trapped within nature" (Ward 120). The pastoral time/space of the Golden Age corresponds then to an inchoate, presymbolic, feminized ideal, deprived of the power of public expression through authorized (national) monoglossia. Chiziane's pastoral problematizes woman's culpability for the Fall, which inaugurates the pastoral by deploying a female pastoral subject whose journey through suffering and life, symbolized throughout by the journeying waters of the River Save, provides the trajectory of exile and displacement between locations that enables pastoral convention to delineate its necessary contrasts. Chiziane has remarked that "aquilo que eu faço em termos de escrita é uma tradução da oratura à literatura" (Owen 1999) but her process of translation and cross-cultural communication between zones is conspicuously, artfully incomplete and can never reinstitute lost wholeness.

Chiziane refuses any form of assimilative, enforced monoglossia, rather emphasizing oral and written heteroglossia as a field of "untranslatability" across systems, marked by inexact symbolic correspondences, deliberate epistemic fracture and ironic double-voicing. By allowing Sarnau as a journeying woman to be both the expressive subject of pastoral nostalgia and the passive object of the "natural" essentialist mythology that the pastoral requires, Chiziane uses the gender hierarchy of the pastoral *topos* to synthesize a deconstructive speaking position for Sarnau, which takes account of specific poetic and linguistic histories of silencing. Thus Sarnau's unfixable voice constantly speaks from two places at once. The novel begins with her explicit declaration of her pastoral positioning, between the "now" and the "then," as she states: "tenho saudades" (9). Looking back to the Eden of her youth by the River Save, she contrasts her past with the present "paraíso de miséria" (9)—

the urban slum of Mafalala where she has a market stall. Expressing Sarnau's successive disillusion with two gender distopias, Christian and Tsonga, Chiziane creates a field of "double vision," a pastoral within a pastoral, contrasting her village childhood among ideal nature, not only with Mafalala in the capital city, but also with the degenerate royal court of Mambone and its corrupt, cumulative polygamy economy based on polygamy and *lobolo*.[13] Thus the novel's double temporality, its present/past dynamic, is chronotopically expressed as a series of shifting, contrasting double spaces and double voices as Chiziane splits and subdivides the pastoral longing for pure maternal wholeness, the fiction of artificial oral monoglossia.

The novel's appropriation of Genesis begins by paradigmatically establishing the impossibility of unitary "maternal" meaning, setting up an ambivalent, centrifugal aesthetic of doubling and splitting in the courtship of Sarnau and Mwando, who are explicitly likened to the original creation couple in the Garden of Eden. Sarnau first falls in love with Mwando following their respective initiation rituals. In Tsonga terms, this is the point at which adult sexual relations between them would normally be sanctioned. Mwando, however, is training for the priesthood in the Catholic seminary. Their burgeoning sexual relationship is therefore dramatized as a linguistic conflict between Christian and Tsonga nature symbolism, between Portuguese writing and Tsonga orature, and between differently authorized definitions of transgression. Sarnau and Mwando disagree in their versions of Genesis as the founding narrative of sexual difference and initiation, and this disjuncture can be traced through the shifting meaning of the snake in their declarations to each other and to g/God.

Sarnau's vision of a spontaneous Paradise is firmly rooted in the beauty of the natural world around her, where human sexuality follows the rhythm of the seasons. Mwando has internalized his Garden of Eden through the scriptural format of the Bible taught at the Catholic college. For Sarnau, nature, not Christianity, is a medium of instruction and an instrument of wisdom, while for Mwando, nature is an unwelcome intrusion on civilization and a threat to the intellect. Indeed, his attraction to the priesthood is neither spiritual nor material but a question of aesthetics, appearances and dominant linguistic ritual as he remarks, "eu quero ser padre, usar batina branca, cristianizar, baptizar" (16). While Mwando associates Sarnau with a snake, awakening him from the "ventre fecundo da inocência" (15), Sarnau does not see the snake as evil, but rather as discrete and passive, since "a serpente junto ao ninho, fecha os olhos, discreta, não vá ela interromper os beijos dos pássaros que se amam, crescem e se multiplicam" (15). Sarnau exculpates the snake, and, by future inference, herself, from occasioning original sin. For Mwando, the serpent is the (feminized) agent of evil in Christian consciousness, and "como o Adão no Paraíso, a voz da serpente sugeriu-lhe a maçã, que lhe arrancou brutalmente a venda de todos mistérios" (15). His troubled conscience is aware of imminent transgression when he asks, "porque é que Deus não protége os seus filhos mais devotos, e deixa serpentes espalhados por todo lado, porquê?" (16). Fearing yet secretly desiring his expulsion from the paradise represented by the gardens of the Catholic college, Mwando remarks, "se o padre descobrir a minha paixão expulsa-me do colégio na frescura do entardecer tal como Adão no Paraíso" (16).

When Mwando is finally won over by Sarnau's physical charms, he commits his feelings to writing. Posturing as a romantic poet, he writes a love letter to Sarnau replete with local, natural imagery for his feelings, even though he knows that Sarnau cannot read it; he begins: "que pena, não saberes ler. Escrever-te-ia uma carta linda, longa" (17). The act of writing is a materializing of Mwando's cultural dilemma, an attempt to assume a Portuguese lyric subject position that ultimately betrays him by occasioning the very thing he had hoped to avoid, when the letter accidentally falls into the hands of the priest. Padre Ferreira uses it as evidence that gives credence to the "línguas de serpente" (17) warning him of sexual misdemeanours in the school. He expels Mwando and his friend Salomão, but not the school cook who he has caught in bed with Salomão. This comically infers the priest's sexual hypocrisy but also, in contrast to Mwando, it underlines his impunity under his own laws.

The conventional treachery of the serpent is transposed onto the civilized literate world of Catholic colonialism, which is exposed as a fraud and a risk for those seeking assimilation to it, precisely because it embodies social law in writing. The serpent meanwhile retains a Tsonga association with the continuity of nature and the forces of love. When Mwando and Sarnau finally make love, Sarnau openly defies the Christian God saying, "a serpente deume uma maçã e o Adão vai trincá-la mesmo debaixo do vosso nariz. Ide, ide queixar-vos a Deus que eu não me importo, as ervas serão nossas confidentes" (19). Mwando's eventual "sin" in Tsonga terms consists precisely in his not keeping faith with the world of the serpent. He breaks his Tsonga commitment to Sarnau after their lovemaking when he does not pay the ritually required dues: "dinheiro, rapé e pano vermelho" (20) to Sarnau's ancestral protector. When he leaves her pregnant so that he can contract a Christian monogamous union, a deadly snake threatens him and Mwando realizes that "os teus defuntos estão contra mim, mandaram esta cobra para me aniquilar, o que significa isto?" (23).

Mwando's masculine identity in the Tsonga patriarchal system draws him into the danger zone of transcultural contact, where imitative colonial power becomes his only mode of survival and yet also his greatest risk. Mwando's risks are always underwritten by the hard labor of Sarnau, however, and, as the text makes clear, she has been "enslaved" by marriage, more effectively and permanently than Mwando will ever be by his corrective labor on the Angolan plantations. Mwando's experience of deportation and corrective labor ultimately provides him with an opportunity to thrive at the expense of his fellow convicts, although it is his liminal position in the contact zone, between Christian colonial literacy and the world of Tsonga orature, which causes his arrest in the first place. Just as Sarnau was initially tricked by Mwando, he too is now deceived when he unwittingly has an affair with a woman whose boyfriend, or possibly pimp, is a *sipaio* who accuses Mwando of theft and rape. As a literate, Christianized, black man, nonetheless refused admittance to full citizenship, it is precisely Mwando's incomplete assimilation, his good Portuguese and his ability to write beautifully, conjoined with the racist stereotype of black sexual monstrosity, which are used to justify suspicion. He receives the excessively harsh punishment of deportation merely because his "caderneta" does not have the right stamps for the "indígena" (93) group in which he is officially classified. His formally perfect but incomplete obedience to the laws laid down by the dominant colonial semiotics, embodied in the "caderneta" law, leaves him in an administrative and linguistic limbo, a victim of assimilative transculturation. At the same time, from a gendered point of view, Chiziane affords a certain poetic justice in that Mwando's misjudged sexual encounter causes him to fall to the wrong side of the very discourse of assimilation that he had previously used to cheat Sarnau of her rightful due when he deflowered her.

Unlike Sarnau, Mwando learns to assimilate the white man's lesson of exploitation and duplicity when he turns deportation into an opportunity for material gain; as Chiziane prophetically notes, "o escravo liberto torna-se tirano" (93). Reinventing himself as "Padre Moçambique" he performs rituals for the dead among his workmates with considerable success because:

> Leu as orações num latim tão perfeito que nem o melhor párroco, dando mais solenidade no acto. Apesar do trabalho forçado, encontrou felicidade no degredo. Finalmente conseguira satisfazer a ambição de usar batina branca, baptizar, cristianizar. (100)

Undercutting the local competition with lower rates for saying mass, he eventually becomes a combination of Padre Ferreira, who educated him in sexual hypocrisy, and the *sipaio* who kept faith with the colonial authorities by having Mwando deported. Echoing the *sipaio*'s role as colonial agent, Mwando comes to be trusted as intermediary between the white colonial powers and the workers, finally earning enough money to return to Mozambique, where he finds Sarnau and claims poverty, obliging her to take him in.

Mwando's multilingual skills, his Portuguese and his spoken Latin, enable him to gain the trust of his fellow convicts, which he then uses to support Angola's white plantation owners. Both languages are shown to be historically masculine prerogatives in the colonial Christian context, although levels of access to them remain racially overdetermined. Specifically, though never totally, empowered under patriarchal culture to move between Tsonga and Christian symbol systems, Mwando's sexual and linguistic duplicity reverses the scapegoating of Eve and the serpent for Man's expulsion from paradise. His gender betrayal at the outset is responsible for the Fall. In an ironic rewriting of Genesis then, already signalled in the youthful sexual/linguistic conflicts between Sarnau and Mwando, Chiziane undoes the mythology of the female translator, the Malinche figure, whose sexual cumplicity is responsible for colonial penetration.[14] Finally abandoning any illusion of pastoral longing, Sarnau concludes "enterrei o passado" (117) as the youthful perspective of "saudade" disappears, to be replaced by a painful and uneasy compromise, the end of a pastoral journey in which no equilibrium can be restored.

Written in a climate of female disillusion with the conditional and contingent benefits of modernity proffered by Frelimo, the dialectic movement of this novel cannot be closed, nor its problematic resolved. Rather, it leaves open women's refusal to embody the contradictions of a false rationalism. The subtext is evident. Marxism, like Mwando, has betrayed women once too often. Further, the depatriarchizing of language and of society will not arise from displacing one monolithic discourse in favor of another. As a critique of Mozambican masculinity under the Christian colonial and "traditional" Tsonga belief systems, syncretically personified in Mwando and

Nguila, *Balada de Amor ao Vento* marks a significant move to depatriarchize the literary and social text of southern Mozambique. Developing a narrative poetics that can account for the gendered power struggles between dominant written and oral media, Chiziane avoids privileging oral narrative as African feminine expression *par excellence* without relinquishing the strategic ability of the oral to remind dominant literary language of its contingently "manufactured" status. One valuable result of this is that Portuguese as the national (literary) language of Mozambique is not artificially reified in the masculine singular. Another is that Chiziane asserts the desiring feminine body (adultery, transgression, illegitimacy and divorce) in terms of an economic materiality, which the traditionally privileged materiality of the Maternal cannot account for, thus denaturalizing women's relegation to a sphere outside of history, progress or the emergence of national literary language(s).

Notes

[1] I would like to thank the Arts and Humanities Research Board for funding my Research Leave in 1998, and the British Academy and Sir Ernest Cassel Educational Trust for funding the research trip to Mozambique in 1999, which enabled me to conduct much of the research for this article. I am also indebted to Paulina Chiziane for her helpful comments and productive discussion in interviews in 1998 and 1999.

[2] See Mary Modupe Kolawole, *Womanism and African Consciousness*, for a discussion of African Womanist as opposed to feminist thinking.

[3] In an interview with Michel Laban, Chiziane provides an interesting biographical insight into her father's attempts during her childhood to confine domestic, oral languages and official, written languages to their appropriate spheres of influence. "O meu pai é muito radical, sim: ele nunca permitiu que se falasse português em casa. Não aceitava. Ele considerava que nós tínhamos obrigação de conhecer a nossa própria língua. Agora, a língua de comunicação, de progresso, isso é lá fora porque em casa não deve ser assim" (977).

[4] As Allen and Barbara Isaacman have noted on the issue of divorce in Tsonga systems of polygamy, "if [the father's lineage] refused to sanction the separation, i.e. to repay her *lobolo* to her husband's lineage, her only option was to flee from her husband's home. Many of the women who migrated to Maputo and congregated in the few low-paying jobs open to women or who practiced prostitution were trying to earn enough money to repay *lobolo* and end their marriages in the only way that the society legally recognized" (4). Taking a specifically historical view, Sihaka Tsemo has argued in a 1992 study for *Estudos Moçambicanos* that dilemmas such as Sarnau's arose in part from the transformation of the southern "lobolo" system when migrant labor to the South African mines established an "economia monetarizada" to which women had little independent access, other than by selling their own bodies. In this context, according to Tsemo, "a impossibilidade de se divorciar do seu esposo sem lhe devolver o lobolo [...] levou em determinadas circunstâncias, certas mulheres à práctica da prostituição" (202).

[5] As Inocência Mata indicates, Chiziane's work moves narrative constructions of the feminine beyond their confinement to objectification in nationalist poetry, which she describes as "[o] discurso que recicla o trabalho poético que edita a imagem da mulher na sua quase exclusiva vinculação ao projecto nacionalista" (36).

6 See Kathleen E. Sheldon, *Pounders of Grain* 195-227. Sheldon concludes regarding the 5th FRELIMO Party Congress, held in 1989:

> In this case, the expansion of FRELIMO membership appeared to appeal to men, and traditional men at that, while requiring women's continued subordination. [...] One explanation was the strength of patriarchal attitudes among male leaders in FRELIMO who apparently saw traditional men as more valuable potential recruits than women. (204)

7 For discussions of women's role as symbolic border guards of culture in anti-colonial nationalism, see Florence Stratton 39-55 and Nira Yuval-Davis 39-67.

8 Pratt defines the contact zone as "the space in which peoples geographically and historically separated come into contact with each other and establish ongoing relations, usually involving conditions of coercion, radical inequality, and intractable conflict" (6). As Chiziane points out in *Eu Mulher,* one of the more "harmonious," non-conflictive contact zones between her own cultural legacies centred on Christian and Tsonga agreement regarding the inferior status of women, as "encontrei harmonia na matéria que dizia respeito ao lugar da mulher na vida e no mundo" (14).

9 As Kathleen E. Sheldon points out, for example, the Swiss protestant missionary and ethnographer, H. A. Junod, relied solely on four male informants for his 1908 study of the practice of widow inheritance among the Ba-Ronga. *Pounders of Grain* 27 and 41, n.143.

10 A classic example of colonial missionary ethnography in Mozambique is Henri A. Junod's *Usos e Costumes dos Bantu.* Far from being a product of the Portuguese colonial system, this two-volume ethnography was written in English and first published in 1912/13, Junod's interest in the then emergent discipline of anthropology having been awakened by contact with British academic pioneers in the field. Significantly, even José Fialho Feliciano's preface to the 1996 edition of *Usos e Costumes,* which otherwise affords necessary context and critique for Junod's work, singles out the fact that Junod "deu valor ao tradicional como uma matriz" (20) as central to his lasting academic value.

11 In *Usos e Costumes dos Bantu. Tomo 1*, Junod projects a pastoral world of lovers and goatherds, "estas raças tanto tempo imobilizadas" (28), threatened by encroaching mercantile "civilization" and the money economy of the Johannesburg mines, which will sexually corrupt the innocent unless they are subject to (his) paternalistic Christian guidance. As Sidonie Smith indicates in her discussion of the pastoral's implication in colonialism, "the lowly are projections of the universal subject's desire for innocence, integrity and uncomplicated meaning" (171).

12 Raymond Williams significantly argues that the city/country divide inherent to the European pastoral finds modern expression in the colony and metropolis relationship, in the post-Industrial era of 19th century European colonialism and its capitalist and imperialist visions of progress. For Williams, then, "one of the last models of 'city and country' is the system we now know as imperialism" (277). On colonialism and the pastoral mode, see also Peter Weston, "The Noble Primitive as Bourgeois Subject" 166-80.

13 In *Eu Mulher em Moçambique,* Chiziane compares women's demonization under Christian Genesis myth with Tsonga mythologies perpetuating the scapegoating of women for drought, crop failure and epidemics. Firmly rejecting both of these overlapping forms of sexual essentialism, Chiziane writes: "as diversas mitologias não são mais do que ideologias ditadas pelo poder sob a máscara da criação divina" (12).

14 See Norma Alarcón, "Traddutora, Traditora: A Paradigmatic Figure of Chicana Feminism" 86-7.

Works Cited

Afonso, Ana Elisa de Santana, coord. *Eu Mulher em Moçambique.* Maputo: Comissão Nacional para a UNESCO em Moçambique e Associação dos Escritores Moçambicanos, 1994. Under Chiziane.

Alarcón, Norma. "Traddutora, Traditora: A Paradigmatic Figure of Chicana Feminism." *Cultural Critique* 39 (1989): 57-87.

Boehmer, Elleke. "Stories of Women and Mothers: Gender and Nationalism in the Early Fiction of Flora Nwapa." *Motherlands: Black Women's Writing from Africa, the Caribbean and South Asia.* Ed. Susheila Nasta. New Brunswick: Rutgers UP, 1992. 3-23.

Chabal, Patrick, et al. *The Postcolonial Literature of Lusophone Africa.* Evanston: Northwestern UP, 1996.

Chiziane, Paulina. *Balada de Amor ao Vento.* Maputo: Associação dos Escritores Moçambicanos, 1990.

Guerreiro, Manuela Sousa. Interview with Paulina Chiziane. *Mozambique. Revista. Literatura* 23 (Dezembro de 1999): 1 http://www.ccpm.pt/paulina.htm.

Isaacman, Allen and Barbara Isaacman. *National liberation and women's liberation: Mozambican women in the armed struggle 1962-1975.* Unpublished paper presented at UNESCO Experts' Meeting on "The Role of Women in Angola, Guinea-Bissau, Mozambique and Zimbabwe." September 1983. 1-71.

Junod, Henri A. *Usos e Costumes dos Bantu. 2 Tomos.* Maputo: Arquivo Histórico de Moçambique. Documentos 3, 1996.

Kolawole, Mary E. Modupe. *Womanism and African Consciousness.* Trenton, NJ: Africa World Press, 1997.

Laban, Michel. *Encontro com Escritores. Moçambique.* Porto: Fundação Eng. António de Almeida, 1998.

Marinelli, Peter V. *Pastoral.* London: Methuen, 1971. 75-82.

Mata, Inocência. "Paulina Chiziane. Uma Colectora de Memórias Imaginadas." *Metamorfoses* 1 (2000): 135-42.

Moreira, José da Silva. "A guerra dos espíritos." *Expresso – Cartaz* 1,450. 12 de Agosto de 2000. 22.

Ong, Walter J. *Orality and Literacy. The Technologizing of the Word.* London: Methuen, 1982.

Owen, Hilary. Unpublished interview with Paulina Chiziane. Maputo. June 1999.

Pratt, Mary Louise. "Transculturation and autoethnography: Peru 1615/1980." *Colonial discourse/postcolonial theory.* Ed. Francis Barker, Peter Hulme and Margaret Iversen. Manchester and New York: Manchester UP, 1994. 24-46.

———. *Imperial Eyes. Travel Writing and Transculturation.* London and New York: Routledge, 1992.

Sheldon, Kathleen E. *Pounders of Grain. A History of Women, Work and Politics in Mozambique.* Portsmouth: Heinemann, 2002.

Smith, Sidonie. *Subjectivity, Identity and the Body. Women's Autobiographical Practices in the Twentieth Century.* Bloomington: Indiana UP, 1993.

Stratton, Florence. *Contemporary African Literature and the Politics of Gender.* London and New York: Routledge, 1994.

Tsemo, Sihaka. "Direitos e Papel da Mulher Africana no Contexto Político-Jurídico Tradicional: Evolução e Perspectivas." *Estudos Moçambicanos* 11-12 (Nov. de 1992): 183-209.

Ward, Cynthia. "Bound to matter. The father's pen and mother tongues." *The Politics of*

(M)Othering. Womanhood, Identity and Resistance in African Literature. Ed. Obioma Nnaemeka. London and New York: Routledge, 1997. 114-29.

Weston, Peter. "The Noble Primitive as Bourgeois Subject." *The Pastoral Mode. Casebook Series.* Ed. Bryan Loughrey. London: Macmillan, 1984. 166-80.

Williams, Raymond. *The Country and the City.* London: Hogarth, 1985.

Yuval-Davis, Nira. *Gender and Nation.* London: Sage. 1997.

Hilary Owen is Senior Lecturer in Portuguese at the University of Manchester. She is the editor of *Gender, Ethnicity and Class in Modern Portuguese-Speaking Culture* (1996) and the author of *Portuguese Women's Writing 1972-1986. Reincarnations of a Revolution* (2000). She has published extensively on modern and contemporary Portuguese women's writing, particularly *Novas Cartas Portuguesas.* She is currently working on a book about feminism and women's writing in Mozambique. Email: hilary.owen@man.ac.uk

Em torno de modelos no romance moçambicano

Ana Mafalda Leite

Resumo. O artigo descreve algumas das especificidades do romance moçambicano, em que os novos autores de ficção, ao recriarem a sua enunciação no terreno das poéticas orais, recorrem ao modelo, iniciado pela poesia narrativa de José Craveirinha, ao *Karingana wa Karingana.* Estes novos narradores, repõem na escrita a arte griótica, e encenam estratégias narrativas que legitimam a enunciação de uma memória, cujos procedimentos retóricos, se inscrevem nas tradições locais.

A prática narrativa em Moçambique

Durante o período colonial, o género literário mais praticado foi a poesia em Moçambique. Muitas razões podem ser evocadas para tentar explicar esse facto. Entre elas, o facto de a elite intelectual ser pouco numerosa, por via de o ensino se ter desenvolvido tardiamente na então colónia. Outra razão, prende-se ao facto de a poesia ser uma forma mais insidiosa de iludir a censura, e de mais fácil publicação, em jornais, revistas, ou antologias.

Alguns anos após a independência começam a surgir vários autores, a maioria oriundos de uma nova geração, que contribuem para o desenvolvimento da prática narrativa.[1] Isto acontece em meados da década de oitenta, passada quase uma década da euforia revolucionária do governo marxista de Samora Machel. Todos estes novos autores escolhem, preferencialmente, como género, o conto ou a crónica, o que é muito significativo.

A arte de narrar oral é um dos aspectos do quotidiano africano. A história é uma espécie de *medium* à conversa e funciona como *exemplum.* Conversar não é apenas trocar ideias, antes contar histórias que exemplificam as ideias. Este acontecimento quotidiano tende a ganhar forma na literatura, como é óbvio. Por outro lado, alguns dos escritores tiveram experiência jornalística e tiraram partido dela para a escrita dos seus livros, como é o caso de Mia Couto, Elton Rebello, Calane da Silva e Albino Magaia.

Outro aspecto que permitirá ainda compreender a escolha do conto como género predilecto, radica-se no facto de o país viver, desde a independência, um processo de transformação tão rápido, e com uma realidade cultural tão multifacetada, que o conto se adapta e se revela como a prática narrativa mais adequada, tendo em conta o seus estreitos laços com a oralidade, mais acessível à edição e à leitura, e ainda, muitas vezes, à representação teatral.

Além dos autores citados anteriormente, publicaram em livro as suas narrativas: Ungulani Ba Ka Khosa, Suleimane Cassamo, Marcelo Panguana, Paulina Chiziane, Lilia Momplé, Aldino Muianga, Isaac Zita, Aníbal Aleluia. Os temas tratados são diversos, mas tentarei dar conta de alguns dos mais significativos. Além do relato de histórias do tempo colonial, o quotidiano da vida é descrito em cenas que colocam em confronto os valores tradicionais do campo, as crenças religiosas, a mundividência mítica, com os comportamentos urbanos da cidade. Outros temas recuperam aspectos da vida moçambicana no imediatamente pós-independência, ridicularizando e criticando certos comportamentos da actuação política. A ambição e a corrupção encontram o seu lugar nestes cenários.

As relações entre homem e mulher, os mais velhos e os mais novos, é um assunto que merece especial atenção, tendo em conta os valores ancestrais e os códigos antigos reguladores da sociedade camponesa, agora por vezes postos em causa por novas ideias e comportamentos menos conservadores. Um dos grandes temas é, sem dúvida, a guerra civil, a miséria e a fome, provocadas pelos muitos anos de sofrimento, e a despersonalização das personagens, a destruição dos laços clânicos pela necessidade de fugirem e se refugiarem em outras zonas. Em simultâneo, o avivar das crenças e dos valores animistas, como último recurso para a esperança.

Observa-se o retrato de uma sociedade em crise nos seus valores fundamentais. Mal saída de uma guerra colonial, entrando numa outra, civil, muitas vezes desconhecendo as causas e o inimigo. No campo foge-se, sem saber de quem exactamente, dos bandidos armados, dos ladrões que assaltam os últimos víveres dos camponeses e muitas vezes os chacinam. As crianças crescem com armas nas mãos, e este estado de sítio, mais ou menos generalizado, por todo o país até meados da década de noventa, transparece, com intensidade, na temática narrativa dos escritores moçambicanos.

Em relação ao uso da língua portuguesa revelam-se maioritariamente duas tendências. Uma, para seguir uma norma relativamente estável do português moçambicanizado, através de alterações sintácticas de menor monta, e de um léxico usado no dia a dia em Moçambique, com algum léxico ronga ou changana. Uma outra tendência é a da invenção linguística, e tem por expoente o prosador Mia Couto, que imprime à linguagem do quotidiano uma dimensão poética, através de múltiplas recriações e de combinações linguísticas. Mia Couto consegue manter a simplicidade dos diálogos das suas personagens, reinventando-lhes a dimensão literária da oralidade.

Paulina Chiziane, Marcelo Panguana e Ungulani Ba Ka Khosa optam pelo recurso a uma escrita oralizada, que tenta recuperar as formas tradicionais da arte de contar, recorrendo ao uso dos provérbios, às imagens muito concretas da natureza, ao exemplos da interacção entre o mundo natural e o humano. Por vezes, o fluxo da linguagem é ininterrupto e encantatório, reaparecendo nele figurado os universos fabulosos e mágicos da imaginação mítica. A língua, apesar de não muito alterada, segue ritmos e uma lógica outra, em que o sonho, o presságio, a profecia e a adivinhação intuitiva reinam na sua lenga-lenga narrativa e na sua oratória de recitação.

Mas há outros exemplos, Suleimane Cassamo e Lília Momplé, por exemplo, investem numa arte do conto concisa e mais fotográfica, numa economia de meios, e assumem a brevidade do conto na sua total apetência. São variadas as formas de escrever ficção no Moçambique actual. A tendência para a arte do conto parece ser o grande denominador comum e o modo como os escritores readaptam a língua portuguesa, moçambicanizando-a, variam também de acordo com a estratégia e a opção de cada um.

Criação de uma tradição da escrita narrativa

A grande diferença em relação ao período colonial manifesta-se hoje pelo maior número de prosadores em relação a poetas. Pode falar-se numa tradição de escrita poética, formulada na encruzilhada entre o cosmopolitismo e a nativização, de que os expoentes serão Rui Knopfli e José Craveirinha. Este último, consagrando uma escrita proteiforme, travejada pelas poéticas orais do sul, ao mesmo tempo que seduzida pelo registo culto. Desta combinatória, resultou, muitas das vezes, uma escrita em que o ritmo narrativo predomina sobre o registo fragmentário da lírica: *Karingana wa Karingana*,[2] era uma vez.

O achamento de uma vertente poético-narrativa, cujos fundamentos se alicerçam nas práticas orais do sul de Moçambique,[3] que o poeta conheceu e aprofundou, contribuíu, pensamos, para o alargamento e a localização de uma escrita, mergulhada, como a parte invisível do iceberg, nesse território cultural/ oral, dinamizador e fundacional da futura escrita narrativa moçambicana.

A oscilação, ou indefinição, das estruturas poético-narrativas, a dominante de uma voz colectiva e laudatória, entre muitos outros aspectos que já tive ocasião de analisar pormenorizadamente, bem como outros investigadores e saliento, em especial, a pesquisa de Gilberto Matusse,[4] explicam esta recorrência à inscrição de modelos orais na poesia moçambicana, que se revela, pensamos, um dos caminhos mais aliciantes, em via de instituição, na prática narrativa pós-colonial.

Com efeito, aparentemente, com uma esporádica tradição anterior[5], os novos autores de ficção, *ao recriarem a sua enunciação no terreno das poéticas orais,* recorrem ao modelo, iniciado pela poesia narrativa de José Craveirinha, ao *Karingana wa Karingana*, capaz de narrar as histórias que se multiplicam, de inverosímeis à mais crua e terrível verosimilhança. Estes novos narradores, repôem na escrita a arte griótica, o maravilhoso do *era uma vez* e, refrânica e encantatoriamente, vêm contar *a forma como se conta*, na sua terra, *encenando as estratégias narrativas*, em simultâneo à narração:

> Escutai os lamentos que me saem da alma. *Vinde,* sentai-vos no sangue das ervas que escorre pelos montes, vinde, escutai repousando os corpos cansados debaixo da figueira enlutada que derrama lágrimas pelos filhos abortados. *Quero contar-vos histórias antigas, do presente e do futuro porque teho todas as idades* e ainda sou mais novo que todos os filhos e netos que hão-de nascer. Eu sou o destino. A vida germinou, floriu e chegamos ao fim do ciclo. Os cajueiros estão carregados de fruta madura, é época da vindima, escutai os lamentos que me saem da alma, ***Karingana wa Karingana.*** (Chiziane, *Os Ventos do Apocalipse*, 9)

É, no entanto, a publicação de diferentes romances, e escolhemos para este trabalho, um da autoria de Ungulani Ba Ka Khosa, *Ualalapi* (1987), outro de Mia Couto, *Terra Sonâmbula* (1992), e ainda *Sétimo Juramento* (2000) de Paulina Chiziane, que me parecem ser demonstrativos de novas propostas formais, reveladoras deste entrecruzamento dos géneros orais, na arte romanesca moçambicana.

Segundo algumas opiniões críticas, refiro-me, por exemplo, a Lourenço do Rosário,[6] o romance é uma arte narrativa com que os moçambicanos lidam com dificuldade, e com menos competência, talvez até inabilidade. Parece-me muito discutível este ponto de vista, uma vez que o "romance" é um género, por excelência, de hibridação de formas, e, provavelmente, os moçambicanos escolhem e optam por "modelos" próprios, em via de formação, diferentes, que escapam a outros, considerados canónicos. Por isso, a leitura do romance moçambicano provoca uma certa perplexidade ou estranheza, uma vez que não se rotula ou encaixa em formas previamente conhecidas, inaugurando outras, experimentais, e menos convencionadas.

Mikhail Bakhtine,[7] no entanto, sublinha o carácter instável do romance como género, hoje em dia, hegemónico; como se sabe, a origem da palavra aparece na Idade Média para designar uma língua vernacular, falada, a língua vulgar, por oposição à lingua latina escrita.

> Á l'heure de sa naissance, le roman ne tire donc pas son identité d'une forme littéraire. D'ailleurs, des récits écrits en langue romane sont très souvent rédigés en vers, comme les poémes hagiographiques (*Vie de Saint Alexis*), les épopées écrites en laisses d'octosyllabes (*La Chanson de Roland*), ou les premiers récits de de style "romanesque" comme *Le Roman de Brut, Énéas, Le Roman de Troie.* (...) L'apparition de la prose ne modifiera pas la nature du "genre". En revanche ce type d'oeuvre, *parce qu'il marque une rupture avec l'oralité, fonde progressivement une rhétorique nouvelle* d'où procédera le roman moderne: recours à des situations quotidiennes, souci de la vraisemblance, priorité de l'individuel sur le collectif, rapidité de la narration, goût de l'amplification. (Stalloni, 2000: 57)

Quero dizer, que os três romances – que vou utilizar neste texto como uma espécie de amostragem – tendem a explicitar "estratégias" narrativas, características da prática do romance moçambicano, cada um à sua maneira, mas convergindo numa reflexão maior sobre a nação, a cultura, as origens e o devir do Moçambique pós-colonial. Revelam, e interessa-me, em especial, este aspecto, formas específicas de formação de modelos, próprios, do romance moçambicano. O que quero com isto dizer?

Género da enunciação, o conto, Género do enunciado, o romance

O conto,[8] pela sua dimensão, é uma sinédoque dos temas maiores, que apenas o romance, dada a sua amplitude de personagens e enredos, mais facilmente preenche. Mas, curiosamente, ainda aqui nos defrontamos com uma surpresa, qualquer um dos dois primeiros autores, organiza os seus romances, tomando como base exploratória de escrita essa unidade menor, o conto. Os capítulos organizam-se com uma quase adaptação do modelo "conto." Por seu turno, a terceira autora, Paulina, usa o conto como forma dilatatória e, em expansão, para a escrita do romance.

Podemos adiantar, o conto parece ser a forma reinvindicativa cultural da oralidade e dos antecedentes da tradição narrativa moçambicana, *que invade os registos genótipos da escrita romanesca.* Embora saibamos também que o romance, enquanto género, ele próprio, tem uma estrutura indefinida, de uma *irremediável* plasticidade: "rien ne l'empêche d'utiliser à ses propres fins la description, la narration, le drame, l'essai, le commentaire, le monologue, le discours; ni d'être à son gré tour à tour ou simultanément, fable, histoire, apologue, idylle, chronique, conte, épopée" (Robert, 1972: 15).[9]

Mas, é uma forma estrategica e ironicamente utilizada, o que confere aos seus autores um enquadramento simultamente pós-moderno e pós-colonial. Há nos três autores essa procura de conciliação harmónica entre o legado das formas orais e a absorção de outros modelos de escrita, como, por exemplo, legado do romance latino e hispano-americano,[10] entre o recurso aos mais velhos detentores da oratura, das lendas e do imaginário mítico e maravilhoso, das estórias fabulosas e didácticas, e aos mais novos, que escrevem em folhas de papel o alfabeto dos novos sonhos.

Os três autores moçambicanos parecem confirmar que a categoria de "género" é uma instituição que funciona como "modelos de escrita" para os autores, e como "horizonte de espera" para os leitores (Todorov, 1978: 53). Por um lado os autores escrevem, fundamentalmente, mas não só, em função do sistema genérico que lhes é conhecido, reabsorvendo as poéticas orais, por outro lado, provocam os leitores potenciais, que irão ler em função do sistema de géneros que melhor re(conhecem).

Como se sabe, a escrita é uma importação dos árabes e dos europeus em África. Maioritariamente, a base da cultura africana pré-colonial assenta na oralidade e no regime de transmissão oral, de geração para geração, e ainda hoje essa situação se mantém nas áreas rurais e suburbanas dos países africanos. Ora, acontece que uma grande parte destes países é rural, e no caso de Moçambique, essa é uma verdade inquestionável, por isso continuam a ser predominantes as práticas da oralidade.

O "Diário de Manua," narrativa incluída em *Ualalalpi* de Ba Ka Khosa, problematiza a valorização do legado oral. Manua é nguni, filho de Ngungunhane. Tirou um curso de artes e ofícios e deixou escrito um diário, do qual o narrador se socorre para nos dar informações. Representa o assimilado, não é reconhecido pelos seus, nem pelos brancos. Transgride os valores e a tradição da sua cultura, e por isso é punido com a morte.

> Manhune transmitira ao filho e ao neto de que Manua fora envenenado pelo pai, pois era uma vergonha para os nguni ver um filho seu assimilar costumes de outros povos estrangeiros(...) Matem-no na próxima oportunidade, disse Ngungunhane num dos encontros que teve com os maiores do reino. (106)

O "conto" de Khosa começa aliando a ideia de decadência do império nguni com o achado do diário. A escrita é aqui o símbolo maior da recusa da cultura tradicional, e do início do colonialismo. Repare-se ainda na referência feita a um árabe, e ao seu testemunho escrito, que complementa os registos de Manua. Estas duas personagens testemunham o início da quebra de uma tradição de oralidade.

> Por entre os escombros daquilo que fora a última capital do império de Gaza encontraram um diário com uma letra tremida, imprecisa, tímida, as folhas amontoadas ao acaso, estavam metidas numa caveira que repousava entre ossadas humanas e animais... Não há referência ao seu autor, mas sabe-se que pertenceu a Manua, filho de Ngungunhane. (97) ... De 1892 a 1985, ano de sua morte, o diário nada diz, pois a folhas foram comidas pelos ratos, as letras que restaram estão soltas. Juntando as cinco letras tem-se a palavra morte. Ou temor. Ou tremo. Kamal Samade, que pela capital passou, deixou as suas impressões em árabe, escritas em folhas desordenadas. (U, 105)

A imposição da escrita numa sociedade de tradição oral, é um elemento sentido como uma forma de desiquilíbrio. Tchicaya U'Tamsi, escritor congolês, afirma: "toda a civilização é um encontro sincrético de dois mundos, tão bárbaros um para o outro, quanto bárbaros um e o outro. E isto tem como resultante um novo bárbaro, tão controverso em si mesmo, que é forçosamente um ser trágico, fatal, porque habitado por duas mortes, a dois dois mundos que o criaram" (Chevrier, 1998: 68).

A implantação da escrita em África não foi um produto da evolução histórica normal e respondeu a uma necessidade imposta pelo exterior. Por outro lado, a desvalorização das formas das culturas indígenas, que caracterizou a política colonial de assimilação, contribuiu para a descaracterização e rasura de valores ancestrais.

A tematização da revalorização da oralidade é uma forma de manifestar uma *recuperação simbólica*, um meio de afirmação de uma cultura, que foi subjugada pela hegemonia da escrita. Neste conto patenteia-se, de forma relativamente explícita, uma espécie de moral: o narrador, ao problematizar o significado da escrita na sociedade moçambicana, denega o seu valor, socorrendo-se parodicamente de uma estratégia temático-formal, a invenção de fontes escritas, o diário achado de Manua e o testemunho do árabe.

Verificamos, por estas razões, que a escrita do romance moçambicano procura "encenar", *territorializar culturalmente*, essa herança, nas várias opções temáticas e formais escolhidas. A surpresa do analista residirá em constatar nítidas convergências na escolha performativa do género, recriado com sabedoria, ao lermos diferentes autores, como é o caso de Paulina Chiziane, de Mia Couto ou de de Ungulani Ba Ka Khosa, e nos depararmos com *uma linha narrativa-motor, genotextual, propulsora, o conto*, ora em prática reduplicada, acrescentada e aditiva, ora num processo de alongamento, em expansão digressiva.

Semelhante característica genótipa do romance moçambicano poderá, eventualmente, confirmar alguma especificidade narrativa da ficção moçambicana, de estratégia oralizante, pela sua tentativa de articulação entre o mundo rural e o urbano, entre a mundividência mítica e a modernidade, entre o mundo fabuloso das tradições e a convivência, trágica e, ironicamente criativa, com as alterações irremediáveis, que as novas mentalidades e os novos tempos trouxeram.

Ualalapi

Ualalapi é uma narrativa organizada em seis episódios narrativos, aparentemente independentes, do tipo conto,[11] e versa sobre a figura do imperador nguni Ngungunhane, que colonizou, no século passado, o que é, actualmente, o sul de Moçambique. Tal como todos os países africanos, também Moçambique viria a herdar as fronteiras coloniais, estabelecidas a partir das decisões da Conferência de Berlim.

Ngungunhane foi o último resistente às campanhas dos portugueses, quando ficou decidido que a posse das colónias deveria ser legitimada pela efectiva ocupação territorial. Este chefe nguni ficou conhecido na história colonial portuguesa, como sendo o emblema da derrota dos negros de

Moçambique. Sobre ele, e as campanhas militares que tiveram lugar no sul do país, há bastante documentação histórica.

Com o advento da independência de Moçambique em 1975, a figura de Ngungunhane foi recuperada como herói nacional e figura mítica, que representava o primeiro resistente moçambicano à colonização portuguesa, anterior à luta de libertação pela independência, levada a cabo pela Frelimo. Na sequência desta reabilitação da personagem, convém destacar, por exemplo, o empenhamento dos moçambicanos na reabilitação do "herói," ao pediram o envio, há anos atrás, aos portugueses, dos restos mortais do imperador, que tinha sido exilado nos Açores, no fim do século passado.

Acontece que o imperador Ngungunhane era um invasor nguni, vindo que é, actualmente, a África do Sul, que ocupou os territórios do sul de Moçambique e escravizava os tsonga, grupos étnicos de Moçambique, quando os portugueses iniciaram o seu próprio processo colonial. Ungulani Ba Ka Khosa ao escrever o seu romance desmitifica e desconstrói esta figura, transformando o mítico herói, naquilo que ele era realmente, um ditador, estrangeiro e prepotente, que manteve sobre o seu domínio, escravizado, uma parte significativa do território moçambicano.

Este é o tema de que trata o romance de Ungulani Ba Ka Khosa. Nesta medida é uma narrativa histórica pós-colonial, que interroga a história pré-colonial e colonial, controversa, do actual país, Moçambique.

Os seis "contos" narram episódios, que marcam o início do reino do imperador até ao seu declínio e exílio. O protagonista só surge no último conto. Até lá, é descrito através de estórias de outras personagens, súbditos ou escravos, que sofrem as sucessivas desgraças que a prepotência do imperador faz recair sobre elas; uma ténue linha diacrónica se desenvolve em torno dos vários contos, criando uma sequência que promove a queda final da personagem. Todas as estórias se alimentam de um mal incontrolável, que anuncia o fim do império. E isto deve-se às sucessivas transgressões do protagonista, que não respeita as tradições da terra que coloniza. Por isso é castigado. Sonhos, pesadelos, visões, sucedem-se em catadupa, tal como fenómenos inexplicáveis da natureza e deformações humanas.

Na narrativa/conto finais, denominado, "O Último discurso de Ngungunhane," somos confrontados com a personagem que, antes de embarcar para a viagem que o levaria ao seu exílio, faz uma enorme profecia sobre todos os males que irão recair sobre os seus antigos escravos. O discurso relata a colonização, os efeitos da assimilação europeia, a conquista da independência e a guerra civil que teve lugar. Esta visão apocalíptica termina, anunciando a necessidade de um recomeço: "E terão que voltar ao princípio dos princípios. Eis o que será a vossa desgraça de séculos homens." (U., 124)

As fontes deste discurso são criadas pelo narrador, no interior da estória, que ouve um velho contar-lhe o discurso de Ngungunhane, que por sua vez ouviu a narração ao avô e, assim, sucessivamente. O narrador escuta este velho, à noite, junto a uma fogueira, com os papéis em que escreve o romance, num processo autoreflexivo do próprio acto de escrita/audição. Oscilando entre as fontes escritas, documentais, e as orais, forjadas ou reinventadas, o narrador, submeteu os seus "contos" à força do sagrado e das normas reguladoras dos tabus da sociedade pré-colonial, reiterando-lhes, na actualidade enunciativa, alguma da sua força e a necessidade do respeito e conhecimento das mesmas.

Trata *Ualalapi* de uma releitura crítica da História, mas, em simultâneo, também a herança cultural, literária e poética, e do seu reajustamento a um novo princípio, não submetido à opressão de modelos, mas à expressão livre das diferenças.

Terra Sonâmbula

Este romance da autoria de Mia Couto tem como pano de fundo a guerra civil que assolou o país até 1992. É uma narrativa que se reproduz em outras histórias. Organizada a partir de uma história matriz, a de um velho e uma criança, abandonados junto a um autocarro, incendiado no meio de uma estrada, alterna essa história com uma outra, a do personagem Kindzu, que vem escrita nuns cadernos descobertos pela criança no interior do autocarro. Cada uma das histórias, a encaixada e a englobante, alternam, capítulo a capítulo em unidades narrativas isoladas, que encaixam ainda outras histórias mais pequenas, mas que sempre se complementam, através dos protagonistas, que as ouvem ou contam.

Pode considerar-se uma narrativa de viagens, as viagens escritas de Kindzu, e as do velho e da criança, através dos relatos de Kindzu. As duas narrativas acabam confluindo, as personagens da história primeira começam a viver os acontecimentos da segunda, as paisagens a misturar-se magicamente, e no final o romance termina unindo-as, ou unindo os sonhos à realidade. Quando digo que o romance é uma narrativa de viagens, confiro-lhe o sentido iniciático de aprendizagem, conhecimento e descoberta. Porque se viaja em *Terra Sonâmbula*? Quem viaja?

A viagem é da própria terra que procura encontrar-se, sonâmbula, perdida, a viagem de um país que a guerra fratricida ocupou de lés a lés. A ausência de espaço seguro e de bússola, percorre as personagens e suas acções. Deparamos, na primeira narrativa, com uma criança, desmoriada e sem identidade, e um velho desaprendido da vida; na segunda, o jovem Kindzu quer tornar-se um guerreiro para lutar pela paz. Assistimos a um cortejo de personagens desesperançados de tudo, no entanto, através de cada pequena viagem, acontece uma nova história, uma iniciação. As diversas histórias que pontuam as viagens são essencialmente aprendizagem e fábula moralizante.

Os velhos ensinam as crenças, fazem conhecer os mitos, acontecem casos extraordinários. Só a palavra mágica parece encaminhar, e os eventos rondam o maravilhoso, a credulidade dos mitos. Os mortos falam, a natureza transmuta-se, os sonhos ganham realidade, bem como os pesadelos.

Na parte final do romance através de um sonho de Kindzu temos acesso à palavra de um feiticeiro, seguido se um séquito de centenas e centenas de pessoas que o ouvem; depois de um longo discurso onde anuncia todo o género de catástrofes, o feiticeiro termina reabilitando um novo tempo, principial, a vir: "No final, porém, restará uma manhã como esta, cheia de luz nova e se escutará uma voz longínqua como se fosse uma memória de antes de sermos gente (...) Essa voz nos dará força de um novo princípio" (*TS* 216). Esta promessa do romance aponta para uma harmonia futura entre mortos e vivos, ou seja entre o passado e o presente, as tradições e os novos tempos.

O romance *Terra Sonâmbula,* na forma como está estruturado, executa como que uma dúplice demanda, a de um caminho narrativo, uma vez que o que se narra se mistura com o "narrado," provando que a arte de contar ensina a viver e a sonhar, tal como acontece na sociedade tradicional, reinvestindo-se da sacralidade intemporal e educativa dos mitos e da plasticidade anímica dos sonhos.

Sétimo Juramento

O romance de Paulina Chiziane de certo modo combina as propostas anteriores; é um romance mítico-histórico e de viagem, perspectivado alegoricamente; ou seja executa um processo de viagem (ou de peregrinação?) iniciático pelos meandros da cultura anímico-religiosa, recuando no tempo, no entanto acrónico, que permanece latente, incrustado no presente.

Uma história de luta entre o mal e o bem, em que as personagens não oscilam em ambiguidades comportamentais, definindo-se pelas suas acções, tal como nos contos maravilhosos; no final o agente do mal é castigado e triunfa o bem.

Um gestor de uma empresa estatal em falência, já no contexto neo-liberal, David, não querendo prescindir do seu novo riquismo, usa a feitiçaria para conseguir os seus intentos. Para tal não se inibe da sacrificar uma parte da família, entrando nos meandros de uma entrega ao mundo das práticas e rituais mágicos. A mulher e o filho apercebendo-se, aos poucos, de alguma anormalidade, que lhes invade a vida, percorrem outro percurso iniciático, voltado para o bem, a fim de combater e exorcizar as práticas de David.

Gera-se uma luta entre os espíritos ndau (a força do mal) e os nguni (a força do bem), e vencem estes últimos, através da aprendizagem a que Clemente, o filho, dedica ao conhecimento das artes mágico-espirituais para defesa da sua família. Esta luta, permite uma insidiosa leitura ideológica da luta de poderes que se trava em Moçambique, tendo em conta a figuração do Centro pelos ndaus e do Sul pelos ngunis; em simultâneo, denuncia e critica os comportamentos da burguesia urbana, que recorre às práticas feiticistas em surdina, e toda a gente sabe disso, simulando muitas vezes alhear-se da tradição.

O mundo do feitiço e dos mitos esteve sempre ligado ao comportamento sócio-cultural da maior parte dos intervenientes activos na nova estória social de Moçambique, ricos ou pobres, urbanos ou camponeses, instruídos ou analfabetos, o moçambicano, de uma forma ou de outrea, conhece-o e envolve-se nele.

As viagens ao interior – e este paradigma *litoral/interior* é significativo na narrativa moçambicana – descritas no romance, metaforizam essa procura de uma representação cultural antiga, longínqua e inacessível; em Massinga, no estranho casarão assombrado e povoado de terror, a noite simboliza a descida ao inferno; quem lá vai à procura de solução para os seus problemas, representa uma elite intelectual e a burguesia com dinheiro: o jipe 4x4, o professor universitário, o padre, o gerente, o político.

Há dois movimentos no romance de Paulina, a entrada do mundo mítico, descendente, a viagem ao inferno ndau, e um outro, ascendente, a subida às montanhas na procura de um espírito nguni muito antigo, que surgem como consequência um do outro. Este movimento alegorizado, mostra que a estrutura narrativa segue uma estrutura ciclíca, aproximável das narrativas orais do tipo conto, e as personagens agem de acordo com funções bem definidas, preenchendo funções de "herói," "agressor," representando qualidades inconfundíveis.

Uma criação romanesca que se fundamenta no conto tradicional, em as personagens cumprem papéis; exemplar, moralizadora, a narrativa deste romance desoculta os imagináros culturais e trata-os, pela escolha narrativa, dentro da sua lógica intemporal, mítica e maravilhosa.

Um romance, conto por conto, ou um conto como um romance

As poéticas de tradição oral incluem pelo menos dois aspectos: as formas e as estruturas das literaturas orais tradicionais,[12] aquilo a que corresponde a noção de género, e o imaginário comum a essas tradições.

Os três romances são organizados a partir de uma estrutura narrativa oral de base, o conto (com variantes tipo fábula, alegoria, mito, provérbio), alicerçando a prática narrativa sobretudo nas *Poéticas Orais* e suas estruturas móveis e comunicantes, promovendo, assim, a incorporação destas poéticas no cânone literário moçambicano.

As narrativas da tradição oral africana têm uma forte componente didáctico-moralizante. Isto[13] reflecte-se na sua estruturação, através do carácter e da sequência das suas transformações. Com efeito, algumas classificações tipológicas, destas narrativas, têm como critério fundamental o sentido da transformação, que altera a situação inicial e determina a situação final da história, e que pode ser de degradação e de melhoramento.

Deste modo, distinguem-se dois tipos básicos de narrativas, que podem combinar-se de forma variada[14]: as de tipo ascendente e as de tipo descendente, conforme apresentem uma transformação de melhoramento ou de degradação, respectivamente. O carácter didáctico das de tipo descendente está na punição do agressor pela transgressão das regras, enquanto que, no caso oposto, na exemplaridade heróica. A recuperação deste modelo, mais ou menos linear, está naturalmente absorvida e retrabalhada de modo poliforme, como viémos observando.

Tematicamente, os romances propõem uma releitura do presente, *Ualalapi* voltando-se para o passado histórico, *Terra Sonâmbula* redimensionando a demanda da nação em viagem, e *O Sétimo Juramento* questionando a situação religiosa, através de um regresso ao conhecimento mítico e cultural. Relatam uma visão desassombrada do país, e suas mutações pós-coloniais, questionando a identidade cultural, avançando no conhecimento dos imaginários míticos.

Os três romances colocam questões fulcrais relacionadas com a manutenção e transformação das tradições culturais e desenvolvem o tema da loucura, ou da quase esquizofrenia, sendo algumas das personagens, símbolos deste estado de perda. A conflitualidade nasce perante a ausência da memória histórica e das práticas ancestrais, fruto das sucessivas colonizações, da guerra, da ocidentalização; as personagens debatem-se com um interior, desconhecido, ocultado, de si.

Um ponto comum parece desenhar-se neste desenrolar de contos/romance: a constatação de uma comunidade que violentamente se confronta com o seu próprio passado, enquanto herança de um desconhecimento de ser, histórico e cultural, que necessita ser preenchido e actualizado.

Parece haver, no propósito dos vários narradores, mais ou menos assumido, um objectivo didáctico e moralizante, tal como na prática comunitária da narração oral, alegorizando-se, com as muitas histórias, entre outras coisas, a crítica aos primeiros anos de independência, que tentaram obliterar as diferenças étnicas e culturais, sobre a égide de uma nação popular, marxista, um pouco alheia ao respeito pelos valores e pela religiosidade das culturas tradicionais.

Confrontos entre os mais velhos e os mais novos. Os mais novos necessitam reaprender a sabedoria transmitida ao longo de gerações, reaprender com o exemplo dos mais velhos, ou da História, e reformulá-la. Precisam de voltar a contar histórias e a entender os sentidos míticos e fabulosos, os *exempla* formadores, capaz de os reintegrar, fundamentando valores éticos e criticando o desregramento social e individual.

Desta forma se pode ler a radicalização comportamental de algumas personagens de Mia Couto, Ungulani Ba Ka Khosa e de Paulina Chiziane: loucura, amnésia, atopia, resultantes de um desiquilíbrio social e cultural. Todavia, em *Ualalapi* e *Terra Sonâmbula*, o apocalipse dá ainda lugar à promessa de regeneração, em o *Sétimo Juramento*, a entrega do espírito às forças desagregadoras do mal é combatida com a vitória.

A moralidade nas três obras parece ser similar: é necessário voltar ao princípio dos princípios, renascer, aprender a contar o presente, *conhecendo o passado*, pois só quem tem histórias para contar é que está vivo e tem memória, saber. Os romances procuram relatar, afinal, a diversidade de uma nação pluriétnica e pluricultural, onde as diferenças se reconheçam, se ajustem, tal como as diferentes histórias, entrelaçadas e nascidas umas nas outras, ou por encaixe, ou por alternância, ou por dilatação sequencial, constituindo-se, na *estrutura manifesta*, em romance.

Talvez a proposta dos autores, se me é permitido utilizar esta imagem, se baseie na formulação de uma espécie de narrativa, alegoria do país, o romance, a narrar-se, a escrever-se, organizado nos múltiplos contos, culturas e histórias. Todos eles diferentes mas, só juntos, ganhando sentido pleno.

Notas

[1] A Revista *Charrua*, fundada em 1984, por Ungulani Ba Ka Khosa, Eduardo White, Hélder Muteia, Marcelo Panguana, Juvenal Bucuane, entre outros, permitiu o desenvolvimento de novas práticas de escrita, não só no campo da narrativa, como também da poesia.

[2] Título do segundo livro de José Craveirinha, publicado em 1974.

[3] No que respeita à oratura moçambicana,como já referi mais atrás, Henri Junod na obra *Usos e Costumes dos Bantos* (1974: 161) refere três tipos diferentes de género ("estilo") no folclore tsonga: a *poesia didáctica e sentenciosa* que se encontra nos provérbios, máximas e enigmas, a *poesia narrativa* nos contos de todos os géneros e *a poesia lírica* nos cantos.

[4] Ana Mafalda Leite, *A Poética de José Craveirinha* (Lisboa: Vega, 1990); Gilberto Matusse, *A Construção da Imagem da Moçambicanidade em José Craveirinha, Mia Couto e Ungulani Ba Ka Khosa* (Maputo: Imprensa Universitária, 1997).

[5] As publicações mais significativas no domínio da ficção no período colonial são os livros de contos de João Dias, *Godido e Outros Contos*, em 1950, de Luís Bernardo Honwana, *Nós Matámos o Cão Tinhoso*, em 1964 e o pequeno romance *Portagem* de Orlando Mendes em 1965. Todos estes livros nos narram histórias que documentam a opressão do colonizado, e se situam no contexto da situação de discriminação racial e económica que então se vivia na colónia portuguesa de Moçambique.

[6] A propósito de *O Sétimo Juramento*, Lourenço do Rosário escreve: "(...) Hesito em classificar a natureza das dificuldades que encontro em Paulina: não sei se situá-las num plano meramente técnico literário dado o género escolhido, o romance, *pois é sabida a dificuldade dos nossos escritores perante o romance.* O ponto forte da nossa literatura situa-se na poesia e nos contos." In *Proler* (Julho/Agosto 2001) 25.

[7] Mikhail Bakhtin, *Esthétique et théorie du roman* (Paris, Gallimard, 1976).

[8] Utilizo aqui a noção de conto como narrativa curta, podendo englobar vários tipos,adequando a designação de provérbio narrativo, utilizada por E Obechina no primeiro capítulo, ou emprego altenativamente a designação conto, história ou narrativa, para designar as unidades narrativas correspondentes ao que se costuma nomear como "conto oral," uma vez que a estrutura de grande parte dos contos, encaixados,desenvolvidos, ou elididos, nos romances, é variável no seu tamanho e espécie.

[9] Marthe Robert, *Roman des Origines et Origines du Roman* (Paris: Grasset, 1972).

[10] Cf. Gilberto Matusse, 1999.

[11] Primeira edição do livro (Aemo, 1987) traz a indicação "contos" na página de rosto, mas a edição de 1991 suprime essa indicação.

[12] O substracto cultural banto do sul de Moçambique tem afinidades entre si; assim algumas das características levantadas por Henri Junod sobre os rongas podem generalizar-se à oratura de outros povos do sul, como os changanas, chopes, suazis, zulus, entre outros.

[13] Cf. Denise Paulme, *La Mère Dévorante. Essai sur la Morphologie des Contes Africains* (Paris: Gallimard, 1976); nesta obra a autora destingue além do conto do tipo ascendente e descendente, o tipo ciclíco, em espiral, em espelho, em ampulheta e o tipo complexo.

Bibliografia

Bakhtin, Mikhail. *Esthétique et Théorie du Roman.* Paris: Gallimard,1976.

Carlier, Christophe. *La Clef des Contes.* Paris : Ellipses, 1998.

Chevrier, Jacques. *Littératures d'Afrique Noire de Langue Française.* Paris: Nathan Université, 1999.

Leite, Ana Mafalda. *A Poética de José Craveirinha.* Lisboa: Vega, 1990.

Loiseau, Sylvie. *Les Pouvoirs du Conte.* Paris: PUF, 1992.

Matusse, Gilberto. *A Construção da Imagem da Moçambicanidade em José Craveirinha, Mia Couto e Ungulani Ba Ka Khosa.* Maputo: Imprensa Universitária, 1997.

Obiechina, Emmanuel. "Narrative Proverbs in the African Novel." In *Oral Tradition* 2 (Oct. 1992).

Paulme, Denise. *La Mère Dévorante. Essai sur la Morphologie des Contes Africains.* Paris: Gallimard, 1976.

Robert, Marthe. *Roman des Origines et Origines du Roman.* Paris: Grasset, 1972.

Stalloni,Yves. *Les Genres Littéraires.* Paris: Nathan Université, 2001.

Todorov, Tzvetan. *Os Géneros do Discurso.* Lisboa: Ed.70, 1978.

Ana Mafalda Leite é Professora da Faculdade de Letras da Universidade de Lisboa. Docência e investigação na área das Literaturas de Língua Portuguesa, nos domínios da história literária, relações comparadas e estudos pós-coloniais. Publicou, entre outros, *A Poética de José Craveirinha* (1990), *Oralidades & Escritas nas Literaturas Africanas* (1998), *Literaturas Africanas e Formulações Pós-Coloniais* (2003).

História literária em Angola e Moçambique e fixação do cânone da crítica

Ana Maria Martinho

Resumo. As literaturas de Moçambique e Angola passaram por um intenso processo de discussão crítica e de fixação canónica, quase sempre de natureza ideológica, que discutimos neste artigo. Uma das dificuldades de entendimento sobre esta problemática reside na própria literatura de transmissão oral. Falar da tradição e do cânone em África é a nosso ver de grande complexidade, pelo facto de existirem duas tradições activas – uma oral e outra escrita – que evoluiram em grande parte em oposição uma à outra e que foram consideradas pela crítica de formas muito diversas.

As literaturas de Angola e Moçambique, tal como se nos apresentam na actualidade, passaram por um intenso processo de discussão crítica e de fixação canónica, sendo esta vista como um imperativo histórico, determinante para a selecção e expurgo de autores e obras, em nome de imperativos de ordem muito diversa, mas quase sempre de natureza ideológica explícita. Foi fundamentalmente a produção das décadas de 50 e de 60 que esteve no centro deste debate, bem como as leituras críticas correspondentes, relidas e muitas vezes corrigidas nos anos 70.

Foram de tal forma determinantes estes debates, que ainda hoje alimentam inúmeras divergências entre os críticos. Quanto a nós, o que consideramos relevante é que, independentemente das motivações dos seus protagonistas, os diversos procedimentos de selecção artística e todo o período que os acolheu, foi responsável pela visibilidade de autores e de textos que geraram movimentos de aproximação e negação de paradigmas visíveis até aos dias de hoje. Passamos a apresentar alguns factos que podem deixar informação significativa sobre esta matéria e terminaremos com a enumeração dos autores privilegiados pela crítica, muitos dos quais ainda hoje podemos encontrar nos textos escolares, o que constitui sempre um indicador não negligenciável na disseminação das preferências oficiais.

Assim, para compreendermos o modo como em Angola e Moçambique se evoluiu no tocante à centralidade de textos e autores nos respectivos sistemas literários, importará lembrarmos alguns dos momentos fundamentais em termos das respectivas histórias literárias e igualmente os condicionalismos que presidiram desde sempre a esse efeito selectivo.

Tais pressupostos são de toda a ordem: cronológicos, temáticos, ideológicos, linguísticos, literários. Traçando uma breve história do que nestas literaturas é comummente apontado como fundamental, importa distinguir sobretudo o que pode considerar-se como definidor de nacionalidade literária do que é, provavelmente, de natureza circunstancial.

Em Angola é habitual situar-se a literatura claramente radicada em termos nacionais a partir do século XIX, com alguma resistência por parte de sectores que a vêem mais como produto da década de 50, pelo surgimento de movimentos literários e programáticos novos. Hoje teremos que aceitar, e parece desenhar-se algum consenso sobre a questão, ou pelo menos pouca resistência à hipótese, que, se já havia escritores angolanos no século XVII em solo angolano, provavelmente a literatura deste país começou desde então, tenha ela as características que tiver.

Com a fixação da imprensa (em 1845 em Angola e em 1854 em Moçambique), foi possível a emergência de produções literárias tanto associadas a periódicos como de autor, em que se destacam José da Silva Maia Ferreira (1827-1881) e Alfredo Troni (1845-1904) no primeiro caso, e Campos Oliveira (1847-1911) e Ruy de Noronha (1909- 1943) no segundo. O facto de se publicar, durante a segunda metade do século XIX, o *Almanach luso-brasileiro de lembranças* (a edição da ALAC, de 1993, inclui textos datados de entre 1854 e 1932), que contava com a participação de escritores de todos os espaços de língua portuguesa, teve igualmente uma importância decisiva, em termos formativos, para várias gerações.

Referindo-se a Moçambique, Manuel Ferreira, procurando enquadrar toda esta produção, bem como a que antecederá as independências, dirá em "Do conceito de literatura moçambicana":

> (...) no período colonial defendemos um critério para a definição das literaturas africanas de língua portuguesa que se baseava, fundamentalmente, na temática e no modo como o sujeito de enunciação se colocava no desenvolvimento textual dos temas. Era a tendência geral para os que se assumiam numa perspectiva anti-colonialista. (...) Constituía, sobretudo, uma reacção contra a Literatura Colonial, incapaz de incorporar uma visão concreta do homem e dos factos culturais, ideológicos ou outros autenticamente africanos. (...) processo colectivo de revelação e valorização do universo especificamente nacional.[1]

Podem por este depoimento depreender-se dois dos critérios fundamentais para a *nacionalização* literária e muito frequentemente recuperados: uma temática consentânea com a opção anti-colonial; escritores motivados a elegerem sujeitos de enunciação não contraditórios em relação a uma escolha de base colectiva, africana por via do empenhamento e do compromisso. O fazer-se depender uma estética africana de uma ética de intervenção implicaria, então, em nosso entender, que a escrita criativa se situaria em níveis facilmente identificáveis pela referencialidade, admitindo-se portanto que a criação pode ser mais discursiva e menos poética sem prejuízo do seu valor dentro do sistema.

O modo que outros críticos encontraram para contrariar ou modalizar esta perspectiva passou pela dotação de um estatuto de dignidade àquela literatura que, mesmo se de sobrevalorização exótica, e por essa via claramente exógena, viria acompanhada de uma aplicação dos elementos colhidos nas culturas de contacto. Por outro lado, procurou-se também chamar a atenção para a necessidade de demarcar qualitativamente as diferentes produções, como forma de recuperar textos e autores que, negados pela África pós-colonial, teriam lugar numa panorâmica histórica das suas literaturas.

Assim, no primeiro caso estamos em presença da definição de um cânone de aferição ideológica, no segundo de um enfraquecimento desse mesmo cânone através da aposição de noções de valor extensíveis a todas as produções de referência africana. Esta problemática parece ser de facto o dado inibidor de uma leitura descomprometida destes fenómenos: atribuir a uma conteudística relacionada com África a responsabilidade de definição e enquadramento nacional e histórico dos diferentes autores que lá nasceram ou por lá passaram, é uma empresa que dificilmente nos permitirá aproximações rigorosas aos factos e às leituras. Se estas preocupações são necessárias à constituição de uma História da Literatura para cada um dos países envolvidos, não deixam de ser um terreno de difícil construção epistemológica pela extensão e diversidade das implicações de natureza ideológica que colocam.

No figurino pós-colonial a literatura angolana acolheu tópicos do pensamento anti-colonial, em face da afirmação de um país renovado politicamente e que procurava encontrar paradigmas literários também novos. Refere-se com muita insistência a importância do grupo "Vamos descobrir Angola!" neste processo; cremos no entanto que teve maior durabilidade na literatura angolana a filiação oitocentista, romântica, de muitos autores. Já durante os anos 60 e 70 houve um efectivo esforço de africanização do discurso, e a tentativa de rupturas visíveis com a literatura intimista ou autobiográfica, embora tal efeito não tenha chegado, em todos os casos, a concretizar-se.

Alguns críticos faziam depender o problema da distinção entre uma literatura de viagens e expansão, de uma outra com raízes editoriais em África, e em que os autores respondiam a critérios de nacionalidade literária de múltipla interpretação (ora marcada pelo nascimento ora pelo percurso biográfico). Em todo o caso, esta leitura era ainda tutelada pelo conteúdo dos seus textos e pela leitura ideológica das suas obras. A importância destes movimentos serem dominantes e a valorização dada a posturas como a de Mário de Andrade (que considerava existirem basicamente três tendências nas literaturas africanas em língua portuguesa: a da *negritude,* a da *diferenciação* e a do *protesto e denúncia*),[2] parece-nos operatória mas insuficiente para entendermos a complexidade de sistemas que contam com proveniências estéticas e éticas de toda a ordem.

O que se passa em Moçambique é relativamente equivalente ao caso angolano, sendo que a obra de autores como Noémia de Sousa e Craveirinha (nascidos respectivamente em 1926 e 1922), facilita a leitura da transição entre estas questões. A lírica de ambos permite-nos definir um eixo de relações entre os mundos africanos e europeus a partir da herança estética de Ruy de Noronha (1909-1943) e por contraste com a diversidade formal do grupo de *Msaho.* Este facto detém algumas semelhanças com o tipo de colaboração que ocorre na *Mensagem* da CEI (Casa de Estudantes do Império) durante os anos 40. Aí, é nítida a diversidade de escolhas formais, a independência temática, a filiação estética multiforme, fácil de comprovar pela leitura de colaboradores como Fernando Bettencourt, Orlando de Albuquerque, António Navarro, Vítor Evaristo, Vítor Matos, entre uma opção europeia e a exortação de traços africanos.

Assumirá, neste contexto, especial relevo a separata "Poesia em Moçambique" datada de Janeiro-Julho de 51.[3] Esta edição foge um pouco à regra que prevalece para os boletins de edição regular durante os anos 50, incluindo autores ligados de alguma forma a Moçambique e procurando dar lugar a muitas e diversas posturas estéticas. Os autores que aí privilegiam tópicos claramente africanos são Fonseca Amaral, José Mathias Ferreira Jr., Orlando de Albuquerque, Ruy de Noronha, Vera Micaia (i.e., Noémia de Sousa), António de Navarro, etc.

Em número de Abril de 63, e confirmando a tendência mais especulativa dos contributos dos anos 60, no texto "A poesia moçambicana e os críticos de óculos," Alfredo Margarido discutirá o conceito de Negritude para Rui Knopfli a partir da sua crítica à edição dedicada à poesia de Moçambique, considerando que ele revelava preconceitos de cor que não lhe permitiam ser mais claro.

A questão não parece ser muito relevante para o segundo; no seu poema "Naturalidade," Knopfli interroga-se precisamente sobre a sua formação europeia e a sua vivência africana. Na continuação do primeiro texto, Margarido invectiva este poeta, (em "do poeta Knopfli à cultura moçambicana"), afirmando que só a literatura comprometida pode definir o ponto de encontro entre as formas da poesia erudita e as da poesia popular.

Datados de 63, textos de Ilídio Rocha ("A Praia") e Craveirinha ("Grito Negro") ilustram a persistência de modelos europeus, híbridos, e de pesquisa africana. O que pontifica nesta colaboração é em boa medida a presença de autores revelados ou participantes do periódico *Itinerário* (1941-1955). Assim, aquilo que veio a surgir em Angola a partir de 48 já se fazia sentir também em Moçambique.

O nacionalismo das publicações periódicas, progressivamente acentuado, não é de estranhar nem deve associar-se exclusivamente a fenómenos emergentes durante os anos 40 e 50; na realidade, existiu sempre nestes países uma tradição jornalística facilitadora desse fenómeno. Terá havido, isso sim, uma actualização das mesmas questões vertidas desta feita para uma linguagem mais marcada por um léxico que se vinha impondo desde o início do século por toda a África e que resultava da relação com os mundos negros de outros espaços.

Não deixa de ser verdade, no entanto, que as literaturas angolana e moçambicana se encontram num quadro formativo que tem suporte, no fundamental, no que ocorreu na *Mensagem* da CEI, publicada entre 48 e 64. O facto de se achar sediada em Portugal terá dificultado até hoje a visão da sua centralidade. Pouco conhecida no seu conjunto, muito comentada em segunda mão, deve merecer uma apreciação mais justa.

Independentemente de a *Mensagem* da Anangola ser tida por africana e africanizante, aqueloutra marcou mais claramente a transição e contactos entre os diferentes universos literários africanos lusófonos, e manteve até ao último número uma relação de compromisso com os diferentes sistemas, antecipando também a consideração, hoje obrigatória, de literatura de diáspora. Em todo o caso, pode dizer-se que os poetas da *Mensagem* de Luanda constituem uma geração independente, vinculada politicamente, nuns casos dentro de um quadro claramente angolano, noutros de prioridade negritudinista. É também consensual que o movimento correspondeu a uma fase de viragem na literatura angolana, quer tal tenha decorrido pela sua natureza intrínseca, quer por necessidade conjuntural de dar início à demarcação clara entre a literatura portuguesa e a produzida em África.

Dentro deste quadro geral, e independentemente da relativa indiferença atribuída a este domínio crítico, a consideração de um cânone dominante nos dias de hoje pode, em nosso entender, retirar-se ainda da existência das matrizes criativas e interpretativas resultantes de uma tradição não-grafada, oral, e sobretudo conhecidas através de traduções, transcrições e do aproveitamento parcial de aforismos e de estruturas marcadas pelas línguas bantu (tanto para a prosa quanto para os textos em verso). Determinadas pelas narrativas e saberes tradicionais, chegam-nos por via de intérpretes que são quase sempre também tradutores; de um modo geral pertencendo à etnia de que falam, constituem interlocutores entre dois mundos e nesse sentido colocam-nos face a verdades que, adaptadas a realidades parcialmente partilhadas com os seus leitores, pressupõem a interpretação e a eleição de discursos de consenso. Trata-se assim de mundos que, pelo facto de serem em si mesmos detentores de uma unidade ética resultante de sedimentações culturais antigas, recolhem o crédito de estarem simultaneamente próximos de dois ou mais contextos culturais sem se comprometerem exclusivamente com nenhum deles. Independentemente dos efeitos de desgaste que sofreu, esta tradição manteve vitalidade e presença indiscutível nos cânones angolano e moçambicano.

Quanto à literatura grafada, há que lembrar a que chegou aos escritores do século XIX, tendo seguido a pesquisa de uma angolanidade e moçambicanidade que se afirmavam frequentemente sem distintivo anticolonial explícito; também esta se viu continuada por autores que já neste século se interessaram por uma norma de radicação *antiga*. Incluem-se neste conjunto nomes de todas as gerações, de Maia Ferreira a Manuel Rui, passando por Alda Lara; de Campos Oliveira a Ba Ka Khosa, passando por José Craveirinha. Aqui se centram as maiores dificuldades de constituição do cânone oficial.

Por outro lado, há que referir, com existência paralela, uma prática marcada pelas vertentes sul-americana e negritudinista. Circunstancial, é sobretudo associável a uma literatura de oposição ao sistema colonial e de guerrilha.

Neste quadro, a novidade irá residir na introdução de uma nova experiência de escrita, regulada por uma herança literária (retórica e discursiva) de língua inglesa, de que o ficcionista angolano Sousa Jamba é um exemplo: aqui reside a nosso ver o primeiro sinal de que há mundos novos em presença. O facto de a produção deste angolano nos chegar por tradução da língua inglesa é desde logo um primeiro sintoma. O segundo é que, pela primeira vez, também não são os mundos urbanos de Angola que determinam as referências literárias. Partindo da realidade da Zâmbia, do exílio em África, abre-se um contexto novo e de algum modo estranho mesmo para os angolanos. A divergência semântica e pragmática que tal facto implica obriga-nos à revisão do que conhecemos sobre esta literatura (parece-nos muito provável que a literatura moçambicana, por outra ordem de razões, associáveis à existência de de um espaço sul africano de interesses comuns, venha a apresentar características de algum modo equivalentes).

De facto, em Moçambique, alguns autores mais jovens aparentam filiação em movimentos exógenos, portugueses e anglo-saxónicos (como Eduardo White, por exemplo) o que tem, segundo cremos, a sua primeira origem dentro da literatura escrita por autores como Rui Knopfli (ou mesmo Grabato Dias e Eugénio Lisboa), marcados por experiências assumidamente cosmopolitas.

Também a narrativa histórica (tanto de base documental explícita como de referência particularizante) vem ocupando um lugar fundamental de reunião de todos estes efeitos: por um lado recupera traços da história nacional e recompõe esses mesmos traços por via de um discurso literário; por outro fá-lo por um olhar endógeno e rectificador. Os casos de Manuel Rui (com *Quem me dera ser onda*) e de Pepetela (com *A Geração da utopia*) são sintomáticos deste efeito. Os jovens poetas angolanos, e nomeadamente os que participam na antologia *No caminho doloroso das coisas*,[4] recuperaram a tradição europeia e brasileira a par de uma afirmação étnica pontual (a lembrar os contributos fundamentais de Arlindo Barbeitos e Ruy Duarte de Carvalho, radicados nas culturas de transmissão oral).

Um crítico que não hesitou em enunciar um cânone preciso de autores foi Amândio César. Fez o levantamento do processo de evolução da literatura produzida em África com a preocupação de não considerar divergências estéticas, preferindo apontar factores de natureza uniformizante. Em relação a Moçambique, valorizou as narrativas de viagens, e os nomes de Almeida d'Eça, de Correia de Matos e de João Dias. Na poesia, referiu António de Navarro para os anos 40. E, sobre Ruy de Noronha, lembrou que em "Quenguêlêquêzê" se teria manifestado como demiurgo da futura expressão poética moçambicana. Na década seguinte, mais importante do que Navarro, serão, em seu entender, A. dos Santos Abranches, ligado em Coimbra ao neo-realismo, e os antologiadores da CEI, Orlando de Albuquerque e Vítor Evaristo.

Um esforço de apreciação distinto será apresentado por diversos outros críticos e de acordo com argumentos mais selectivos e menos panorâmicos. É fácil de reconhecer, por exemplo, que muitos dos textos escritos durante o período colonial se revelaram pelo excesso místico e exótico, havendo críticos que distinguem nesse contexto os contributos de Vieira da Cruz e de Bessa Vitor, indicando que terão concorrido para a definição de uma poética angolana contemporânea. Assis Junior, Óscar Ribas e Castro Soromenho são, por outro lado, responsáveis por uma ficção com equivalentes pressupostos. Apresentam-se todos eles, *grosso modo,* como autores em que, por via de uma afectação à terra angolana (determinante nos motivos seleccionados) e da ausência de rupturas com o paradigma europeu, se revela uma literatura marcada pela síntese dos diferentes mundos em presença.

Entre a aparente contradição de escritores negros a exaltar os mundos criados pelo colono, e a de portugueses radicados a preferirem como veículo de expressão um discurso híbrido, em que é patente o esforço de mimetização de línguas e hábitos locais, o resultado é com certeza o de uma acentuada complexidade ética que não exclui os mundos tradicionais embora se demore por vezes na dificuldade da sua compreensão.

Mário de Andrade, no seu *Caderno de poesia Negra de Expressão Portuguesa,* de 1953, lembrará como autores fundamentais: de Angola, Agostinho Neto, António Jacinto e Viriato da Cruz; Noémia de Sousa, de Moçambique; Alda do Espírito Santo e Francisco José Tenreiro, de São Tomé e Príncipe. Considera-os representantes da "vanguarda literária desses países, tanto pelo conteúdo dos seus poemas como pelo papel desempenhado nos movimentos culturais de carácter nacionalista."[5]

A explicitação do cânone pós-independência estará ligada ao peso de actos políticos determinados. Assumindo uma perspectiva também claramente ideológica, Antero Abreu, em representação da União de Escritores Angolanos, referirá, na sessão inaugural da VI Conferência dos Escritores Afro-Asiáticos (que decorreu entre 26 de Junho e 3 de Julho de 1979 em Luanda), momentos e nomes que vê como fundamentais. E lembra, uma "(...) linhagem que vem já do século XVII e principalmente do XIX," reconhecendo que a literatura negra angolana é das mais antigas na África negra. Para ele, "(...) em Angola, ser escritor é ser nacionalista e revolucionário," evocando, além dos nomes de Cordeiro da Matta e Paixão Franco (responsável pela formação da Associação Literária Angolense), Castro Soromenho, também precursor, o movimento Anangola, *Mensagem - a voz dos naturais de Angola,* 1950 (que a seu ver determinou o início da época moderna da literatura angolana, e através do qual surgem Agostinho Neto, António Jacinto, Viriato da Cruz ("A partir da Mensagem, podemos dizê-lo, a actividade literária desemboca na actividade política e com ela se confunde.").[6]

Para aquele crítico, a CEI corresponderá a um processo de consciencialização com responsabilidade na publicação da *Mensagem*, de Lisboa, e da *Meridiano*, de Coimbra, onde se revelam novos valores e se sagram outros. Em 61, a Sociedade Cultural de Angola, com *Cultura*, terá contribuido para a afirmação de Luandino, Arnaldo Santos, António Cardoso. Considera também fundamentais os escritores da guerrilha – Costa Andrade, Nicolau Spencer, Gasmin Rodrigues, Emanuel Corgo, Pepetela, e os da prisão – Agostinho Mendes de Carvalho, Manuel Pacavira. E continua: "Outros tinham dado ou continuaram a dar o seu contributo para uma literatura nacional," como são os casos de António Assis Junior, Aires de Almeida Santos, Alda Lara, Alexandre Dáskalos, Óscar Ribas, Manuel Rui, Jofre Rocha, Boaventura Cardoso.

As palavras que cita de A. Neto confirmam a sua opção pelo cânone enunciado: "(...) a literatura de Angola e, podemos estender um pouco mais dizendo que a arte em Angola, esteve sempre ao serviço da revolução."[7] Criada logo a seguir ao próprio processo de independência nacional, a UEA (União de Escritores Angolanos) tornou-se um dos pilares do sentido revolucionário que a sociedade procurava tomar.

Procurava-se assim afirmar a literatura pelo lado revolucionário, e o cânone que por esta via se constituiu, tanto nos seus representantes *protocanónicos* como *deuterocanónicos,* revela o contributo interno para a constituição de um efeito de identidade que passava pela necessidade de transformação e correcção sociais. Este processo relaciona-se ainda com o que diz A. Neto: "O que devemos fazer para conservar a nossa cultura? (...) devemos é retirar daquilo que resultou do contacto entre diferentes povos o necessário para o progresso actual da nossa própria cultura,"[8] assim definindo a exigência de uma elite e da própria noção de expurgo ("Nós sabemos que uma cultura de carácter nacional sairá deste confronto quotidiano, confronto onde se encontram o velho e o novo, o produto de qualidade superior, como as obras de alguns escritores, como o folclore de alguns grupos, como os trabalhos de alguns pintores, de alguns músicos, etc., com os produtos fáceis e de baixa qualidade dos restantes. Mas essa curva sinusóide é justamente a curva matemática do início do processo, e quanto maior for a amplitude dos baixos e dos altos, mais profundo será o resultado obtido.").[9]

As noções de criatividade e a representatividade deduzem-se deste quadro e dependem directamente de um projecto que é revolucionário e político. Dado confirmado sobejamente por E. Ferreira, em *A crítica neo-realista:*

> A literatura e a arte, como formas ideológicas, estão abrangidas nesta lei da evolução social. (...) A literatura e a arte são determinadas, assim como todas as formas ideológicas, por condições objectivas de criação e desenvolvimento. (...) A literatura é uma forma ideológica integrada numa ideologia, isto é: num conjunto de ideias formando um sistema, uma teoria, uma cultura. A literatura é a expressão de uma cultura.[10]

Ao referir-se à metodologia da crítica neo-realista, lembra que "(...) no reflexo estético o particular constitui o ponto de encontro dos dois movimentos. Movimento do particular para o universal e do universal para o particular. Movimento do particular para o singular e do singular para o particular. Em ambos, é conclusivo o movimento para o particular."[11] A tónica neste efeito de particularização, resulta, em nosso entender, numa hipótese limitativa de enquadramento da tradição, uma vez que radica numa forma de determinismo que impede a possibilidade autónoma do individual e destaca processos de filiação prioritariamente social. Assim sendo, as próprias oraturas teriam que ser avaliadas à luz de imperativos revolucionários, o que naturalmente lhes limitaria as virtudes construtivista, mágica e ritual.

É relativamente fácil enumerar alguns factos e referências que nos revelam indícios de uma enorme diversidade na análise e selecção de autores e textos ao longo do tempo, mas o que parece mais difícil, senão impossível, é organizar um cânone de consenso, quer ele tenha as características de uma pesquisa de valor monumental quer procure a validação de cânones móveis.[12] Nesse particular, cabe à literatura de transmissão oral a responsabilidade pela impossibilidade de organização desse consenso e não exclusivamente às diferenças de natureza epistemológica que encontramos na crítica à literatura escrita. É aliás significativo que não exista praticamente nenhuma crítica sistemática sobre a oralidade angolana ou moçambicana.

Falar da tradição e do cânone em África é a nosso ver de grande complexidade, pelo facto de existirem duas tradições activas – uma oral e outra escrita – que evoluíram em grande parte em oposição uma à outra e que foram consideradas pela crítica de formas muito diversas. Esta oposição, sobretudo retórica, que radica em diferentes formas de recuperação do passado, implica similitude funcional (na aproximação à disciplina e ao poder; na centralidade argumentativa e morigeradora; na eleição de transmissores da palavra escrita ou oral; na preservação dogmática), mas não hermenêutica. E esse é talvez o dado mais inibidor de uma discussão conclusiva sobre autoria e identidade cultural em Angola e Moçambique.

Notas

[1] Cfr. Ferreira, Manuel, *O mancebo e trovador Campos Oliveira* (Lisboa: INCM, 1985, Escritores dos Países de Língua Portuguesa 2), 27-30.

[2]Cfr. Andrade, Mário de, *Antologia temática de poesia africana*, vol.1: *na noite grávida de punhais* (Lisboa: Sá da Costa, 1976, Vozes do Mundo 5), 7-10.

[3] Teve a organização de Orlando de Albuquerque e Vítor Evaristo e incluía em boa parte poemas retirados do periódico *Itinerário.*

[4] Pode ler-se na abertura a esta antologia que os dezanove poetas representados têm em comum o serem "(...) Autores de um discurso legítimo e íntimo quanto o povo, poetas com o coração na Língua que lhes cabe ampliar e enriquecer. Numa só perspectiva, nacionalizar." (cfr. p.12). Aí se exaltam também a diferença e a legitimidade de uma poética nova que têm como pano de fundo a expectativa de transformações sociais e culturais, mas de prioridade totalmente artística.

[5] Organizado em parceria com Francisco J. Tenreiro, foi editado em Lisboa pela Escolar, antecedendo um conjunto de publicações similares.

[6] Cfr. a publicação da União de Escritores Angolanos, *Teses Angolanas – documentos da VI conferência de escritores afro-asiáticos I* (Estudos, 1981).

[7] Cfr. *op.cit.*, 23.

[8] Cfr. *op.cit.*, 73.

[9] Cfr. *op.cit.*, 74-5.

[10] Cfr. 3ª ed., UEA, Lavra & Oficina 27, Jan. 1980, 8-9.

[11] *Id., ibidem,* 17-31, 22.

[12] Enumeramos a seguir os autores nomeados pela crítica, ou por vozes oficiais, como pertencentes ao cânone.

Angola:

A) *O cânone* (não consensual) *da crítica* (*História Geral das Guerras Angolanas; Almanach de Lembranças;* Cordeiro da Matta; José da Silva Maia Ferreira; Pedro Félix Machado; Tomaz Vieira da Cruz; Assis Junior; Óscar Ribas; Castro Soromenho; Geraldo Bessa Victor; Maurício Gomes; Viriato da Cruz; Mário Pinto de Andrade; Agostinho Neto; António Jacinto; Alda

Lara; Alexandre Dáskalos; Ernesto Lara Filho; Aires de Almeida Santos; Mário António; *Mensagem*; Arnaldo Santos; David Mestre; LuandinoVieira; Manuel Rui; Pepetela; Ruy Duarte de Carvalho; Arlindo Barbeitos).

B) *O cânone oficial* (Cordeiro da Matta; Assis Junior; Óscar Ribas; Castro Soromenho; Viriato da Cruz; Agostinho Neto; António Jacinto; Alda Lara; Alexandre Dáskalos; Aires de Almeida Santos; *Mensagem*; Arnaldo Santos; LuandinoVieira; Manuel Rui; Pepetela; Paixão Franco; *Meridiano*; *Cultura;* António Cardoso; Costa Andrade; Nicolau Spencer; Gasmin Rodrigues; Emanuel Corgo; Agostinho Mendes de Carvalho; Manuel pacavira; Jofre Rocha; Boaventura Cardoso).

Moçambique:

A) *O cânone* (não consensual) *da crítica* (Campos Oliveira; João Dias; Ruy de Noronha; José Craveirinha; Noémia de Sousa/Vera Micaia; Orlando Mendes; Fernando Bettencourt; Orlando de Albuquerque; António Navarro; Vítor Evaristo; Vítor Matos; Fonseca Amaral; *Mensagem/Poesia em Moçambique*; Rui Knopfli; Ilídio Rocha; Eugénio Lisboa; Grabato Dias; Mutimati Barnabé João; A. dos Santos Abranches; Alberto Lacerda; *Itinerário; Msaho;* Marcelino dos Santos; Reinaldo Ferreira; Sérgio Vieira).

B) *O cânone oficial* (não identificável).

Bibliografia

Andrade, Mário de. *Antologia temática de poesia africana*, vol.1: *Na noite grávida de punhais.* Lisboa: Sá da Costa, 1976, Vozes do Mundo 5.

César, Amândio. *Novos parágrafos de literatura ultramarina.* Lisboa: Sociedade de Expansão Cultural, 1971.

Feijoó K., Lopito (dir., org.). *Antologia de jovens poetas angolanos – no caminho doloroso das coisas.* Luanda: UEA, 1988.

Ferreira, Eugénio. *A crítica neo-realista.* 3ª ed., UEA, Lavra & Oficina 27, Jan. 1980.

Ferreira, Manuel (dir.); Moser, G., (sel.). *Almanach de Lembranças – 1854-1932.* Linda-a-Velha: ALAC, 1993.

Ferreira, Manuel. *O mancebo e trovador Campos Oliveira.* Lisboa: INCM, 1985, Escritores dos Países de Língua Portuguesa 2.

Martinho, Ana Maria Mão-de-Ferro Martinho. *Cânones literários e educação – os casos angolano e moçambicano.* Lisboa: FCG/FCT, 2001.

Mensagem, ACEI, Lisboa, s/d; policopiado.

Mestre, David. *Nem tudo é poesia.* 2ª ed., Luanda: UEA, 1989, Estudos.

Oliveira, Mário António Fernandes. *Reler África.*

Salvato Trigo. *Ensaios de literatura comparada afro-luso-brasileira.* Lisboa: Vega, s/d, Universidade.

União de Escritores Angolanos. *Teses Angolanas – documentos da VI conferência de escritores afro-asiáticos I.* Estudos, 1981.

Ana Maria Martinho é docente na Universidade Nova de Lisboa. Coordenadora de Mestrado em Culturas, Línguas e Literaturas Africanas. Professora de Literaturas Africanas e de Literatura Brasileira. Membro de conselho europeu de investigadores no âmbito das culturas e línguas africanas. Algumas Publicações: "A Mulher Escritora em África", in *Santa Barbara Portuguese Studies* (1999); *Cânones literários e educação em África (Angola e Moçambique)*, edição da FCG/FCT (2001); CD sobre Bibliografia em Português sobre Línguas Africanas (2001). E-mail: anaferro@iol.pt; estudosafricanos@hotmail.com

Mozambique in Transition in the Narratives of Lília Momplé

Claire Williams

Abstract. Without over-dramatizing and without sentimentalizing, Lília Momplé has managed to portray a multi-layered portrait of Mozambique and its people through the enormous strains and upheavals of its history over the last seventy years. Above all her texts foreground a wide range of Mozambican characters intent on preserving not only their families and their country, but also their own self-respect. It is Momplé's concerns about education and learning from the past, as well as her portrayals of women that will be discussed in the course of this paper, after an overview of her work and her stylistic tendencies.

> Eu própria, Lília Momplé, escrevo sobre tudo o que me tem impressionado, no dia-a-dia, ao longo da vida.
> Lília Momplé[1]

Unlike the sad fables of Luís Bernardo Honwana, the horror of the testimonials collected by Lina Magaia, or the sweeping tragedy of Paulina Chiziane's epic novels, unlike the magical realism and wordplay of the internationally known Mia Couto, Lilia Momplé's stories describe Mozambique's history and the traumatic experiences of her countrymen and women without explicit criticism or excessive lyricism but instead by presenting facts and events and describing her characters with subtle touches that emphasize their tragic situation.[2] Her eye for detail, turns of phrase and sensitivity to emotion combine in her depiction of characters who represent a wide variety of participants in the country's long and painful transition from Portuguese colonial territory to independent state. Although they deal largely with the same topics—the Mozambican struggle, and Mozambicans' struggles, for identity under different regimes—her works differ from those of her contemporaries in their apparent objectiveness and simplicity yet their powerful emotive human force.[3]

Momplé has published three books to date: two collections of short stories and a novella, all of which deal with the reality of Mozambican life.[4] Her stories have won recognition in the form of prizes, not only within Mozambique (the story "Caniço" won first prize in the literary contest marking the centenary of the capital city Maputo) but abroad ("Celina's Party" ["O Baile de Celina" (OCV)] was runner-up in the 2001 Caine prize for African literature, along with a story by Mia Couto), and her work has appeared in anthologies of Mozambican literature, African literature and African literature by women.[5] *Neighbours*, her novella, was translated into English in 2001.[6] She has lived in Lisbon, London, São Paulo and Bahia, returning definitively to Mozambique in the early 1970s to work in the Ministério de Cultura.[7] As well as being Secretary General of the Associação de Escritores Moçambicanos, Momplé has also represented her country as a member of UNESCO.

This role as "ambassador" for her country and spokesperson for her craft as a writer is paralleled in the allegories woven through her fiction, whereby characters can be seen to embody their sex, class, racial group, regional identity, and position in the family unit, as well as symbolizing Mozambique itself on many occasions. Since colonial literature began, conquered lands have been described in terminology that refers to the female body, penetration and domination of it, and paternalistic patriarchal control and occupation of it by the invader. In Momplé's works several characters, (and, by extension, her country) are raped and/or murdered by the colonizers (Suhura, "Ninguém Matou Suhura" [NMS]; the hotel staff in "O Último Pesadelo" [NMS]), mutilated or killed by RENAMO rebels (characters in *Os Olhos da Cobra Verde* and *Neighbours*), or exploited and humiliated during the neo-colonialism of the 1980s (the teacher, "Stress"; Ana Maria and Lola, "Um Canto Para Morrer" [OCV]). Once tended and nourished by its inhabitants, the country is abused by successive waves of oppressors, including its own inhabitants. Momplé's stories lament this self-destructive betrayal of the motherland, "tão duramente libertado do jugo colonial" (OCV 54), and the damage to future development of its citizens who need to fight against the threat of "recolonização."[8]

The breadth of historical and subjective experience and geographical and social type covered in Momplé's stories is impressive. She writes about Mozambique in the 1930s and 40s under the colonial yoke of Portuguese rule; in the 1960s and 70s during the fight for independence, finally gained on 25 June 1975. Furthermore, she also sets stories during the period when the FRELIMO government was under constant threat of RENAMO guerrilla action and destabilization by South African terrorists. The sixteen-year-long so-called civil war was fuelled by FRELIMO's anti-*apartheid* stance and sympathy towards the ANC, including the harboring of ANC members. It is this latest period that most concerns the author (although she does identify the roots of some problems further back in time through flashbacks and tracing family trees) because it was then that the socio-cultural organization of her country was effectively ruined.[9] Her most recently published stories deal with Mozambican society immediately after a peace agreement was signed in Rome between FRELIMO and RENAMO in 1992, ushering in a new era of hope and relative stability.

Momplé's stories are poignant chronicles of life under a series of brutal oppressive systems or in perilous and precarious situations: colonial (and subsequently neo-colonial) rule, traditional patriarchal tribal customs, the continuous threat of rebel attack, the struggle to combat natural disasters. She focuses not on leaders, politicians, or key historical figures in Mozambican history, but on humble people—often country folk, often women—caught in the crossfire and bearing the brunt of racism, oppression and violence. Thus she highlights the fact that each person who died at the hands of *sipaios*, murdered by *matchangas*, blown up by mines, or burnt alive, was an individual with their own life and their own history, emotions, and motivations, extending the emotional dimension of the text by the use of flashbacks.

Momplé places a strong emphasis on the reality behind her fiction: these terrible things did take place, as testimonial accounts and histories of the country prove.[10] In the afterword to *Ninguém Matou Suhura* the author explains: "Estes contos são baseados em factos verídicos, embora os locais e as datas nem sempre correspondem à realidade" (V). In the short introduction to *Neighbours*, she claims that the book was "inspirado em factos reais" (5).[11] There are no framing authorial asides in *Os Olhos da Cobra Verde*, maybe because the stories speak for themselves, but instead an epigraph that sums up Momplé's wider project of learning from suffering and transforming anguish into energy for positive ends: "Feliz do povo que sabe transformar o sofrimento e o desespero em arte e amor" (5).

In the preface to her first collection of stories, Luís Bernardo Honwana confirms that the author is tapping her people's collective grief, alluding to events and details that fellow Mozambicans will recognize all too clearly:

> Efectivamente, Lília Momplé conduz-nos a um passado que é próximo à experiência da generalidade dos moçambicanos de hoje não só porque é recente como até, e mais importantemente, porque constitui um dos pontos de referência do processo moçambicano [...] convidando o leitor à reanálise do nosso quotidiano. (NMS, i)

In a perceptive essay on the story "Stress" (OCV), Phillip Rothwell suggests that Momplé attributes to her characters the symptoms of melancholia in order to signal a betrayal of and by the mother country whereby globalization brings with it a loss of identity.[12] I feel that by appealing to a common grief and a shared past in which they were unable to envisage life "sem o pano de fundo da guerra omnipresente" (OCV 33) she is offering Mozambicans a channel for their traumatic memories and inviting them to participate in a multiple exorcism.[13] By expressing the attitudes and impulses behind characters' actions she attempts to explain why such things may have happened and praises the resourcefulness and perseverance of those who survived.

Ana Maria Martinho describes Momplé's technique as approaching the journalistic or documentary, noting the author's tendency to emblematize:

> Este princípio coloca o escritor como figura que, entre o poder e o povo, garante a transmissão de um vínculo com o passado ao mesmo tempo que retira efemeridade aos acontecimentos relatados. E é precisamente nessa medida que os textos de Lília Momplé se afastam da crónica: não fazem o comentário datado ou pouco definido de episódios reais; não são explicitamente críticos ou só sobre costumes. São, antes, como o conto, narrativas aplicáveis a parcelas do universo, susceptíveis de generalizações *exemplares*.[14]

Although used illustratively, the characters do not lose their individuality.[15] On the contrary, in several stories the author analyses the points of view of several protagonists to provide a balanced picture of a particular situation. This is most obvious in "Ninguém Matou Suhura" (NMS), which is divided into three parts: *O dia do Senhor Administrador*, *O dia de Suhura* and *O Fim do Dia* (which is also the end of Suhura). The first two sections record the actions of the eponymous characters up to the moment they meet, and the last describes their encounter and its fateful consequences. This device allows the narrator to compare and contrast the lifestyles and attitudes of the narcissistic, opportunist Administrador and the innocent peasant girl Suhura. Their living conditions, food, and daily customs are juxtaposed for implicitly critical effect and the halfway house where they meet represents the site of relations between the sexes and races. Suhura's refusal to succumb to the Administrador's demands can only end in tragedy and erasure, counteracted by the defiant use of her name in the title of the story and the whole collection.

A similar effect, whereby the environment explicitly reflects social inequality, is used in "Caniço" (NMS) where Naftal, the central character, works for a white family and travels from his shack in the slums to a smart neighborhood every day:

> Apesar da hora matinal, o [seu] bairro já apresenta um aspecto desolador. O sol é ainda fraco mas já fustiga as palhotas indefesas [...]. Moscas invadem as ruelas de areia solta, zumbindo à volta dos montes de lixo espalhados por toda a parte. [...] Um cheiro a miséria envolve todo o bairro. [...] A cidade se transforma gradualmente à medida que os bairros dos negros vão ficando para trás. [...] Ao aglomerado de palhotas de caniço, seguem-se os casinhotos de madeira e zinco dos mulatos e indianos, de mistura com modestas casas de alvenaria. [...] Finalmente, nos bairros onde só residem colonos, erguem-se apenas prédios e vivendas de alvenaria, ladeando ruas e avenidas verdejantes. E o suave aroma dos jardins e das acácias em flor vai substituindo o cheiro da miséria. (26-7)[16]

The injustice of the situation is underlined by the fact that Naftal has to do the shopping and buy goods his family could never afford: "um regalo para os olhos e um tormento para a alma" (27). Furthermore, he has to water all the beautifully decorative but useless plants in the garden, while his family cannot cultivate enough food to live on. In the face of the cruel irony toiling hard for only a pittance, and even more unjustly, of being wrongly accused of stealing and actually being punished, Naftal has become used to gritting his teeth and accepting that "Tudo faz parte do destino dos negros" (26). His unbearable situation as presented in the story is more than enough reason for the bitterness of the black Mozambicans and justification for their passionate fight for independence.

The use of multiple points of view is clearest in *Neighbours*, in which the lives of a small number of characters interlink on one night in central Maputo, in May, in the mid-1980s. At the climax of the novel, all the protagonists are involved in an armed raid on a flat in the Avenida Emília Daússe—either as victims, perpetrators, or witnesses. The structure of the text, whose chapters relate the events happening simultaneously in three different households in Maputo at 7 p.m., 9 p.m., 11 p.m., 1 a.m. and 8 a.m., match the jigsaw-like fitting together of stories that comprise Momplé's works as a whole. It provides tension and dimension, explaining the motivations and beliefs of each character, as well as capturing their philosophy of life; setting them all out before the reader in equal measure and inviting comparisons. As a microcosm of this technique, the five very different men in the gang preparing for the raid are analyzed one by one to show how they have reached the current state of affairs and why they are prepared to kill innocent people. The reactions of each of them to Mena, their beautiful mulatta hostess, are described. All of them find her attractive, except the evil, aloof South African Boer, for whom she "não passa de uma sombra, alguém que existe apenas para servir os brancos" (N 88). When Momplé does not show the alternative perspective(s), it is because that perspective is obvious. This is usually the case with stereotypical characters like the racist Portuguese colonials of "O Último Pesadelo" (NMS), or the stubborn husband and father figures.

This democratic voicing of those involved fits in with the portrayals of individuals, challenging the stereotypes common in African literature. For example, not all the white characters are paternalistic racist rapists and bullies (although most of them are), notable exceptions being Eugénio ("O Último Pesadelo" [NMS]) and Alberto Cereja ("Era uma Outra Guerra" [OCV]). Not all the colonial wives are idle, vain and narrow-minded like those in "Caniço" (NMS) and "Ninguém Matou Suhura" (NMS); some, like Ana Maria ("Um Canto Para Morrer" [OCV]), Dona Florinda (N) and Assunção ("Era uma Outra Guerra" [OCV]), love their adopted country and try to help its people.[17] Not all the African wives are submissive workers and mothers, not all the African husbands stray after other women, not all the women are young and beautiful but have other valuable qualities instead.[18] Therefore Salimo, the RENAMO soldier who returns to his family in "Xirove," hoping to be greeted as a prodigal son but instead having to face a humiliating ritual of cleansing of sin, gets a brief chance to explain why he colluded in atrocities against his countrymen. He does have the excuse of having been snatched from his village when still a child, and having been inculcated with anti-government ideology. When challenged by his outraged brother, Salimo stammers out his reasons, as he must have been taught: "Mas [...] era preciso [matar e roubar] para termos agora a democracia, acabar com as aldeias comunais, as guias de marcha" (OCV 73). Their aged mother realizes that he is not able to articulate any further: "Só lamentava [ela] que Salimo não estivesse ainda preparado para corresponder com igual franqueza e tentasse, a todo o custo, justificar as atrocidades praticadas em nome de ideias que ele próprio não devia compreender" (OCV 74). Salimo recognizes his estrangement from family and community and leaves home once again, significantly without completing the ceremony that would grant him reintegration as well as symbolic forgiveness.

When looking at her works as a whole, the range of characters represent the multicultural mixture of Mozambican society both racial (European Portuguese and South African whites, Indians, Mauritians, as well as *mestiços*), regional (from the northern interior, the coastal regions, the Ilha de Moçambique and Maputo; from both inner city and shanty town) and political (Frelimo sympathizers, those who uphold the Portuguese regime, Renamo rebels, South African terrorists). She depicts characters of all ages, male and female. If the early stories allow for simple structuralist analysis based on the contrast of behaviors in women and men, blacks and whites, colonials and freedom fighters, this becomes more complicated in the later stories.

In fact, the characters can be seen as parts in the jigsaw of Mozambican society and the sum of Momplé's work seen as a series of interlinking segments. Frustrated Naftal ("Caniço" [NMS]) could grow up to be a revengeful Frelimo guerrilla in another story. Salimo in "Xirove" (OCV) could have been responsible for the murder of Januário's parents in *Neighbours* or the teacher's grandfather in "Stress" (OCV). Someone just like Januário could have taught Alima "O Sonho de Alima" (OCV). Many of those who drift to the cities in the wake of rural atrocities could be displaced members of Vovó Facache's scattered family ("Os Olhos da Cobra Verde" [OCV]).

This impression is strengthened upon consideration of Momplé's first and most bitter collection of stories: *Ninguém Matou Suhura*. They make explicit reference to the political situation, favoring Frelimo actions, and mentioning the harmful effects of Portuguese propaganda. The stories in this collection are dated not according to when they were written but as a subheading indicating the historical and geographical context: Junho de 1935 (the year

Momplé was born); Lourenço Marques, Dezembro de 1945; Lourenço Marques, Dezembro de 1950; Ilha de Moçambique, Novembro de 1970; Luanda, Abril de 1974. Over almost forty years, the author seems to be saying, nothing changed in terms of the colonizers' attitudes towards the colonized in the major cities of Lusophone Africa. The passing of time is also conveyed through the presentation of several generations of one family and the stunted or truncated futures of the younger characters (Naftal, Aidinha, Celina, Suhura) who are prevented from getting an education (in the Western sense of instruction and qualifications) or from achieving equal social status to their white counterparts. In the same collection, the racial situation is shown to be unbearably oppressive for black Mozambicans, yet the revolution is only glimpsed as rumors and distant reports of terrorist activity. This hearsay mars the otherwise comfortable lifestyle of the white colonials. *Neighbours* is clearly set in Maputo in the mid-1980s, right in the middle of the South African destabilization campaign. The stories of *Os Olhos da Cobra Verde* show the consequences of the Acordo Geral de Paz, which should guarantee future peace. It brings liberation to some but tragedy to others in practical as well as psychological terms, due to the large numbers of refugees and landless, and the struggle to find accommodation and rebuild villages.

The reactions of Momplé's characters to the systems of oppression are varied. Some succumb to death or violence as a way out: violence directed against themselves (Mussa Racua, "Aconteceu em Saua-Saua" [NMS]), against others (the teacher, "Stress" [OCV]; Atumane, "Xirove" [OCV]); or against objects (Celina, "O Baile de Celina," [NMS]). However, the overwhelming response is a numb acceptance that matches the powerlessness of the common people, living in a constant state of shock. Wrongly punished Naftal "caminha como um sonâmbulo, sem consciência de si próprio. [...] não quer nada, não deseja nada, não tem vontade de nada" (NMS 30, 31); Celina, not allowed to attend her school's party for final-year students because of her mixed blood, "move-se numa semi-inconsciência de pesadelo" (NMS 46); Suhura, summoned to meet the lecherous Administrador, does so because "não há outra saída [...] não vale a pena resistir. [...] caminha sem ver, indiferente a tudo que não seja o medo incontrolável do que a espera" (NMS 68).[19]

A large part of the contained frustration of these sleepwalking characters concerns the bitter irony that hard work brings no rewards but only further hardships. The waste of life and potential is excruciatingly tragic. Enthusiastic, optimistic characters like Léia and Januário (N), who want to build a new Mozambique, are murdered in a terrorist attack. Others, because of their race or sex, are restricted access to an education, which could provide them a better future. Momplé's positive presentation of teachers and keen learners is an encouragement to her readers to improve their prospects and also their self-respect through education. This backfires for Celina, whose mother's life becomes a quest to ensure that her daughter never suffers like her but achieves "um mínimo de aceitação por parte dos senhores da terra, ou seja, os colonos" (NMS 41), a mission which entails the best education available to mixed-race children and a process of assimilation to the Portuguese language and way of life. D. Violante insists: "Estude filha! Só a instrução pode apagar a nossa cor" (42), but her sacrifices are in vain because racism is too deeply rooted for her daughter to be welcomed into white society.[20]

In later stories, set after Independence, the results are more encouraging. Alima, in "O Sonho de Alima" (OCV), is determined to study in order to "levantar o véu que encerra um mundo de infinitos horizontes" (45), experiencing "momentos de plenitude e triunfo" upon receiving her fourth grade certificate. Her case demonstrates the obstacles faced by African women wanting an access to education because she is hindered firstly by her father's beliefs and then by her husband's:

> Na sua infância e juventude o facto de ser Negro condenava [o pai de Alima] de antemão a permanecer analfabeto. E, mesmo quando, devido ao avanço da guerra de libertação, foi permitido aos seus filhos estudar, jamais sentiu curiosidade em saber o que eles aprendiam naqueles complicados livros, escritos em português, língua que nunca dominou. Quanto à mãe de Alima, o estudo sempre lhe causou uma espécie de temor porque se lhe afigurava pertencer a um universo do qual, por razões várias, fora sempre excluída. (41)

Again, the mother's thwarted life is not to be repeated by the daughter. Alima's husband, although willing to go against tradition for her by not taking another wife in order to produce the children Alima cannot have, becomes "louco de ciúme e furor machista" (42) when she insists on taking evening classes. Another character, Muntaz (N), challenges tradition by effectively choosing university instead of marriage and children. She does so to the despair of her mother, Narguiss, who "como uma 'verdadeira mulher,' quer dizer, dentro de casa e no quintal [...]. Jamais frequentou a escola [...]. Aprendeu, sim, a cozinhar primorosamente com o supremo objectivo de agradar ao homem que um dia a escolhesse" (74). Nevertheless, her training proved unsuccessful in perpetuating either of her marriages, both to unfaithful rogues.

Luckily, there are teachers like Januário (N), who take a real pride and satisfaction in their work, even considering that remuneration is minimal. His zest stems from his love of reading, and it is infectious:

> O seu entusiasmo não podia deixar de se transmitir aos alunos. Estes são, na sua maioria, homens e mulheres ensonados por um dia inteiro de trabalho, cronicamente insaciados pela monotonia da ushua e do repolho diários, abatidos pela perspectiva de ter que regressar a pé às suas suburbanas casas onde nada os espera, além das preocupações do dia seguinte. Apesar disso, Januário consegue levá-los a maravilhar-se com a oculta lógica da gramática, o ritmo de um verso ou a beleza de uma frase, despertando-lhes o gosto de dominar uma lingual que não beberam no leite das suas mães.
>
> Estes pequenos sucessos acordaram nele a iniciativa criadora, adormecida por anos de trabalho rotineiro, o que lhe permite desenvolver métodos de ensino verdadeiramente originais. (N 80)

Januário's positive outlook in spite of the traumas he has suffered and the day-to-day hardship he endures is a sign that people's resistance and strength will triumph. Love between husband and wife, maternal devotion, and the support provided by networks of family and friends are seen as powerful forces. The bleakness of *Neighbours* is countered by the fact that Mena acts to save others and manages to save herself from an abusive marriage. She reclaims her independence and takes her first steps into "um novo e imprevisível destino" (N 105).[21] Female characters in particular are seen to represent the future because woman has always been, in Momplé's words, "a principal difusora e transmissora de valores culturais, tradições e ritos [...], de usos e costumes [...], formas de arte."[22] The author's determined, forward-thinking *moçambicanas* are important for developing a feminist consciousness in her readers, as a scholar of African literature declares:

> The study of images [...] represents the first realization that something is wrong [...]. Beyond that it becomes a challenge to established male writers to recognize distortions just as it is for racist writers to recognize and correct racial caricatures. For women writers the "woman as victim" character performs a political function,

> directly stimulating empathetic identification in the readers and in a sense challenging them to change. [...] A positive image, then, is one that is in tune with African historical realities and does not stereotype or limit women into postures of dependence or submergence. Instead it searches for more accurate portrayals and ones which suggest the possibility of transcendence. [...] Included here is also making visible the "invisible woman," or audible, the mute, voiceless woman, the woman who exists only as tangential to man and his problems.[23]

Such positive models help to counteract the negative self-image that centuries of racial and patriarchal oppression have fostered, the conviction of "a inferioridade da sua própria raça" (NMS 44) or, more dangerously, the hatred for one's own race that constant abuse promotes in Aidinha ("Caniço" [NMS 24]) and Romu (N 65-8).

Momplé does use her female characters to refer to the traditions, rituals, and beliefs with which African women have had to contend as well as fighting against colonial oppression: lack of education, *lobolo* ("bride price"), polygyny, serial infidelity, the favoring of sons, initiation rites involving genital mutilation, abusive husbands, expectations linked to marriage and child-bearing. She creates women who stand up for themselves, even if it means flouting convention: Manuela, the Administrador's daughter ("Ninguém Matou Suhura" [NMS]), shocks and shames her parents by declaring that she would consider marrying a black man. Likewise, financially independent tia Mariamo ("Os Olhos da Cobra Verde" [OCV]) "decidiu ficar solteira" (OCV 28), in spite of having children by several men. Facache, Mariamo's niece, admires her courage and learns from her "o espírito independente e lutador e a firme convicção de que, na vida, é preciso contar com as próprias forças" (28). This strength enables her to start up and run her own successful business.

The stories of *Os Olhos da Cobra Verde* refer back to the days of struggle for independence but focus mostly on the problems of reconstructing the country, denouncing the administrative chaos and corruption and the disillusionment of those who had been euphoric and optimistic. Nevertheless, the green snake in the story that gives its name to the collection is a sign of good luck and good news. These later stories illustrate Momplé's championing of those who stand up for their rights and their self-respect even against the odds. Most survive, but casualties are inevitable. Although melancholic, Momplé's narratives are also an encouragement not to admit defeat, a rallying cry that raises consciousness and boosts confidence. She always includes characters committed to building a better future for their country, with energy and optimism, who maintain their dignity in the face of overwhelming discrimination and humiliation.

Notes

[1] Lília Momplé, "A Mulher Escritora e o Cânone – Aproximação e Ruptura," 32.

[2] Luís Bernardo Honwana, *Nós Matámos o Cão-Tinhoso*; Lina Magaia, *Dumba Nenque, Run for Your Life: Peasant Tales of Tragedy in Mozambique* and *Delehta: Pulos na Vida*; Paulina Chiziane, e.g., *Balada de Amor ao Vento* and *Ventos do Apocalipse*; Mia Couto, e.g., *Vozes Anoitecidas* and *Cada Homem é uma Raça.*

[3] Nelson Saúte, "Identidades em literatura (Espaço público, literature e identidade)." See also Fátima Mendonça, "Literatura Moçambicana: o que é isso?"; and Nelson Saúte, *As Mãos dos Pretos: Antologia do Conto Moçambicano.*

[4] Lília Momplé, *Ninguém Matou Suhura*; *Neighbours*; *Os Olhos da Cobra Verde*. For convenience, references to these editions will be made in the texts and the titles abbreviated to NMS, N and OCV respectively.

[5] "Stress," in *Opening Spaces: An Anthology of Contemporary African Women's Writing*, ed. Yvonne Vera; "Celina's Banquet," in *The Picador Book of African Stories*, ed. Stephen Gray; "Stress," in *As Mãos dos Pretos: Antologia do Conto Moçambicano*, ed. Nelson Saúte.

[6] *Neighbours: The Story of a Murder.*

[7] In a 1992 interview with Michel Laban she explains how the experience of travelling abroad was an extremely valuable experience, but that she can only write fiction successfully *in* Mozambique (in Laban, *Moçambique. Encontro com Escritores*).

[8] Lília Momplé, in Laban, 588.

[9] Momplé describes the situation in "A Mulher Escritora."

[10] See, for example: Anabella Rodrigues, "Mozambican Women After the Revolution"; Stephanie Urdang, "Women in national liberation movements" and *And Still They Dance: Women, War, and the Struggle for Change in Mozambique.*

[11] Stephanie Urdang reports a similar attack that took place in Maputo on May 29th 1987 when Afrikaans-speaking terrorists broke into a flat across the hall from some South African exiles (*And Still They Dance*, 40). Momplé makes further comments on the testimonial nature of her writing in her interview with Michel Laban.

[12] Phillip Rothwell, "Momplé's Melancholia: Mourning for Mozambique."

[13] Nelson Saúte identifies the cathartic nature of much Mozambican literature and its function as an "exorcismo dos demonios" that also attempts to "debelar os fantasmas nacionais": Prefácio, *As Mãos dos Pretos*, 18, 19.

[14] Ana Maria Mão-de-Ferro Martinho, *Contos de África escritos por Mulheres*, 107-8.

[15] This concept of "pluralism without hierarchy" is identified by Ana Teixeira as an Afrocentric concept particularly useful when analyzing Mozambican literature. Her insightful thesis, "Building a Bridge: Reconciling European and African World-Views in the Works of Contemporary Mozambican Women Writers," is one of the very few studies in English to deal with Mozambican women's writing.

[16] Similar descriptions of the division of the city into zones according to social status (linked to race) and in particular the problems in supplying accommodation for refugees and landless citizens in Maputo are provided in the stories "Stress" and "Um Canto Para Morrer" (OCV).

17 On stereotypical white characters, see Mineke Schipper's comments: the men "are rapists (in Africa the colonial men took at will the local African women or children). Their rude behaviour is uncivilized, they steal (emptying Africa of its riches); they are lazy (Africans do all the work for them and are paid very little). [...] The image of the white man, just like its counterpart, consists of numerous observations that are indicative of mistrust and misunderstandings, dividing black from white. The most striking thing about the white characters in a number of African novels, in addition to their superiority complex, is that they exhibit pathological greed: they are eternally hungry for money, more property and more power. [...] The white colonial woman as a character in African novels rarely has a status of her own; she has no occupation and is totally dependent on her husband and his position. [...] The problem that seems to occupy much of her time is her appearance: her complexion, her figure, her clothes, her jewellery. [...] Another favourite pastime is exchanging critical comments on Africa and the Africans" (38-9, 51, 54).

18 On stereotypical images of women in African literature, see Deidre LaPin, "Women in African Literature"; and several of the essays in *Ngambika: Studies of Women in African Literature*, eds Carole Boyce Davies and Anne Adams Graves.

19 This atmosphere was encountered by Stephanie Urdang on her fieldwork in Mozambique in the mid and late 1980s, in the book *And Still They Dance*. She noted a strange calmness in a village under the constant threat of bandit attack (52-3), and an "absence of expression" on the faces of women in a northern refugee camp, their eyes "empty of existence" (89).

20 Another way out for black and mulatto women is sex—as prostitutes or the lovers of white men. Aidinha's resentment of the discrimination that limits her living a decent life leads her to become a prostitute: "farta da miséria, sendo negra, não tinha outro caminho. O ódio que a rapariga sentiu por toda a vida passada, abrangia a mãe também" (NMS 24). She can feel superior when white South Africans fight for her favors. Attractive mulatta Leonor ("O Baile de Celina" [NMS]), is proud of having seduced many white husbands away from their wives.

21 Momplé describes how Mena was a particularly "stubborn" character to write: "a princípio eu queria que fosse uma mulher sem carácter, que só pensava em coisas fúteis, e no fim é ela que faz com que se descubram os assassinos. Eu não queria que fosse aquela mulher, queria que o romance seguisse outro trilho. E ela não quis!" (in Laban, 586).

22 Lília Momplé, "A Mulher Escritora...", 31.

23 Carole Boyce Davies, "Introduction: Feminist Consciousness and African Literary Criticism," 14-5.

Works Cited

Chiziane, Paulina. *Balada de Amor ao Vento*. Lisbon: Caminho, 1990.

———. *Ventos do Apocalipse*. Lisbon: Caminho, 1999.

Couto, Mia. *Vozes Anoitecidas*. Lisbon: Caminho, 1987.

———. *Cada Homem é uma Raça*. Lisbon: Caminho, 1990.

Davies, Carole Boyce, "Introduction: Feminist Consciousness and African Literary Criticism." *Ngambika: Studies of Women in African Literature*. Eds. Carole Boyce Davies and Anne Adams Graves. Trenton, NJ: Africa World Press, 1986. 1-23.

Gray, Stephen, ed. *The Picador Book of African Stories*. London: Picador, 2001.

Honwana, Luís Bernardo. *Nós Matámos o Cão-Tinhoso*. 3rd ed. Porto: Afrontamento, 1988; col. Fixões. 18.

Laban, Michel. *Moçambique. Encontro com Escritores.* 3 vols. Porto: Fundação Eng. António de Almeida, 1998.

LaPin, Deidre. "Women in African Literature." *African Women South of the Sahara.* Eds. Margaret Jean Hay and Sharon Stichter. London: Longman, 1984. 102-18.

Magaia, Lina. *Dumba Nenque, Run for Your Life: Peasant Tales of Tragedy in Mozambique.* Trenton, NJ: Africa World Press, 1987.

———. *Delehta: Pulos na Vida.* Maputo: Viver, 1994.

Martinho, Ana Maria Mão-de-Ferro. *Contos de África escritos por Mulheres.* Évora: Pendor, 1994; col. Ao Sul. 2.

Mendonça, Fátima. "Literatura Moçambicana: o que é isso?" *Estudos Portugueses e Africanos* 7 (1986): 153-7.

Momplé, Lília. *Ninguém Matou Suhura.* Maputo: Associação dos Escritores Moçambicanos, 1988; col. Karingana. 8.

———. *Neighbours.* Maputo: AEMO, 1995; col. Karingana. 16.

———. *Os Olhos da Cobra Verde.* Maputo: AEMO, 1997; col. Karingana. 18.

———. "A Mulher Escritora e o Cânone – Aproximação e Ruptura." *A Mulher Escritora em África e na América Latina.* Ed. Ana Maria Mão-de-Ferro Martinho. Évora: NUM, 1999. 31-4.

———. "Stress." *Opening Spaces: An Anthology of Contemporary African Women's Writing.* Ed. Yvonne Vera. London: Heinemann, 1999. 100-13.

———. "Celina's Banquet." *The Picador Book of African Stories.* London: Picador, 2001.

———. *Neighbours: The Story of a Murder.* Trans. Richard Bartlett and Isaura de Oliveira. London: Heinemann, 2001.

Rodrigues, Anabella. "Mozambican Women After the Revolution." *Third World – Second Sex.* London: Zed, 1983. 127-34.

Rothwell, Phillip. "Momplé's Melancholia: Mourning for Mozambique." *Portuguese Studies Review* 10.1 (2002): 185-193.

Saúte, Nelson. "Identidades em literatura (Espaço público, literature e identidade)." *Identidade, Moçambicanidade, Moçambicanização.* Dir. Carlos Serra. Maputo: Livraria Universitária, Universidade Eduardo Mondlane, 1998. 79-97.

———. *As Mãos dos Pretos: Antologia do Conto Moçambicano.* Lisbon: Dom Quixote, 2000.

Schipper, Mineke. *Imagining Insiders: Africa and the Question of Belonging.* London: Cassell, 1999.

Teixeira, Ana. "Building a Bridge: Reconciling European and African World-Views in the Works of Contemporary Mozambican Women Writers." Unpublished doctoral thesis, Temple University, 2001.

Urdang, Stephanie. "Women in national liberation movements." *African Women South of the Sahara.* Eds. Margaret Jean Hay and Sharon Stichter. London: Longman, 1984. 156-69.

———. *And Still They Dance: Women, War, and the Struggle for Change in Mozambique.* London: Earthscan, 1989.

Vera, Yvonne, ed. *Opening Spaces: An Anthology of Contemporary African Women's Writing.* London: Heinemann, 1999.

Claire Williams lectures in Lusophone language, literatures and cultures at the University of Liverpool. Her research has focussed largely on the narratives of Lusophone women writers, in particular Clarice Lispector and Maria Gabriela Llansol. Recent publications include a co-edited volume of essays on Lispector, *Closer to the Wild Heart* (Oxford: Legenda / European Humanities Research Council, 2002) and the forthcoming *The Encounter Between Opposites in the Works of Clarice Lispector* (Bristol: HiPLA Monographs, 2003).

Remembering the First Multiparty Elections

The following are memorabilia from the first multiparty elections to take place in Mozambique. They include a famous painting by one of Africa's most important contemporary artists, the Mozambican Malangatana, entitled "Já Votei" (1994), reproduced with his permission and that of Caminho publishers. The painting captures the excitement and attempted inclusion of Mozambican civil society in the elections. One of the figures holds up an ink-stained index finger, a sign that he has performed his civic duty. Each elector was stained in this way on voting as a means of avoiding electoral fraud.

Also included are various political posters used during the election campaign, and copies of the ballot papers for the congressional and presidential elections (from the Gaza electoral circuit).

Malangatana, "Já Votei," 1994.

1994 Election Posters and Ballot Papers

AFONSO DHLAKAMA
VOTA

VOTA
RENAMO
viva a vitória!

Vota
CHISSANO

Vota
FRELIMO
O FUTURO MELHOR

VOTE X
MÁRIO CARLOS MACHEL
CANDIDATO A PRESIDENTE DA REPÚBLICA
PAZ, AMOR E PROGRESSO
DEFENSOR DA DIGNIDADE MOÇAMBICANA

COMISSÃO NACIONAL DE ELEIÇÕES
ELEIÇÃO DA ASSEMBLEIA DA REPÚBLICA

ALIANÇA PATRIÓTICA	AP		
UNIÃO NACIONAL MOÇAMBICANA	UNAMO		
PARTIDO TRABALHISTA	PT		
FRENTE UNIDA DE MOÇAMBIQUE/PARTIDO DE CONVERGÊNCIA DEMOCRÁTICA	FUMO/PCD		
PARTIDO FRELIMO	FRELIMO		
PARTIDO SOCIAL-LIBERAL E DEMOCRÁTICO	SOL		
PARTIDO INDEPENDENTE DE MOÇAMBIQUE	PIMO		
RESISTÊNCIA NACIONAL MOÇAMBICANA	RENAMO		
PARTIDO DO CONGRESSO DEMOCRÁTICO	PACODE		
PARTIDO DO PROGRESSO DO POVO DE MOÇAMBIQUE	PPPM		
PARTIDO DE CONVENÇÃO NACIONAL	PCN		
UNIÃO DEMOCRÁTICA	UD		

COMISSÃO NACIONAL DE ELEIÇÕES
ELEIÇÃO DO PRESIDENTE DA REPÚBLICA

MÁXIMO DIOGO JOSÉ DIAS

CARLOS JOSÉ MARIA JEQUE

CASIMIRO MIGUEL NHAMITHAMBO

MÁRIO FERNANDO CARLOS MACHELE

CARLOS ALEXANDRE DOS REIS

AFONSO MACACHO MARCETA DHLAKAMA

JACOB NEVES SALOMÃO SIBINDY

PADIMBE MAHOSSE KAMATI ANDREA

DOMINGOS ANTÓNIO MASCARENHAS AROUCA

VASCO CAMPIRA MOMBOYA ALFAZEMA

WEHIA MONAKACHO RIPUA

JOAQUIM ALBERTO CHISSANO

Reviews/Recensões

Vinte e Nove Assaltos ou os *Novos Pactos, Outras ficções: Ensaios sobre literaturas afro-luso-brasileiras*, de Laura Cavalcante Padilha. Porto Alegre: EPIDUCRS, 2002. Coimbra: Imbondeiro, 2003.

Margarida Calafate Ribeiro

Depois de tão originalmente trabalhar a obra de Eça de Queirós em *A Ilustre Casa de Ramires: o espaço do desejo* (1989) e a ficção angolana em *Entre Voz e Letra – O Lugar da Ancestralidade na Ficção Angolana do Século XX* (Nitéroi: EDUFF, 1995), em *Novos Pactos. Outras ficções: Ensaios sobre literaturas afro-luso-brasileiras*, Laura Cavalcante Padilha oferece-nos em vinte e nove ensaios uma viagem dialogante por entre algumas das obras basilares da cultura lusófona, utilizando um manancial teórico que desde logo desafia o 'cânone ocidental' branco e masculino ao fazer dialogar, lado a lado, os grandes teóricos ocidentais, mas também os africanos de língua portuguesa, francesa ou inglesa e os brasileiros, pelas privilegiadas vozes de Antônio Cândido, Alfredo Bosi, Silviano Santiago, Leda Martins ou Vera Queirós. 'Fará a África parte do Ocidente?'(p. 241), interroga Laura Padilha. Parodiando o 'olhar sphyngico e fatal' de Pessoa, pelo que ele deixa de fora, Laura Padilha persegue as criações desses lugares outros ou desse 'entrelugar onde a fala própria interage com a alheia, criando-se a terceira margem' (p. 241) ou, por outras palavras, onde se tecem outras vozes em diferença. Mas a indagação da ensaísta vai mais longe ao interrogar também o incipiente 'canône' africano lusófono estabelecido, lido e codificado pelas obras pioneiras de Manuel Ferreira, Gerald Moser ou as conhecidas entrevistas de Michel Laban. Em 'A diferença interroga o cânone' a pergunta perturba: onde estão as mulheres, onde estão os negros ? Será este 'canône' reprodutor do tal outro ocidental masculino, branco, revestido de vestes e vozes africanas? Por que razão se insiste em apontar um centro que apaga as diferenças? Daí a pertinência da frase de Paula Tavares em entrevista a Michel Laban, citada pela ensaísta: 'Eu sinto-me melhor quando grito' (p. 169).

As questões levantadas por Laura Padilha não são, portanto, meramente teóricas ou literárias. São literárias, teóricas, políticas, históricas e sociais e têm a espessura de séculos. Questionam o(s) centro(s) a partir das margens, pois é lá que, nas leituras da ensaísta, se afirmam as diferenças e se depuram as identidades.

Como a autora informa no prefácio que dedica à obra, a reflexão ensaística aqui publicada é fruto de um trabalho de dez anos de participações em congressos, colóquios e outras conversas. A apresentação expressamente fragmentária que este tipo de livro encerra é contornada pela autora ao agrupar as suas tessituras textuais usando as ligações que os textos em análise sugerem, destacando três grandes grupos: 'Dobras narrativas,' com textos dedicados essencialmente à ficção angolana (de Assis Júnior e Alfredo Troni ou Castro Soromenho a Pepetela, Boaventura Cardoso ou Sousa Jamba), mas também a *Partes de África*, de Helder Macedo, a Mia Couto e às 'casas' queirosianas, todos unidos na sua diversidade de dizer África; 'Novas fiandeiras de palavras,' constituído por seis excelentes ensaios integralmente dedicados a sujeitos autorais e poéticos femininos para que assim se ouça 'o grito diferente e, através dele, a fala dos excluídos dos rituais canónicos': Alda Espírito Santo, Alda Lara e Noémia de Sousa são lidas nas suas vozes rasgadas contra o(s) colonialismo(s), mas também Odete Semedo, Vera Duarte e marcadamente Paula Tavares; e finalmente a terceira parte: 'Diálogos, reconversões, contaminações,' composta por dez ensaios, de que destaco os dedicados à poética de Edmilson de Almeida Pereira, na sua forma de dizer África no Brasil e estudado comparativamente com duas grandes vozes africanas: Francisco José Tenreiro e Ruy Duarte de Carvalho.

Assim o livro ganha organicidade e unidade, destacando a navegação surpreendente e ambiciosa que Laura Padilha nos oferece da ficção e da poesia produzida em língua portuguesa. Ora trabalhando os textos portugueses, angolanos, moçambicanos, sãotomenses ou brasileiros per si, ora analisando as margens dos universos literários, onde situa as escritas regularmente silenciadas das mulheres africanas ou dos negros no Brasil, ora ainda usando a dimensão comparativa como, por exemplo, nos pertinentes cruzamentos entre as vozes poéticas de Alda Lara e de Florbela Espanca, de Edmilson de Almeida Pereira e de Ruy Duarte Carvalho, de Edmilson de Almeida Pereira e de Francisco José Tenreiro e, de um ponto de vista ficcional, entre Helder Macedo e Mia Couto, Pepetela e Manuel Rui ou Pepetela e Boaventura Cardoso, Laura Padilha dá-nos a possibilidade de pensar criticamente o universo lusófono. Universo composto por 'partes sem todo,' no conhecido verso de Alberto Caeiro, certamente inspirador das *Partes de Africa* de Helder Macedo, que Laura Padilha elege como um texto português seminal para o diálogo inter-cultural em que as partes africanas, portuguesas, brasileiras que compõem o universo em análise não são mais vistas sob o olhar português como um percurso de saudade, mas como um percurso identitário múltiplo a construir num constante movimento impulsionado teórica e textualmente pelos 'não canônes' (se me é permitida a expressão) do sul.

Partindo do princípio teoricamente muito bem fundamentado de que a ficção contemporânea de Angola e de Moçambique constitui um terreno fértil e impossível de ignorar, para quem se interessa pela construção das identidades nacionais destes países, Laura Padilha aborda, ao longo de vários ensaios e de forma bastante diversa, dois elementos que me parecem muito pertinentes: por um lado, e particularmente em relação ao imaginário angolano, a importância da reinvenção mitopoética de Luanda e da Lunda, espaços que, nas palavras da ensaísta, constituem 'metáforas da existência de duas Angolas' (p. 27) em permanente tensão, e a reinvenção/recuperação da tradição nestas literaturas, em especial a combinação e a convivência entre o texto tradicional oral e o escrito, o que inevitavelmente traz em si a questão da língua portuguesa.

Relativamente ao primeiro aspecto partiria do ensaio 'Ficção angolana pós-75 processos e caminhos,' em que a autora nos dá conta dos trilhos seguidos pós-independência das 'Angolas' desenhadas por Luandino Vieira – a Luanda dos musseques, nas também do cimento, com a mão do colonizador e a sua ocidentalização urbana — e por Castro Soromenho a Lunda, 'berço de Lueji' e 'forma de condensação imagística de outras realidades angolanas onde, (...) avultaram senzalas e quimbos, como negros sinais' (pp. 27-28). Duas Angolas que a independência não desfez e que, de outras formas e noutras representações, terá até acentuado (p. 28), como mostra Laura Padilha na profunda leitura que faz das obras de Pepetela, Manuel Rui e Boaventura Cardoso ao longo de vários ensaios. Na leitura de Laura Padilha das obras dos referidos autores e na sua análise em relação ao retorno às raízes que todas oferecem, empenhadas em reconstruir as pontes entre estas duas realidades, concluí-se que o maior traço de união é a 'língua de todos,' o português, mas dita na forma em que a 'letra abraça a voz' (p. 30).

A 'semântica da diferença' que, na óptica da ensaísta, estas literaturas exprimem acontece a partir de 'falas-em-diferença' enunciadas em português (p.37). Tal diferença inscreve-se na ruptura com os padrões estéticos do ocidente branco, europeu, tornando-se capaz de criar o lugar imaginado, onde o homem africano luta por se tornar sujeito do seu próprio destino, da sua história e da sua língua. Obras como as de Luandino Vieira, Pepetela,

Ungulani Ba Ka Khosa, Manuel Rui e Mia Couto são objecto de exemplo e de estudo pelas diversas leituras que oferecem da riqueza do processo linguístico e da crueza do processo histórico. A forma mais explorada de tentativa de superação desse processo histórico toma como ponto de partida a recuperação, no universo narrativo escrito, da tradição africana e portanto da oralidade, como Laura Padilha demonstra na análise comparativa que nos oferece de obras como *Terra Sonâmbula*, de Mia Couto e *O Desejo de Kianda*, de Pepetela. Assim, a autora mostra como a língua portuguesa se dobra aos contornos africanos e ganha novas cintilações. Esta 'dobragem' da língua portuguesa aos seus múltiplos utilizadores torna-se 'ela própria um instrumento que se volta contra o processo de dominação, abrindo-se para o dialogismo cultural que passa a veicular' (p. 51). É assim que vemos como a sua posse se torna parte do processo de reivindicação identitária, nos textos africanos pré-independência. Nos textos pós-75 tudo sofre uma viragem, pois o projecto político, social e cultural é fruto do anterior, mas é já outro. Contudo, os textos continuam a sua aposta na desterritorialização. A intenção didáctica e lúdica que permeia o texto oral, transfigurada em texto escrito, mantém-se, mas a cenarização, como mostra Laura Padilha na senda de *Sim, Camarada*, de Manuel Rui, é outra: os portugueses saem de cena, ou seja, nas palavras de Laura Padilha, 'os que se enfrentam metonimicamente em forma de nós e eles já não são mais os angolanos e os portugueses, mas tão somente os angolanos, dolorosamente incluídos e excluídos' (p. 52), mostrando desde o início uma nação emergente plena de fissuras ameaçadoras e geradora de uma nova semântica da diferença: as novas guetizações geradas na Angola independente em que os excluídos ou dominados são identificados como inferiores das tais 'duas,' ou mais, 'Angolas,' de que falávamos inicialmente. Neste contexto, e como nos textos pré-independência, a tradição continua a ser o imaginário da alteridade. Por isso, e como muito bem enunciou Laura Padilha, 'Recuperar, pois, a tradição significa trazer para a cena do texto a marca da alteridade, para com ela atingir-se, a um só tempo, a modernidade e a descolonização da fala literária' (p. 49).

De tradição e de oralidade 'fantasiada de escrita' nos falam as vozes de Noémia de Sousa, Alda Lara e Alda do Espírito Santo, cujos poemas Laura Padilha lê admiravelmente como gritos poéticos individuais e colectivos, explorando não apenas a questão da raça, mas também a questão do género. Ligações possíveis são estabelecidas com os continuados gritos das mulheres africanas mais jovens e as suas novas modelações, nomeadamente em Paula

Tavares, cuja voz poética seduz, merecidamente, a ensaísta. Ainda 'a última que é a última entre os negros que já são últimos na concepção dos demais povos civilizados' (nas palavras de Alda do Espírito Santo citadas por Laura Padilha (p. 180), a mulher é, em Paula Tavares, a maior vítima dos senhores da guerra, mas também o maior foco de resistência, pois são elas que inventam a vida, continuando a nação nas suas tarefas tradicionais que a guerra insiste em desfazer e destruir. Mas, como Laura Padilha tão bem mostra, a mulher é também corpo numa relação de cinco sentidos com a terra africana por si semeada de palavras portadoras de uma voz e de uma sensualidade outra, geradoras de uma utopia outra, de uma vida outra, que afirma a diferença num terreno pleno de falos e de morte numa nação adiada.

Para terminar não poderia deixar de referir a gloriosa tarefa de Laura Padilha de, ao indagar os canônes, a origem das teorias e a sua aplicabilidade ou falência face ao universo literário africano, nos proporcionar um diálogo único entre as várias correntes e estudiosos que têm animado a crítica ocidental e os outros, os do sul, africanos ou brasileiros, ao mesmo tempo que nos instiga a reflectir sobre a necessidade de um corpo crítico e teórico para pensar o universo literário africano. Esta é, nas palavras de Laura Padilha 'uma das obsessões fantasmáticas dos estudiosos brasileiros dessas literatura' (p. 331), de que a inquietação crítica de Laura Padilha é seguramente líder. Assim, no entender da ensaísta, estaríamos realmente descolonizados e capazes de analisar as especificidades deste vastíssimo universo, não como um apêndice da crítica ocidental ou um parente pobre que aproveita os restos de teorias sobre uma modernidade que não é africana, mas de uma leitura crítica dialogante com o exterior, que não ofusque ou não refira outros pensadores que até pela língua em que se exprimem acabam por ser marginalizados ou mesmo desconhecidos. É neste aspecto fundamental o diálogo que Laura Padilha estabelece entre uns e outros mostrando-nos a pertinência e a originalidade do pensamento de uns e outros.

Pensar o universo lusófono à altura da excelência da sua variedade e da sua produção estética é o sonho, realizado neste livro e a continuar, de Laura Padilha, guetizá-lo ou torná-lo satélite de outros sempre em busca de algo que não é nosso, ocultando ou rasurando o nosso, é o seu receio e a razão da sua luta. Os ensaios de Laura Padilha pela sua provocação ideológica, pela sua belíssima leitura crítica comparativa e pela excelência do seu texto instigam-nos a dialogar, instigam-nos a responder.

Margarida Calafate Ribeiro Centro de Estudos Sociais, Universidade de Coimbra.

Luís Adriano Carlos (ed). *Árvore: Folhas de Poesia.* Facsimile. Porto: Campo das Letras, 2003.

Daniela Kato

A passagem de cinquenta anos sobre a extinção da revista *Árvore* proporciona um excelente pretexto para revisitar uma década inegavelmente importante, ainda que atravessada por contradições várias, para a poesia portuguesa. Uma década vivida não só sob o peso opressivo da ditadura salazarista, mas também, num plano mais vasto, na sombra das consequências desastrosas da segunda guerra mundial e das tragédias de Auschwitz e Hiroshima. A ambos os contextos os poetas da *Árvore* respondem com uma poesia que negoceia de forma decisiva os legados modernista e neo-realista das décadas anteriores e que abre importantes caminhos às gerações seguintes na sua revalorização do rigor retórico da palavra e numa clara tendência anti-discursiva. Com efeito, ainda que de existência efémera – da revista apenas foram publicados quatro fascículos, entre o Outono de 1951 e a Primavera de 1953, altura em que o regime salazarista lhe decretou a morte – *Árvore* cria um espaço renovado para uma praxis poética que dá a lume nomes como António Ramos Rosa, Raul de Carvalho, José Terra, Albano Martins, Luís Amaro, Egito Gonçalves e Cristovam Pavia, para além de chamar a si colaborações importantes de Eduardo Lourenço, Vergílio Ferreira, Jorge de Sena e Eugénio de Andrade e de incluir ainda traduções de poemas de Rilke (de Paulo Quintela), Stephen Spender e W. H. Auden (de Jorge de Sena), René Char, Paul Éluard e Henri Michaux (de Ramos Rosa).

Numa época caracterizada por um *ethos* pessimista e céptico, em que a confiança num progresso da história em direcção aos "amanhãs que cantam" se torna dificilmente sustentável, não surpreende que esta nova sensibilidade poética se afirme ao arrepio dos aspectos mais radicalmente ideológicos e panfletários da estética neo-realista dominante na década de quarenta. Como refere Luís Adriano Carlos na sua excelente introdução a esta edição facsimilada dos quatro números da revista, o projecto de *Árvore* marca o recrudescimento de uma consciência modernista que a *Presença* tinha reavivado e que os poetas associados aos *Cadernos de Poesia*, com destaque para Jorge de Sena, converteram numa forma de resistência às tendências anti-modernistas de certo neo-realismo (x). Porém, ao contrário das orientações lírico-expressivas do grupo ligado à *Távola Redonda* – outra revista coeva que reage ao legado neo-realista, mas que se localiza bem mais à Direita do espectro polítco – os poetas de *Árvore* não descartam o discurso social da poesia, buscando antes um compromisso nem sempre fácil entre a autonomia estética do poema e uma dimensão ética atenta às contingências da realidade.

Este novo programa poético constitui-se assim como charneira entre o esteticismo e o realismo de cunho existencialista, dando lugar ao que Adriano Carlos apelida de "um realismo fenomenológico mais realista do que os realismos convencionais" (xi) – um realismo enraízado nas exigências do real humano, mas que não deixa de aspirar a um universalismo de dimensão cosmológica. Veja-se, a propósito, o belíssimo ensaio de António Ramos Rosa no derradeiro número da revista e que significativamente se intitula "A Poesia É um Diálogo com o Universo." E talvez valha a pena citar aqui alguns passos, pelo que neles há de demanda exemplar de uma cultura de resistência num tempo de censura e silêncio forçado bem diferente do nosso, mas ainda assim uma cultura de sobrevivência intelectual e criativa cuja necessidade não deixa hoje de ser menos premente para fazer face a um outro tipo de silêncios e conformismos:

> É raro encontrar em Portugal estas grandes ondas de fraternidade que fazem da solidão uma habitação humana e onde os câmbios espirituais frutificam em estímulos, orientações e obras. (...) A poesia como exercício espiritual permanente é ainda alguma coisa que a maior parte dos poetas portugueses ignora, seja porque são assoberbados pelas condições miseráveis da sua vida, seja porque lhes atribuam uma primazia e uma fatalidade que elas espiritualmente não têm. (...)
> Com razão se fala no individualismo dos portugueses: e esta incapacidade para a unidade na generosidade, (...) para o diálogo, enfim, parece-nos ser uma das mais calamitosas deficiências do português, que oscila entre o indiferentismo e o fanatismo. (...)
> Teremos nós força e alma suficientes para imprimir no nosso meio estas energias revoltadas generosas que não se compadecem com a abdicação e o funcionamento arbitrário da angústia e crêem na possibilidade de uma renovação espiritual promovida pela poesia? (*Árvore,* 1, vol. II: 12)

Uma questão para a qual o leitor encontrará algumas respostas nas folhas e ramos de poesia desta *Árvore.*

Daniela Kato é licenciada em Direito pela Universidade Católica e em Línguas e Literaturas Modernas – Estudos Portugueses e Ingleses pela Faculdade de Letras da Universidade do Porto. Actualmente prepara a dissertação de doutoramento em Literatura Inglesa nesta Faculdade, sendo bolseira da Fundação para a Ciência e a Tecnologia. Tem como principais interesses de investigação a poesia do modernismo; teoria dos géneros e poética comparada; nacionalismos e etnias na literatura inglesa do séc. XX; orientalismo. Email: ytd.kato@mail.telepac.pt

Silvina Rodrigues Lopes. *A Inocência do Devir*. Lisboa, Vendaval, 2003.

Pedro Eiras

Desde o título *A Inocência do Devir* até à citação final de Nietzsche sobre a possibilidade de dizer um "sim" absoluto à existência, Silvina Rodrigues Lopes define, neste excelente ensaio sobre a poesia de Herberto Helder, um repto: assumir uma leitura do poema como dicção de uma metamorfose em acontecimento. Recusando o essencialismo do dizer poético que impera em Platão e Hegel (44-47), Silvina Rodrigues Lopes pensa a poesia herbertiana a partir de uma contínua auto-interrogação pela qual a escrita coloca em dúvida os seus próprios pressupostos teóricos. O devir consiste pois (mas que *consistência* pode haver no *devir*?) na leitura do poema como acontecimento de "ritmo," "movimento," "circulações" (7), pluralidade de leituras possíveis e formação de diferentes objectos textuais, revisão pela qual o poema testa a sua própria legibilidade. Que o *devir* do texto seja ainda *inocente*, conforme sugere o título, diz ainda que esta compreensão não essencialista da *poiesis* não pode deixar de se descrever em termos éticos. Se o gesto de interrogação da legibilidade pela assunção de um devir de radical "desenraizamento" (11) pode lembrar o gesto nietzschiano de defesa da filosofia heraclitiana do devir contra o essencialismo de Parménides (*A Filosofia na Idade Trágica dos Gregos*, 1873), por outro lado esta releitura de Herberto Helder pede a última transformação do "altivo leão" em criança que, segundo *Assim Falou Zaratustra* (1883-5), alcança um estádio ético de "novo começo, jogo, roda que gira por si própria, primeiro móbil, afirmação santa" (citado por Silvina Rodigues Lopes, 86).

Para dizer uma poética que não se pauta por categorias fixas mas por um movimento de criação e auto-revisão contínua, Silvina Rodrigues Lopes reformula o próprio vocabulário crítico de trabalho. Cito alguns termos técnicos que surgem nas primeiras páginas do ensaio: devir, articulação, fluxo, dispersão, agregação, ruptura, divergência, entrelaçamento, linha, nó, ferida, troca, união, atracção, repulsa. Alguns destes termos têm forte ressonância deleuziana (como "agenciamento," ou "desenraizamento," que lembra "desterritorialização") e a própria palavra "rizoma" parece subjazer a toda a leitura. Este vocabulário muitas vezes metafórico permite codificar fenómenos tão dificilmente definíveis na leitura de poesia como o ritmo (aqui, um acontecimento muito mais complexo do que qualquer mensurabilidade métrica). De facto, a teoria da literatura não possui qualquer gramática do ritmo ou da metamorfose; as "redes de atracção e simpatia" em Silvina Rodrigues Lopes (99) podem, portanto, descrever estruturas de puro devir que sejam, mais do que meros quadros de sentido ou ligações entre objectos definidos, operações de transformação.

Por isso esta análise recusa a "continuidade totalizadora, como a do discurso lógico, ou do teológico," que "exclui o descontínuo" (14-15), mas sem sacrificar a "ideia de poema como organização diferencial de forças-sentidos que produz ou despoleta ressonâncias, rompendo a superfície e abrindo-a a uma *continuidade subjacente*" [itálicos meus] (24). Por isso se torna necessário reformular o vocabulário de análise: a poética de inspiração aristotélica-horaciana dificilmente permite tratar a excepção, o fragmentário, o monstruoso; o desafio herbertiano aqui aberto implica descrever uma construção a partir do que não cabe nas categorias estéticas clássicas. E se *A Inocência do Devir* deixa o desejo de vermos mais definidas ou sistematizadas as ferramentas de trabalho (o que é uma "atracção?" o que é uma "simpatia?" que relação ao certo estabelecem entre elas?), constituindo-se afinal as figuras de uma gramática do ritmo, o mesmo ensaio adverte ainda para o perigo de qualquer definição ou sistema. Nesta saudável impossibilidade de fixar a leitura do devir em "gramáticas," Nietzsche volta a ecoar: "A vontade de sistema é uma falta de honestidade," escreve algures.

O poema herbertiano e o ensaio de Silvina Rodrigues Lopes comungam portanto de estratégias para impossibilitarem a formação do sistema ou da leitura sistemática. A ironia de Herberto Helder, especialmente em *Photomaton & Vox*, onde todas as leituras, incluindo as que o próprio texto propõe, ficam dubitadas ou impossibilitadas, impede de encontrar qualquer instância de verdade interior ou exterior ao texto: "E leia-se como se quiser, pois ficará sempre errado" (*Photomaton & Vox*, 3ª ed., 1995: 162). *Double bind*: obedecer ao texto, lê-lo, implica compreender que ele é ilegível, e por isso a própria afirmação de ilegibilidade não implica nenhuma verdade como fundamento da ilegibilidade. Silvina Rodrigues Lopes mostra que na poesia herbertiana uma voz "recusa Deus como causa, admitindo-o no entanto como potência" (78): é que "Deus como causa garantiria a estabilidade do sentido, isso mesmo que a *figurabilidade do discurso poético* põe em questão. Com efeito, a figurabilidade é aquilo que abre na linguagem o processo de translação ou trânsito do sentido" [itálicos meus] (79). Pode dizer-se, pois, que *há* sentido, mas não há *um* sentido, *há* sentido que é a divagação do próprio sentido inagarrável, em metamorfose. A autora mostra como a metamorfose não é estranha a Hegel, mas subordina-se ali a uma teleologia, um unificador e sistemático "sentido da História" (46) que o poema herbertiano substitui por uma livre, inadivinhável variação sem degradação, sem superação (47) e sem *telos* (56): "Se admitirmos que a mudança não está pré-determinada, estaremos dispostos a olhar o monstruoso das narrativas míticas sem o reduzir à ilustração de uma degradação" (63). Note-se que a recusa de uma ética (avaliação da metamorfose em termos de decadência e castigo, como tantas vezes, mas não sempre, em Ovídio) não implica a rasura radical de toda a ética. Releia-se o título: o devir é *inocente*.

Ao admitir que "Contra o fim, *pelo recomeço como experiência da finitude*, HH interroga a história da *poiesis*, o seu poder de metamorfose, o desejo de perfeição sem conteúdo que a anima, o contacto, a inscrição das mãos no objecto fabricado" [itálicos meus] (99-100), Silvina Rodrigues Lopes parece enunciar, no fim-tornado-recomeço do seu ensaio, um objecto principal da sua própria leitura: a interrogação de uma *poiesis* que está em devir no próprio instante em que é interrogada. Fazer é re-colocar em movimento a escrita, libertá-la de automatismos (sistemas, categorias), observar uma pluralidade de sentidos do texto irredutível ao monologismo, abdicar de um princípio de verdade independente da escrita para fundamentar a sua legibilidade. Silvina Rodrigues Lopes realiza estas operações mostrando que não há nelas qualquer negatividade (abdicar de um princípio de verdade não é uma perda, o que confirmaria ainda um axioma tácito de privilégio ontológico do verdadeiro, mas uma leitura primeira do texto literário). *A Inocência do Devir* ilustra, pois, aquilo que a autora defende magistralmente em *A Legitimação em Literatura* (1994) a partir de uma inspiração derridiana: não há *um* fundamento da literatura (da sua produção, da sua recepção, da sua teorização), mas a literatura promove a experiência plural de fundamentos e / ou o abandono da própria ideia de fundamento.

Em *A Legitimação em Literatura*, Silvina Rodrigues Lopes cita um excerto de Herberto Helder onde se define toda a "experiência" como "invenção" (460). *A Inocência do Devir* considera também o poema como invenção de um mundo que devém próprio: "Há no poema uma transfusão de memórias da 'mitologia' universal para a 'mitologia pessoal,' digamos, recordando Schelling (...). Trata-se de convocar o mítico como multiplicidade contraditória para a transfusão texto a texto" (94). O pensamento do devir não anula, portanto, a resistência ou permanência de uma individualidade, mas esta "mitologia pessoal" não é senão texto(s): "Não há outro protagonista, porque o poeta que escreve é já, ou é apenas, o poema escrito" (19). Que esse poema, por sua vez, se dê numa leitura em devir, e que essa leitura, decorrendo, obrigue sempre a rever as certezas adquiridas, que a escrita nasça numa *tabula rasa* onde o leitor deve reaprender as leis ou as excepções a cada momento, é, neste ensaio fundamental sobre Herberto Helder, o próprio princípio da legibilidade e de um dionisíaco entendimento do fazer poético.

Pedro Eiras está preparando uma dissertação de doutoramento na Faculdade de Letras, na Universidade de Porto. É autor de *Antes dos Lagartos*, peça de teatro estreada na Mostra de Dramartugias Contemporâneas em 2001, e *Estiletes*, um livro de contos. E-mail: pedro_eiras@hotmail.com

Elizabeth Travassos. *Modernismo e música brasileira.* Rio de Janeiro: Jorge Zahar, 2003 (1ª ed., 2000).

Pedro Meira Monteiro

Modernismo e música brasileira, de Elizabeth Travassos, pertence a este gênero curioso dos pequenos livros de divulgação, voltados para um público não especializado, mas que podem perfeitamente servir de guia e estímulo a estudantes universitários iniciantes e, talvez mesmo, a pesquisadores mais maduros.

Nas suas setenta e cinco pequenas páginas (mais ilustrações), a autora enfrenta com segurança a tarefa espinhosa de situar o modernismo brasileiro, em suas discussões musicais, entre os extremos do cosmopolitismo e do nacionalismo, do erudito e do popular.

Assim sendo, compreende-se a razão pela qual sua atenção recai especialmente sobre a obra complexa de Mário de Andrade. Nela, afinal, os anseios renovadores dos modernistas parecem encontrar seus limites e seu alcance, porque exatamente nela, em toda sua extensão e potência, vemos o pesquisador sistemático entregar-se à busca do "popular," nem sempre consciente de que talvez perseguisse uma miragem.

Esta não é uma conclusão do livro, que se atém otimamente à perspectiva panorâmica (sem demasiada pretensão especulativa), mas é porventura a conclusão a que pode chegar o leitor, se souber atentar para a densidade de sua discussão – densidade que todo bom texto didático deve dissimular, precisamente como faz a autora deste *Modernismo e música brasileira.*

Iniciando com uma "pequena digressão" sobre a troca de nomes, Elizabeth Travassos nos faz pensar na opção de Francisco Mignone ou Guerra-Peixe, em épocas diversas, por resguardar-se sob o pseudônimo com que assinaram sua obras "de caráter popularesco." Eis armado o paradoxo: inspiravam-se no "popular," mas era preciso dele separar-se, marcando os limites simbólicos que os tornavam, senão superiores, ao menos diferentes do populacho. Mas é fascinante que a indústria do entretenimento, e depois o mercado fonográfico, criassem zonas de contato entre músicos de origens sociais diversas, o que tornava ainda mais complexos os mecanismos de representação e diálogo no meio musical e artístico. Não que esboroassem as barreiras entre a alta e a baixa cultura, mas o terreno certamente era mais movediço do que deixam ver as análises apressadas. A entrada da música no mundo industrial, de toda forma, ameaçava a figura do indivíduo criador, artesão de seu próprio trabalho. Havia, além disso, como lembra a autora, o mundo boêmio em que se encontravam "intelectuais" e "artistas populares."

Certamente pensando em estudos recentes que apontam a importância dos "mediadores" culturais na configuração de um cenário de que emerge o "popular," Elizabeth Travassos termina por sugerir que as fronteiras entre gêneros e entre o "erudito" e o próprio "popular" eram sempre mais tênues do que se crê normalmente, embora existam, historicamente marcadas e construídas.

É interessante que neste livro seja lembrada a tese de que a história musical brasileira, em sua vertente erudita, conheceu um "atraso" e um "descompasso entre [a] evolução musical e [a] literária," já que os questionamentos do sistema tonal apareceriam no Brasil tardiamente, com a difusão do dodecafonismo apenas após a Segunda Guerra. Assim, enquanto na França o Grupo dos Seis combatia o impressionismo musical, os músicos brasileiros, em sua maioria, não pareciam aptos a realizar o programa de Graça Aranha, de "ultrapassar Debussy."

Villa-Lobos aparece aí, entretanto, como voz algo dissonante. É contudo fascinante que a autora se afaste, com delicadeza, da simples exaltação da "genialidade" do grande músico modernista, abstendo-se de avaliá-lo categoricamente, reconhecendo a complexidade de sua fatura musical, simultaneamente "moderna" e "antiga," segundo o gosto moderno europeu. Sem esquecer, é claro, que o mais moderno era, então, o primitivismo que os trópicos pareciam gratuitamente oferecer. Sem esquecer, tampouco, que muitos dos procedimentos harmônicos característicos do século XX podiam confundir-se a uma "fluência" que a crítica freqüentemente associa aos chorões, como o próprio Villa-Lobos. Mas a diligência da estudiosa da história musical brasileira permite relativizar o caráter autóctone do "modernismo" musical de Villa, sugerindo que as influências e o contato com a moderna música européia seriam mais intensos e anteriores ao que ordinariamente se supõe.

Talvez um traço esquemático surja, é verdade, no momento em que o modernismo nacionalista de Mário de Andrade é posto em cena. A autora não parece desvencilhar-se de todo da idéia do modernista campeão do popular, como se no fundo não houvesse, antes desse intelectual amoroso do povo, mais que uma lógica republicana estritamente europeizante. Não se trata – claro fique – de reputar um pendor para o popular em autores muitas vezes inequivocamente elitistas, mas sim sugerir que a atenção sobre o elemento do povo não é apanágio exclusivo dos modernistas, ainda que eles – e Mário de Andrade à frente – tenham de fato promovido o "resgate" de cantos tradicionalmente relegados aos espaços menos visíveis (para as lentes ilustradas) da sociedade.

Mas é inegável que Elizabeth Travassos ilumina, tão bem em texto tão curto, o que foi a incorporação menos "epidérmica" de padrões musicais "populares" à linguagem codificada dos concertos. A presença de novos timbres com a introdução de instrumentos tradicionalmente estranhos à orquestra sinfônica, por exemplo, é uma inovação fundamental de Villa-Lobos. Mas, como alerta a autora, "o período modernista não inventou o nacionalismo musical," o que a faz lembrar o caso notável de Alberto Nepomuceno.

É interessante que os modernistas quisessem superar, do ponto de vista musical, as "citações," tornando invisíveis ou imediatamente inaudíveis os elementos nacionais, absorvendo-os "no tecido das obras," sublimando-os, finalmente. Mas o que separaria o exotismo, que é a simples citação musical, da profunda incorporação formal do popular? A autora responde com cautela: "a fronteira que separa exotismo da incorporação profunda da música popular era difícil de traçar."

O problema da efemeridade e inconstância das cantigas brasileiras deixa ver, ademais, o drama do folclorista moderno, ansioso pelo registro, de que Mário fora ele mesmo promotor, em sua famosa viagem como turista aprendiz, no final da década de 1920, e que promoveria à testa do Departamento de Cultura de São Paulo, entre 1935 e 1938. Ou ainda, de que seria promotor, quando gravou inúmeras tradições brasileiras no interior de sua rapsódia macunaímica.

O que buscava Mário de Andrade seriam bem mais as "comoções" que a cultura popular poderia causar. Nesse sentido, a aposta no canto popular e seu fator dinamogênico não esconde o caráter propositivo, quase cívico, do projeto modernista. Sem contar, é claro, que o transporte (co-moção) do individual ao coletivo significava, no limite, a apropriação consciente da música gestada na "inconsciência do povo," transportando-a para um outro plano, inegavelmente (do ponto de vista modernista) superior.

Difícil projeto, cuja impossibilidade e alcance encontram-se na obra de Villa-Lobos, que Mário de Andrade admirava e criticava, não sem esconder o incômodo com o individualismo do compositor das *Danças africanas*. Assim, parece que a recusa parcial de Villa ao receituário nacionalista de Mário o tornava, paradoxalmente, desejado e rechaçado. Em Villa-Lobos, o "nós" dos nacionalistas não se resolvia de todo, porque o músico não completava com isenção (a expressão a serviço de algo mais-que-individual) o círculo que perfaz a comunidade, deixando que um "eu" dissonante desafiasse o projeto nacionalista. Paradoxalmente, ali está o maior dos compositores brasileiros, nem por isso infenso ao encantamento da mobilização popular, cujos rasgos fascistas tanto preocupam a crítica, e com razão.

O incremento de uma incipiente indústria cultural complicava especialmente a localização do "popular," fazendo com que o "autêntico" nacional se tornasse mais e mais inidentificável, ou inalcançável. Num mundo artístico já ligado à urbe e ao mercado, onde buscar essa fonte de que jorra a verdadeira cultura popular? A pergunta é moderna e desconcertante, afinal a crença na verdadeira tradição nacional, ou popular, parece colidir com a constatação de que a pureza há muito se perdera (e evidentemente somos levados a perguntar se um dia existiu) e de que, portanto, o folclorista se encontra sempre na encruzilhada de tempos e tradições vivas e fugidias, o que não o exime daquela tarefa documental, que Mário parece ter realizado com competência e profundidade, deixando, significativamente, não mais que o plano de uma obra magna, *Na pancada do ganzá.*

A sugestão de que a "paisagem sonora" brasileira se apresenta na ensaística do autor do *Macunaíma* é fundamental, mas será então importante que o leitor atente para o fato de que ela se presentifica fragmentariamente (eis os "ecos [...] da paisagem musical urbana" que a autora identifica nos textos modernistas), como se resisitisse ao espírito de sistema de que um projeto folclórico nacionalista se nutre.

Enfim, da música nacionalista à música nacional há um largo espaço, que o pequeno livro de Elizabeth Travassos franqueia à nossa imaginação de leitores que, uma vez concluída a leitura, dificilmente nos furtaremos ao prazer de mergulhar mais fundo nas dubiedades do projeto modernista, não apenas em sua vertente musical.

Resta uma sugestão: imagine o leitor qual seria a atuação de Mário de Andrade se tivesse sobrevivido à "fratura no bloco nacionalista fortalecido no modernismo," que foi o aparecimento do Música Viva de Koellreutter, em 1946. Pode-se muito bem ler com ironia as palavras finais deste *Modernismo e música brasileira* – "as chamadas 'polêmicas dodecafônicas,' as conversões ou reconversões de compositores ao nacionalismo e tudo quanto se seguiu são outra história." Serão mesmo?

Pedro Meira Monteiro é professor-assistente de Literatura Brasileira, Department of Spanish and Portuguese Languages and Cultures, Princeton University. É autor de *A queda do aventureiro: aventura, cordialidade e os novos tempos em Raízes do Brasil* (Campinas: Editora Unicamp, 1999) e *Um moralista nos trópicos: o visconde de Cairu e o duque de La Rochefoucauld* (São Paulo: Boitempo, 2004, no prelo). Prepara, com Vera Neumann-Wood, o volume da Coleção Correspondência de Mário de Andrade (IEB/USP), contendo as cartas trocadas entre o autor de *Macunaíma* e o historiador e crítico literário Sérgio Buarque de Holanda, entre 1922 e 1944. E-mail: pmeira@princeton.edu

David Brookshaw. *Perceptions of China in Modern Portuguese Literature: Border Gates.* Lewiston: Edwin Mellen Press, 2002.

Claire Williams

The tiny enclave of Macau has, for four and a half centuries, been a conduit for commercial and cultural encounters between China and Europe. A prosperous and strategically placed marketplace on the distant fringes of the empire and a multicultural melting pot where East and West blend, it came to represent the ultimate colonial fantasy for the Portuguese. Yet Brookshaw's illuminating study is the first attempt to consider modern literature in Portuguese about Macau (as a gateway to China). It focuses on themes of "exile, memory, adaptation, hybridity and identity" (x) in texts ranging from the last decades of the nineteenth century (Pessanha and Eça de Queiróz's *O Mandarim*), to the flurry of "Livros do Oriente" publications that came out between 1987 and the handing back of the colony to China in 1999.

The author refers to theoretical concepts put forward in a number of key texts of contemporary postcolonial theory (by Bill Ashcroft, Nestor García Canclini, Doris Sommer, and Robert Young) that were originally used to chart developments in cultures elsewhere in the world, illustrating the global applications of postcolonialism. He explains just how the case of Macau differs from that of Portugal's other ex-colonies, largely because of the enclave's fierce and continual loyalty to the homeland. Brookshaw's study might be seen as a microcosm of the colonial experience and the literary reactions inspired by it, varying between fear, fascination, superiority, empathy, nostalgia and celebration.

The choice of texts (novels, essays, articles, short stories and poems) enables the author to explore these reactions and consider the motivations of the writers: the perpetuation of Orientalist myths, colonialist agendas, fascination with an ancient foreign culture, nostalgia for a bygone age, and the idea of the exotic country as Edenic refuge or mystery to be solved. Among the cast of writers discussed are the Portuguese who has "gone native" (Pessanha), the naval officer (Jaime do Inso), the foreign language teacher (Maria Ondina Braga), the journalist (Deolinda da Conceição), the backpacker (Cláudia Ribeiro), the Chinese academic (Yao Jingming), and the authentic, nostalgic Macanese (Henrique Senna Fernandes); including both insiders and outsiders to compare and contrast their views.

Brookshaw raises the question of Macanese identity and how it has been represented by these writers, through the differing approaches to issues of hybridity and miscegenation; the rejection of roots by some characters as opposed to the "re-ethnification" of others; the interweaving of symbols and allusions to Chinese and Portuguese cultures; and the reference to or avoidance of the actual political situation.

Particularly interesting is the significant presence of women writers in the literature of Macau, from the tragic tales of Deolinda da Conceição (1950s), to the insistent curiosity of Maria Ondina Braga's narratives (1960s), Fernanda Dias's poetry (1990s) and the travel literature of Cláudia Ribeiro (2001).

David Brookshaw has published major contributions to the critical material available on literature from Brazil and Lusophone Africa and this study is another important work in the field of Portuguese Studies: a fitting start to the new Edwin Mellen Press series "Studies in Portuguese Literature."

Claire Williams lectures in Lusophone language, literatures and cultures at the University of Liverpool. Her research has focussed largely on the narratives of Lusophone women writers, in particular Clarice Lispector and Maria Gabriela Llansol. Recent publications include a co-edited volume of essays on Lispector, *Close to the Wild Heart* (Oxford: Legenda/ European Humanities Research Council, 2002) and the forthcoming *The Encounter Between Opposites in the Works of Clarice Lispector* (Bristol: HiPLA Monographs, 2003). Email: cleliwel@liv.ac.uk

Kathleen E. Sheldon. *Pounders of Grain: A History of Women, Work and Politics in Mozambique.* Portsmouth: Heinemann, 2002.

Hilary Owen

This history of women in Mozambique, seen through the lens of women's work and political activism over the last century, represents a very valuable resource for anyone working with feminism and gender issues in the fields of literature, cultural studies, women's studies, history, politics or anthropology in southern Africa. Sheldon's central premise, using a materialist feminist approach, is to explore how women as workers wove "the fabric of Mozambican nationhood" (xxiii). Although research on gender issues in Mozambique has proliferated over the decades since national independence, this has tended to be dispersed across edited volumes, political pamphlets and humanities journals. Sheldon's volume provides the first comprehensive full-length study available in English of women's working patterns, poverty, economic survival and political movements in Mozambique. Representing the fruit of more twenty years research, the book is divided into seven chapters, some of which are based on work previously published in journals or edited volumes. The ordering of the chapters follows a chronology from the early colonial period at the end of the nineteenth century, through to the 1990s with the post-Peace Accord transition to democracy, structural readjustment and the effects of globalization.

The opening chapter provides a valuable context for the rest of the study by reviewing women's work in the early colonial period in terms of the complex ethnic and cultural interrelations between the matrilineal traditions of the northern and central regions, and the patrilineal societies of the south. Taking issue with the contention that "women have no tribe" (2), Sheldon compares different regions, focusing on the material effects of these kinship arrangements for women's work, land tenureship and family life. She thus demonstrates how the cultural practices surrounding kin and inheritance are dynamic and changeable in relation to shifting historical and economic circumstances. Chapter two looks at urban and rural contexts, exploring the changing circumstances of women workers in relation to the impact of Portuguese colonialism. Starting from the Conference of Berlin, this chapter charts the increase in European trading companies and the involvement of women in the *prazos* holders' revolts against them. Tracing the intensification of settler colonialism during the Salazar dictatorship, Sheldon reviews the effects of *chibalo*, the colonial forced labour policy on African women and their families, as well as discussing the consequences for women of male labor migration to the South African mines, and noting women's role in urban agriculture, alongside their limited opportunities for waged work under colonialism. Chapter three provides an account of women's experiences in mission education, tracing the history of mission schooling from the 1880s to the 1960s and contrasting the cultures of Portuguese Catholic and Swiss and English Protestant mission schools, as they related to women's opportunities. This section discusses the construction of idealized Catholic domesticity for African women under the Portuguese colonial system at the same time as it observes how the mission schooling system provided new skills and increased opportunities for a very small number of African women.

Chapter four explores the role of women in the Armed Struggle for Independence, the theorizing of their position in the revolution, and their involvement in building the new Marxist-Leninist state. It looks at the birth of Frelimo women's organizations, such as LIFEMO and subsequently OMM, at the OMM's negotiation of women's rights within Frelimo and at the focus on women's liberation through waged work. This chapter discusses the difficulties arising from the patriarchal culture within Frelimo and offers a valuable critical perspective on the conflict between the benefits of modernity and the loss of women's traditional rights and privileges, which was a particularly marked issue for matrilineal northern cultures. Chapter five reviews the major shifts in women's rural and urban working practices brought about by the Frelimo commitment to emancipation through economic independence, requiring the integration of women into the workforce. Comparing the Beira and Maputo experiences, Sheldon explores the famous Green Zones initiatives centred on and led by women, which transformed their involvement in urban agriculture. It notes the positive changes brought about by Frelimo rule in some workplaces, such as increased childcare provision and maternity leave, and it makes the case for women's success in actively influencing key aspects of Frelimo policy on work. At the same time, Sheldon notes the difficulties that arose from attempting to alter traditional male attitudes towards women in the workplace, and demythologizes the popular image of the new woman under socialism routinely taking on conventionally male-gendered work.

Chapter six looks at the impact of the post-Independence war and South African destabilization tactics, which severely damaged much of the Frelimo social and physical infrastructure from which women specifically had stood to gain. It looks at women's experience of rape and sexual abuse in the Renamo camps, at the same time as it notes the evidence of some female leadership within Renamo. It also reviews the effects of internal displacement and loss of community on women's involvement in family agriculture, and their ability to sustain their families. Frelimo policy changes in the wartime context are explored with particular attention paid to the controversial 1989 decision to extend membership rights to polygamous men. There is a discussion of the 1994 elections (for which Sheldon was a UN observer) leading to an analysis of women's representation in the new government, and the issues that were prioritized by women in this context, focusing on two particularly symptomatic debates about sexual harassment and the laws pertaining to land ownership rights. The chapter concludes with a section on women's organizations, reviewing not only the work of the OMM and its changing relations with Frelimo, but also the growth of new campaigns and women's interest groups such as the Fórum Mulher coalition.

Chapter seven provides a detailed critique of the ways in which the structural adjustment programme implemented by the World Bank and IMF in the 1990s led to a general increase in poverty with particular implications for women. It notes the loss of work opportunities, child care and social services which had benefited women under state socialism, as well as the disregard for women's legal rights as firms became privatized. It also points to an increase in urban women surviving through work as street vendors. The rise of independent trade unions and the industrial action of the early 1990s are covered, and although women's involvement in strikes is hard to ascertain, it is noted that women continued to remain active in workers' organizations. A case study of women in the newly privatized cashew processing industry is used as specifically symptomatic of how IMF policy indirectly created unemployment for women. The chapter ends by exploring women in agriculture in the 1980s and 90s, noting the difficulties they continued to experience in earning income to supplement their traditional survival through family food cultivation. The conclusion of the volume, written after the catastrophic floods of 2000, points to the patterns of repetition and change, which have characterized the history of Mozambican women's work over the last century to affirm that women's "inclusion will determine the success of any project" (269) in the country's future development.

Sheldon has clearly conducted painstaking archival research as well as extensive oral interviewing, in order to reconstruct the histories of women's lives, which are often obscured by fragmentary sources or lost in the small print of mainstream historical accounts. Sheldon's overall validation of Frelimo's policy on women during the Marxist period is evident, but the study makes an honest endeavour at striking a balanced position, and does not shrink from providing necessary and nuanced critique. This book is certainly a must for university libraries. It will provide a defining point of reference for serious scholars and researchers in the field, as well as a useful learning resource for students.

Hilary Owen is Senior Lecturer in Portuguese at the University of Manchester. She is the editor of *Gender, Ethnicity and Class in Modern Portuguese-Speaking Culture* (1996) and the author of *Portuguese Women's Writing 1972-1986. Reincarnations of a Revolution* (2000). She is currently working on a book about feminism and women's writing in Mozambique. Email: hilary.owen@man.ac.uk

João Costa (ed). *Portuguese Syntax: New Comparative Studies*. Oxford: Oxford UP, 2000.

José Elías Ulloa

Portuguese Syntax: New Comparative Studies is one of very few works available in English that deal with the particularities of the syntax of Portuguese. The theoretical approach adopted by the essays in the collection is that of Generative Grammar and follows the model outlined in "The Theory of Principles and Parameters" (Chomsky and Lasnik 1993) and *The Minimalist Program* (Chomsky 1995). The book successfully presents an overview of the current theoretical issues that Portuguese syntax raises as well as enlarging the empirical scope of modern comparative syntax. The nine articles deal variously with clitics, V-movement, richness of inflection and functional clausal structure.

Manuela Ambar's article "Infinitives Versus Participles," drawing on her previous work on infinitival and participial structures that under her approach have Tense, tries to answer the question of why these structures have different behaviors. Her argument focuses on the value of tenses, agreement, case, word order, passive voice, negation and cliticization of Portuguese.

Pilar Barbosa, in her article "Clitics," studies the behavior of subjects in Null Subject Languages (NSL). Barbosa challenges the claim that subjects in NSL are ever raised to a preverbal A-position. She argues that there are important structural differences between preverbal subjects in Portuguese/Italian/Catalan and preverbal subjects in French or English. She further argues that the real A-position for lexical subjects in NSL is the post-verbal position and that Clitic Left Dislocation (CLLD) and A'-movement are responsible for instances of overt subject initial constructions.

In his article "Word Order and Discourse-Configurationality in European Portuguese," João Costa studies the different properties subjects in European Portuguese show according to their position in the different word orders Portuguese allows. He studies what position the subjects occupy in these orderings due to discourse factors as well as the intuition that European Portuguese is basically SVO in spite of allowing many different orderings but excluding SOV.

Inês Duarte and Gabriela Matos, in "Romance Clitics and the Minimalist Program," examine the syntax of clitics in European Portuguese. They study why clitics behave differently than DPs and suffixes with regard to syntactic movement and what makes the clitics surface in different positions from one language to another and even within the same language.

Charlotte Galves, in "Agreement, Predication and Pronouns in the History of Portuguese," studies the development of Portuguese from Classical Portuguese until its split into different grammars: Modern European Portuguese and Brazilian Portuguese. She is particularly interested in the correlation between the licensing of subjects and the licensing of clitics and weak pronouns. Following Chomsky (1995) and based on her research on the development of Portuguese, she argues that that correlation follows from viewing agreement not as a syntactic category but as a feature.

Ana Maria Martins, in "A Minimalist Approach to Clitic Climbing," studies the phenomenon of clitic climbing in Romance languages. She shows that the movement of clitics out of an infinitival clause is in certain instances needed, even though *The Minimalist Program* (Chomsky 1995), in which she couches her analysis, assumes that movement is driven only by morphological necessity.

Sérgio Menuzzi, in "First Person Plural Anaphora in Brazilian Portuguese," studies the binding properties of the first person plural anaphora *a gente* in Brazilian Portuguese, which has an intriguing pattern in which it can be the antecedent of a first person plural pronoun only if the dependency is not "local." He argues that Binding Theory has two agreement-like requirements: Agreement-on-Chains and the Feature-Compatibility Condition on Indexing.

Gertjan Postma, in "Distributive Universal Quantification and Aspect in Brazilian Portuguese," studies the properties of the quantifiers *todo+sg* and *cada+sg* of Brazilian Portuguese and discusses their properties compared to the existing literature on universal quantification. In particular, Postma focuses on the relation between aspect and argumental quantification and draws conclusions on why the quantifiers *all*, *every* and *each* behave so differently across languages with different aspectual systems.

The final article in this worthy collection of essays, Eduardo Raposo's "Clitic Positions and Verb Movement," studies enclisis in European Portuguese. Raposo argues that enclisis in European Portuguese and in other Romance dialects is a side effect of the movement of inflection containing the verb to the specifier position of a phrase called FP, and to which the clitic is left-adjoined.

The volume is an invaluable addition to comparative syntax, and will prove useful to all those interested in theoretical linguistics as well as those drawn to the study of Portuguese or, more generally, Romance-language syntax.

José Elías Ulloa is a graduate student in the Department of Linguistics at Rutgers University, New Brunswick. He is particularly interested in the study of the Pano-group of languages, having conducted fieldwork in the Amazon region of Peru. Email: joselias@rci.rutgers.edu

Luitgarde O.C. Barros. *A Derradeira Gesta: Lampião e Nazarenos Guerreando no Sertão*. São Paulo: Muad, 2000.

Maria-Eugênia D.C. Freitas

Nesta obra, a Dra. Luitgarde O.C. Barros conta através de uma linguagem clara, precisa e de tal modo poética, que se pode dizer que canta os dezenove anos de luta entre Ferreiras e Nazarenos, no sertão nordestino, no início do Século XX. Mais que a luta entre Lampião (Ferreiras) e Nazarenos, mais que a história do cangaço, ela canta o sertão nordestino, sua cultura, seus valores, seu povo, as transformações sociais de um período. Como ela mesma diz, a luta entre Lampião e Nazarenos é uma alegoria às tranformações vividas pela sociedade sertaneja no período estudado. O livro *A Derradeira Gesta* ficou entre os finalistas ao Prêmio Jabuti de 2001.

A antropóloga, Dra. Luitgarde O.C. Barros, professora na Universidade Estadual do Rio de Janeiro, após um período de 30 anos de pesquisa, reuniu em sua obra uma significativa documentação sobre o cangaço, sobre a história daquele sertão, enfim, sobre a cultura sertaneja. O livro é embasado em uma invejável documentação, que conjuga uma vasta bibliografia existente, as entrevistas que a autora colheu nos Estados de Sergipe, Alagoas, Bahia, Ceará e Pernambuco, documentos e notícias de imprensa. A obra é de grande importância tanto para o estudo das ciências sociais e história, como para áreas ligadas à literatura, uma vez que o livro ao mesmo tempo que se beneficia da literatura para entender aquela cultura, ajuda a dar embasamento para uma leitura mais completa dos universos descritos e criados por autores que escreveram sobre o sertão, como Raquel de Queiroz, Graciliano Ramos, Euclídes da Cunha e, principalmente, Guimarães Rosa.

A questão do cangaço, no livro, é abordada por uma perspectiva diferente da adotada pela mídia, pelo *mainstream* de maneira geral, que muitas vezes vê Lampião como vítima, um bandido social, que entrou no cangaço para vingar a morte de seu pai, uma espécie de resistência à violência e corrupção da polícia daquele período. Idéia que a autora explica ter-se desenvolvido por livros, relatos dos descendentes, protetores e protegidos de Lampião. Essa, contudo, não é a opinião aceita pela maioria da população local.

A literatura de cordel faz parte da documentação em que a obra se embasa, e nesses versos, "filhos das gestas medievais" (4), Barros encontrou respostas para entender o linguajar mais sofisticado que aquele povo, normalmente de uma fala mais econômica, usou muitas vezes ao relatar a sina dos que viveram a saga daquela região. E a gesta, feito histórico, canção de gesta, "constituída de fatos históricos, de elementos lendários e de ficções poéticas" (30) é parte do título do livro, introduzindo o leitor no seu objeto de estudo que é histórico, mas que já foi mitologizado no imaginário de um povo, de sua tradição oral e escrita. E é particularmente em relação ao falso mito de que Lampião entrou no cangaço para se vingar de seu pai, que a autora se refere no título de seu texto.

No resgate dessa história, Barros discorda do conceito de história desenvolvido por Maurice Halbwachs, em sua visão de que se deve esperar que grupos antigos e suas memórias não estejam mais presentes, para que se possa fazer a história, usando documentos da época, mas sem deixar-se guiar pela idéia dos respectivos conterrâneos. Ela, justamente, vai em busca dos depoimentos e opiniões destes, para resgatar o clima daquele sertão, e os choques de opiniões entre grupos adeptos e inimigos do cangaço. *A Derradeira Gesta* é um livro de memórias, de relatos: escritos e falados. Consciente das armadilhas da memória, trabalhando com esta na perspectiva de Henri Bergson, atenta ao fato de que as lembranças se alteram com a percepção e interesses dos agentes na sociedade e no papel que exercem na história contada, além do fato de que Bastos trabalha com a história de personagens já muito explorados na literatura, no cinema, televisão, o que ajudou na costrução de uma memória coletiva que quase calou memórias pessoais, a Professora Luitgarde C.O Barros enfatisa a necessidade de se colher depoimentos detalhados e cruzá-los sistematicamente, para que se possa encontrar os pontos recorrentes e coinscidentes dos relatos.

A origem alagoana da autora, e como ela diz, sua "experiência pessoal de vida sertaneja até os 20 anos de idade" (44), dá a ela uma intimidade com o universo sertanejo, que permite uma análise de seu objeto de estudo, de quem conhece o assunto de dentro, entendendo a cultura e o povo estudado. Sua própria mãe fora seqüestrada por Lampião, antes de a autora nascer. Apesar de tal proximidade, Barros mantém um rigor analítico e científico em sua análise.

Ao longo do livro dividido em 1) Introdução; 2) Cangaço e Memória; 3) Valentia e Identidade Cultural; 4) Ferreiras e Nazarenos – uma História do Sertão; 5) O Sertão Fragmentado; e 6) Conclusão, Barros introduz o leitor na história sócio-econômica da região, de seus valores, a nova classe social a que Nazarenos e Ferreiras pertencem. Ela apresenta as dimensões, espacial e temporal (cronológica e da transtemporalidade do imaginário) em que a história se desenrola, sempre a relacionar esses áspectos com a identidade cultural do sertanejo. Nesse processo, ela explica a divisão geo-política da região; explora o significado do termo "sertão," seu uso em documentos do período colonial, textos jornalísticos, autores como Euclídes da Cunha e Guimarães Rosa. Na visão de Manuel Antonio de Castro, o sertão rosiano, é o mais completo. No processo de investigação da identidade cultural do sertanejo, Barros considera também a questão da alimentação, embasando-se em Levy Strauss e no importante trabalho de Josué de Castro, que relaciona o clima, a flora, fauna e a repercussão destes sobre a população e sua alimentação. Desse ponto, ela aborda a questão da economia de subsistência local, a policultura do sertanejo, que forneceu os nutrientes necessários para que esse povo enfrentasse a vida dura da região.

Nesse entender do significado do sertão, o que é o sertanejo, a autora mostra a maneira como as classes mais baixas se organizaram ativamente, num movimento de reação em movimentos como a cabanagem e Canudos. Este, aliás, é o tema central de um outro livro da autora *A Terra da Mãe de Deus*. Essa organização, reação ativa de certas camadas da população, muitas vezes, consideradas passivas por certos teóricos, é também um dos focos centrais em *A Derradeira Gesta*, onde os Nazarenos, que simbolizam os estratos dominados da sociedade, se organizam e lutam contra o cangaço. Sobre o movimento de Canudos, Barros escreve "esses fenômenos demostram nitidamente uma dinâmica social mais rica, dela emergindo sujeitos históricos capazes de enfrentar não só o poder local, mas o poder central constituído, do qual aquele era apenas uma representação do modelo de governo, de uma concepção de Estado violento na exclusão das camadas sociais mais pobres" (59).

Barros também enfoca a maneira como as classes dominantes se posicionaram em relação ao cangaço, e mais especificamente, em relação a Lampião: parte dela combatendo o cangaceiro e outra parte protegendo-o e sendo beneficiada por ele. Ela ainda, através da análise das ações dos cangaceiros, das volantes e das autoridades, explica a posição dos coiteiros (informantes), que, juntamente com suas famílias, foram uma das maiores vítimas da guerra do cangaço.

Virgulino Ferreira (Lampião) nasceu de uma família de pequenos proprietários. A professora Luitgarde O.C. Barros, em seu livro, mostra e comprova com registros que Virgulino já flertava com o crime em sua adolescência, e começara sua vida de crimes, antes da morte de seu pai. Ela descreve o Coronel Lucena também sendo frio e cruel, mas lutando no lado oposto do de Lampião. Barros abre as cortinas do jogo de interesses, em que Lampião e a elite daquela região eram beneficiados. O cangaceiro atacava os inimigos de seus protetores, que depois, acabavam comprando as terras atacadas por um preço muito baixo. Com o dinheiro dos roubos, Lampião comprava armas de seus protegidos. A elite, de forma geral, não apoiou a luta contra o cangaço.

A autora em seu livro reescreve a história do Sertão, derrubando o mito de Lampião como um bandido social, e mostrando as cartas do jogo, em que o cangaceiro estava ligado às camadas mais altas do poder, num jogo de interesses.

Maria-Eugênia D.C. Freitas é bacharel em Comunicação Social, mestrado em Roteiro, e atualmente está fazendo doutorado em Communication Studies na University of Liverpool. Foi coordenadora da parte de filmes do Odyssey Group. E-mail: m.duarte-cunha-freitas@liverpool.ac.uk

Ana Paula Ferreira (ed). *A Urgência de Contar: Contos de Mulheres dos Anos 40*. Lisboa: Caminho, 2000.

Kathryn Bishop-Sanchez

The publication of *A Urgência de Contar: Contos de Mulheres dos Anos 40,* by Ana Paula Ferreira, is representative of the author's dedication to the phenomenon of the rise of the "woman writer" in Portugal during the Estado Novo and in particular during the 1940s. The anthology brings together the works of fifteen women authors who, for the most part, have been widely neglected by the critical establishment of Portuguese literature. Alongside the unquestionable merit of making these works accessible to a broader public, the anthology provides a succinct yet thorough contextualization of the corpus and an in-depth reading of the socio-political factors that influenced the themes and the experience inherent in these women's writing. As such, the book aims to bridge a gap in Portuguese literary criticism concerning literature written by women, and further opens the way for a much-needed social history of women writers in Portugal.

A Urgência de Contar consists of a substantial introduction, eighteen short stories that constitute the main corpus of the anthology, followed by a valuable appendix that includes a list of twenty-six women writers who published fiction in the 1940s, a list of short stories and short novellas published in the 1940s, and concise, informative bio-bibliographic notes on each of the fifteen authors included in the volume.

Ana Paula Ferreira's introduction to the texts in this volume addresses the question of the blatant absence of women from literary criticism of the 1940s. With the exception of Paula Morão's pioneering work on Irene Lisboa, the general silence of literary critics in regard to the work of women from this period is all the more unjustifiable given the fact that, as Ferreira amply discusses, from the end of the 1930s to the end of the 1940s there is the first important wave of female authors in Portuguese literature, comparable only to the emergence of women writers in the later part of the 1970s following the overturn of the Fascist regime. Ferreira suggests that, in part, the lack of academic perspectives centered on the category of "women writers" stems from the fact that this literature is marginalized and marked as "feminine literature," entailing a lack of cultural and literary credibility. After a brief introduction to the engendered notion of literary acceptance and status, Ferreira continues with a more detailed analysis of the situation of these Portuguese women. Her analysis approaches the different generations of writers from the 1920s through the 1940s yet without collapsing the authors into indistinct groups.

Ferreira begins by drawing attention to the women writers under the First Republic, many of whom were also translators, journalists and publicists whose works centered on the "woman question," and as such were also often affiliated with the Conselho Nacional das Mulheres Portuguesas, a national organization dedicated to women's issues. Some of the literary tendencies of this first group of writers can be characterized as neo-romantic, and even melodramatic, at times coupled with moralist penchants.

Female writers of the second group that Ferreira discusses are the new voices appearing in the second part of the 1930s. Among these women are writers such as Irene Lisboa, Maria Lamas, Alice Ogando, Rachel Bastos and Maria Archer, many of whom began writing poetry before turning to prose fiction. Ferreira emphasizes in particular the work of Maria Archer and the themes that are characteristic of her writing.

The third and most important group of women writers for the anthology under study corresponds to the female authors who published novels and short stories during the 1940s. Ferreira couches her presentation of this generational group in the sense of community that binds these women around the weight of cultural, moral and socio-economic injustices. From this group of prolific women, for the most part completely forgotten nowadays up unto the publication of this volume, only two women writers became widely acknowledged authors: Natália Correia and Agustina Bessa Luís.

After having mapped the general lines of the woman writer's experience during the first decades of the Estado Novo, Ferreira further develops the socio-historical and literary contexts of these writers in relation to the overtly masculinist Neo-Realist movement and the position of women in Portuguese society at the time. In particular, Ferreira engages with the critical work of João Gaspar Simões and his discussion of literature as "high culture" in relation to the status of women. What is also certainly admirable is Ferreira's discussion of writers in Portugal in light of other European writers and critics. As such, Ferreira succeeds in placing the Portuguese women writer's impasse within a wider socio-cultural perspective, foregrounding the condition of professional women around the general notion of "feminine literature."

Given the fact that this anthology is a collection of short stories written by women in the 1940s, Ferreira pertinently discusses the criteria for working with this literary genre, as well as the writers' possible preference for the short story. As the organizer of this book states, the texts included in this anthology are meant to be considered as a representative sample of the fiction by women of this period and their political, social and ideological preoccupations. Particularly noteworthy is the fact that the organization of the stories included in this anthology was planned and carried out with extreme care. The criteria for both the inclusion and order of the short stories is detailed in the organizer's introduction, making the corpus as a whole even more coherent and emblematic.

As the title indicates, Ana Paula Ferreira's work resurrects the urgency of the messages of these mostly forgotten women authors and is in and of itself a much-overdue critical statement in Portuguese literary studies. This urgency, both then and now, points to the ongoing women's question and in particular to the place of women in literary traditions. More than half a century later, Ferreira's research makes a symbolic stand and opens up the field for further research in this area. Given the fact that gender studies are only just developing in Portugal, this project was without doubt as urgent as it was challenging. The depth of Ferreira's research is visible in the thorough introduction to the present anthology and pertinent related themes, the inclusion of valuable explanatory notes, important bibliography and further reading suggestions, as well as the coherently organized corpus, combining all the necessary conditions for these women's voices to at last be heard.

Kathryn Bishop-Sanchez is Assistant Professor of Portuguese at the University of Madison-Wisconsin. Her research interests include nineteenth and twentieth century Luso-Brazilian narrative and contemporary women writers. She recently completed a manuscript entitled *Utopias desmascaradas: O mito do bom selvagem e a procura do homem natural na obra de Almeida Garrett*. Email: ksanchez2@wisc.edu

María Xosé Rodríguez Galdo and Daniel Varela-Suanzes-Carpegna (orgs). *Galicia & América: Cinco Siglos de Historia*. Coruña: Consello Da Cultura Galega, 1992.

Yeon-Soo Kim

This book is a scholarly attempt to commemorate the role Galicia and its people played in the building of a transatlantic relation between Europe and America, since the time of Christopher Columbus's encounter with America to the present day. The multidisciplinary volume offers a comprehensive vision of how Galicia has come to serve as a crucial intermediator in the reciprocal cultural exchange between the two continents, ever since it received the first ship returning from America in its port of Baiona in 1493. *Galicia & América* consists of fifty-two monographs, written in Castilian and divided into six chapters (Departure, Arrival, Sons of Galicia, The Fifth Province, Exile and Return). Issues dealt with are diverse, covering the participation of Galicians in Columbus's mission, the Galician diaspora in the late eighteenth century, the cultural and political impact Galicians played in the constitution of Latin American countries, the political exile of Galician intellectuals to Latin America during the Civil War, and the contribution of Galician émigrés in the resuscitation of a Galician national conscious.

The first chapter (Departure) documents the history of Galician immigration to Latin America from the end of the fifteenth century to the twentieth century. This section pays special attention to the social debates concerning immigration and its impact on Galician society from the nineteenth century onward. The discussion includes the root causes, remedies for immigration, travel conditions of the immigrants, the opposition to the central government restrictions on Galician immigrants and concerns about the massive demographic loss. Luís Alonso Alvarez accounts for the scope of this phenomenon by pointing out that the transportation of Galicians, by the mid-nineteenth century, replaced that of African slaves (31).

The second chapter (Arrival) deals with the process of adaptation of immigrants to different cultures, languages, clothing and food. While they had to speak Castilian (except those who went to Brazil where the linguistic affinity between Portuguese and Galician facilitated their adaptation), they were united by the shared goal of returning one day to their homeland. One article indicates that while Galicians played a limited role in the participation of the Spanish construction of Empire, their religious symbol, Santiago the Apostle, was appropriated by indigenous popular tradition, in particular, in Mexico and Guatemala. Another article argues that Galician immigration reached its peak after the dissolution of Spanish colonialism and contributed to the demographic growth of Latin America.

Chapter three (Sons of Galicia) examines the role Galicians played in religion, education and the production of colonial literature through which the knowledge of cartography and translation of indigenous languages into Castilian was advanced. Several studies are dedicated to an investigation of the political presence of Galicians from the emancipation of Latin America from the Spanish Empire in the nineteenth century to the political positions held by them across the continent, and their prominence in diverse commercial sectors. Another topic highlighted in this section is their contribution to Latin American literature, their portrayal in it, and their involvement in arts and popular culture.

Chapter four (The Fifth Province: Associationism and the Culture of Immigration) focuses on the contexts in which Galician cultural centers throughout the continent were founded, evolved to serve social causes in their host countries and preserved a cultural attachment to the homeland. It also discusses the role *Congresos de emigración gallega* played not only in reconsidering Republican political ideology but also in consolidating immigrants as a political voice in Galicia. The rest of the chapter investigates the Galician presence in different parts of Latin America as a heterogeneous socio-cultural phenomenon.

Chapter five (Exile: A New Presence of Galicia in America) constitutes a brief report of how Galician exiles formed an intellectual community in foreign lands.

Chapter six (Return: Influence of America in Galicia) looks into the many ways in which Galician immigration has benefited Galicia. During the colonial period, new agricultural products such as corn, potatoes, tomatoes, pepper and tobacco were introduced in Galicia, and from the mid-nineteenth century, Galicians returning from America (*indianos*) brought back different cultural ideas and flavors in architecture, literature (both in Galician and Spanish), natural sciences, music, dance, gastronomy as well as fashion. Several monographs detail the contribution of *indianos* to Galician industrialization and their financial commitment to education, social welfare and religious foundations. This chapter also explores how immigrants took political initiatives in Galicia from America, especially in the construction of Galician nationalism and agrarian reform, influenced by socio-political reforms that were taking place in Latin America.

Galicia & Amércia is a truly resourceful study for scholars working on topics related to transatlantic studies, immigration, colonial history, postcolonial theories, Galician nationalism as well as Iberian cultural studies. Its emphasis on mutual influence in the cultural contact between Europe and Latin America provides a new perspective from which the current European "problem" of African immigration can be reflectively handled. Furthermore, as Manuel Rivas argues in his prologue, the long history of immigration enabled Galicia to construct a nationalist stance, open and tolerant to other cultures.

Yeon-Soo Kim is Assistant Professor of Spanish at Rutgers University – New Brunswick. She specializes in Spanish Cultural Studies. Her forthcoming book, *The Family Album: Histories, Subjectivities and Migration in Contemporary Spanish Culture*, interrogates the role of the family album as a critical and ethical tool through which to reevaluate the complexities of twentieth-century Iberian history. Her current project analyzes the different moral weights assigned to Asians and Arabs in the contemporary Iberian cultural imaginary. E-mail: ykim@spanport.rutgers.edu

Portuguese Literary & Cultural Studies

www.plcs.umassd.edu

Portuguese Literary & Cultural Studies 1
Fronteiras/Borders.

Portuguese Literary & Cultural Studies 2
Lídia Jorge in other words / por outras palavras.
Guest Editor: Cláudia Pazos Alonso, Oxford University

Portuguese Literary & Cultural Studies 3
Pessoa's Alberto Caeiro.

Portuguese Literary & Cultural Studies 4/5
Brazil 2001. A Revisionary History of Brazilian Literature and Culture.
Guest Editor: João Cezar de Castro Rocha, Universidade do Estado do Rio de Janeiro

Portuguese Literary & Cultural Studies 6
On Saramago.
Guest Editor: Anna Klobucka, University of Georgia

Portuguese Literary & Cultural Studies 8
Cape Verde: Language, Literature & Music.
Guest Editor: Ana Mafalda Leite, Universidade de Lisboa

Portuguese Literary & Cultural Studies 9
Post-Imperial Camões.
Guest Editor: João Ricardo Figueiredo, Universidade de Lisboa

Portuguese Literary & Cultural Studies 10
Mozambique.
Guest Editor: Phillip Rothwell, Rutgers University, New Brunswick

Forthcoming

Portuguese Literary & Cultural Studies 7
Contemporary Portuguese Poetry.

Portuguese Literary & Cultural Studies 11
Vitorino Nemésio.
Guest Editor: Francisco C. Fagundes, University of Massachusetts Amherst

Portuguese Literary & Cultural Studies 12
Facts and Fictions of António Lobo Antunes.

Adamastor Book Series

Eduardo Lourenço. *Chaos and Splendor and Other Essays.*
Edited by Carlos Veloso, New York University
ISBN: 0972256113

Forthcoming
Transdisciplinary Readings of Garrett's Travels in My Homeland.
Edited by Victor J. Mendes

The Later Eça Revisited.
Edited by Frank F. Sousa

Eça de Queirós. *The Relic.*
Trans. Aubrey F.G. Bell. Preface by Harold Bloom

Camões. *Sonnets and Other Poems.*
Translated by Richard Zenith

Fernando Gil and Helder Macedo.
The Traveling Eye: Retrospection, Vision, and Prophecy in Portuguese Renaissance.

Uprooted from One's Own Land: An Anthology of Brazilian Essays.
Edited by João Cezar de Castro Rocha,
Universidade do Estado do Rio de Janeiro

Maria Alzira Seixo, Universidade de Lisboa
António Lobo Antunes. The Art of the Novel.

Materialities of Communication in Portuguese.
Edited by Hans Ulrich Gumbrecht, Stanford University

Portuguese Language Textbooks Series

Francisco Cota Fagundes. *Mais Um Passo No Português Moderno: Gramática Avançada, Leituras, Composição e Vocabulário.*

The Portuguese in the Americas Series

Portuguese-Americans and Contemporary Civic Culture in Massachusetts.
Edited by Clyde Barrow, Center for Policy Analysis,
University of Massachusetts Dartmouth.
ISBN: 0972256105

Forthcoming

Charles Reis Felix. *Through a Portagee Gate.*
ISBN: 0972254148

Jerry R. Williams. *Portuguese Immigration from the Azores to the United States.* 2nd edition. Edited with preface by Andrea Klimt.

Alfred Lewis. *Sixty Acres and a Barn: A Novel.*

Donald Warrin. *The Portuguese and Cape Verdeans in American Whaling.*

The University of Massachusetts Dartmouth Center for Portuguese Studies and Culture

Founded in 1996 by a group of faculty from four different colleges, the University of Massachusetts Dartmouth Center for Portuguese Studies and Culture is a multidisciplinary international studies and outreach unit dedicated to the study of the language, literatures and cultures of the Portuguese-speaking world. The Center is designed to be the liaison between the University of Massachusetts Dartmouth and other institutions involved in Portuguese studies both in the United States and abroad. The Center aims to develop pedagogical materials to aid in teaching and learning the Portuguese language and cultures at all levels of education, and also supports the development and dissemination of knowledge regarding the Portuguese-speaking communities in the United States. The Center for Portuguese Studies and Culture promotes outreach efforts in areas such as, but not limited to, the arts, education, economic development, health and politics related to the Portuguese-speaking communities in the Commonwealth of Massachusetts and throughout the United States.

The Center for Portuguese Studies and Culture includes the Summer Program in Portuguese, which was founded in 1994. This program has become the largest of its kind in the United States, with over 100 students from 10 different states in 2002. The Center also launched the Summer Program in Portuguese for Children in 2000. In the same year, the Center led the effort to create a separate Department of Portuguese. In fall 2002 the Department had 325 students and 46 majors, both numbers doubling those of 1999. And in fall 2001, the Center led the way to the creation of the Hélio and Amélia Pedroso/Luso-American Foundation Endowed Chair in Portuguese Studies. Prof. Donald Warrin of the University of California, Berkeley, a renowned expert on Portuguese-American Literature and History, taught a course on the Portuguese and Cape Verdeans in Local History. Prof. Warrin is the first Visiting Distinguished Professor to occupy the Chair. He has also agreed to publish a book-length manuscript on the Portuguese and Cape Verdeans in American whaling in the Portuguese in the Americas Series, in 2004.

In 1998, the Center launched the semiannual scholarly journal, *Portuguese Literary & Cultural Studies (PLCS)*, which has published essays by such eminent scholars as Harold Bloom, Hans Ulrich Gumbrecht, Luiz Costa Lima, and Helen Vendler. *PLCS* has been very positively reviewed in the *Times Literary Supplement* of London (November 8, 2002). Recently the Center launched three new publications: the Portuguese in the Americas Series (the first volume, *Portuguese-Americans and Contemporary Civic Culture in Massachusetts* was published in January 2003); the Adamastor Book Series (the first volume, *Chaos and Splendor and Other Essays* by Eduardo Lourenço, Portugal's most celebrated cultural critic, was published in January 2003); and the Portuguese Language Textbook Series, whose inaugural volume is precisely this work.

The Center also sponsors and organizes colloquia, concerts, art exhibitions, dance performances and theatrical productions, in addition to visits by distinguished authors and critics. With the Center's support, José Saramago, the 1998 Nobel Laureate for Literature, was awarded an honorary degree in 1999 and returned to UMD in 2002 to be the keynote speaker in a similar ceremony for Harold Bloom, America's premier man of letters. In the same month of April 2002, the Center co-organized and co-sponsored events with José Saramago at the prestigious New York Public Library Bartos Forum (Prof. Bloom presented Saramago) and the John F. Kennedy Library, the latter in partnership with the Massachusetts Foundation for the Humanities. In fall 2002 the Center hosted Dr. José Ramos-Horta, Foreign Minister of East Timor and the 1996 Nobel Laureate for Peace. In April 2001, the Center organized a colloquium and launching of an issue of *Portuguese Literary & Cultural Studies*, subtitled "Brazil 2001: A Revisionary History of Brazilian Literature and Culture" at the Library of Congress in Washington, DC., and will do the same for volume 8 ("Cape Verde: Language, Literature & Music") and 10 ("Reevaluating Mozambique") on February 4, 2004.

Future projects include the publication of studies on the Portuguese-American communities and the further development of the Portuguese-American Archives, located in the University Library Special Collections. In addition, the Department of Portuguese is currently developing a Graduate Program in Portuguese Studies to be launched in fall 2004. Finally, the Center and Department are working together to develop a scholarship program to promote the study of Portuguese at the undergraduate and graduate levels.

The varied activities of the Center for Portuguese Studies and Culture have been made possible by the commitment and generosity of numerous supporters. A gift from Frank B. Sousa, Chairman of the UMD Foundation Board of Directors, enabled the launching of the summer program, and subsequent major grants from the Luso-American Foundation of Lisbon and the Government of Portugal contributed significantly to the development of the Center for Portuguese Studies and Culture and the Department of Portuguese. Other grants from the Camões Institute and the Calouste Gulbenkian Foundation have supported the Summer Program in Portuguese and the organization of major international conferences. Portuguese studies at UMass Dartmouth have also benefited from the generous financial support of Anthony Andrade, Dennis Rezendes, the Citizens Financial Group, and the Portuguese-American legislative delegation led by State Representative Robert Correia. The Hélio and Amélia Pedroso/Luso-American Foundation Endowed Chair in Portuguese Studies was made possible by the generous support of Luis Pedroso, the Luso-American Foundation, Anthony Andrade, Maria Dulce Furman, Frank B. Sousa and Manuel Fernando Neto.

Portuguese Literary & Cultural Studies Subscription
Center for Portuguese Studies and Culture
University of Massachusetts Dartmouth
North Dartmouth, MA 02747 USA
Tel. (508) 999 9270 Fax (508) 999 9272 E-Mail greis@umassd.edu

Name

Address

City **State** **Zip**

Country

- ☐ **Annual Individual Subscription $40 (2 issues)**
- ☐ **Annual Institutional Subscription $80 (2 issues)**
- ☐ **Single Issue $25 (Issue Number __)**

Outside of the USA add $12.00 for shipping and handling

Payment enclosed
☐ **Check** ☐ **Visa** ☐ **Mastercard**

Credit Card Number **Expiration Date**

Signature **Date**

NOTES

NOTES